Political Parties and the Internet

Net gain?

Edited by Rachel Gibson, Paul Nixon and Stephen Ward

Routledge
Taylor & Francis Group

LONDON AND NEW YORK

First published 2003 by Routledge
11 New Fetter Lane, London EC4P 4EE

Simultaneously published in the USA and Canada
by Routledge
29 West 35th Street, New York, NY 10001

Routledge is an imprint of the Taylor & Francis Group

Typeset in Baskerville by Wearset Ltd, Boldon, Tyne and Wear
Printed and bound in Great Britain by The Cromwell Press,
Trowbridge, Wiltshire

British Library Cataloguing in Publication Data
A catalogue record for this book is available from the British Library

Library of Congress Cataloging in Publication Data
Political parties and the Internet : net gain?/edited by R.K. Gibson,
P.G. Nixon, and S.J. Ward
    p. cm.
  1. Political participation–Computer network resources. 2. Political
parties–Technological innovations. 3. Internet. I. Gibson, Rachel
Kay. II. Nixon, P.G. (Paul G.), 1957– III. Ward, Stephen, 1965–
    JF799 .P638 2003
    324.2′0285′4678–dc21
                                                    2002152775

ISBN 0-415-28273-X (hbk)
ISBN 0-415-28274-8 (pbk)

Contents

Illustrations

Contributors

Gabriel Badescu is Associate Professor in the Department of Political Science at Babes-Bolyai University Cluj, with research interests in political culture, social capital, public administration, citizenship and democracy. He is editor of the social capital series of the Centre for Publishing Development, Budapest, co-director of the Romanian National School of Social Statistics (1998–2001) and a member of the European Science Foundation 'Citizenship, involvement, democracy' scientific network.

Julian Bowers-Brown is a PhD student of Politics at the European Studies Research Institute, University of Salford. He is currently undertaking a comparative study of political parties and online political marketing in the UK and the Netherlands.

Nigel Copsey is Senior Lecturer in Modern and Contemporary History at the University of Teesside. He has published widely on the subject of the extreme right and his most recent publications include *Anti-Fascism in Britain* (2000). He is currently working on a book on the history of the British National Party and its struggle for political legitimacy.

Carlos Cunha is Professor and Chair of the Political Science Department at Dowling College (Oakdale, NY). Author of *The Portuguese Communist Party's Strategy for Power, 1921–1986* (Garland, 1992), he has published numerous articles and book chapters on various aspects of Portuguese politics, and especially on the Portuguese Communist Party. He is also a member of an EU COST A14 Working Group examining the use of ICTs by political parties.

Rachel Gibson has recently completed a TMR research scholarship at the Mannheim Centre for European Social Research (MZES), University of Mannheim, and is currently Deputy Director of the ACSPRI Centre for Social Research and Fellow in the Research School of Social Sciences (RSSS) at the Australian National University, Canberra. Her research interests include the impact of the Internet on politics, particularly on participation and campaigning and extreme right-wing parties. She has published widely on both the Internet and politics and extreme-right parties. She is working (with Stephen Ward) on a major research programme examining participation, political organisations and the impact of new ICTs funded by the Economic and Social Research Council's Democracy and Participation programme.

Rod Hague is Senior Lecturer in Politics at the University of Newcastle upon Tyne, specialising in comparative politics, policy-making and public opinion. Recent publications include *Comparative Government and Politics: An Introduction* (5th edition, Palgrave, 2000), co-authored with Martin Harrop, and *Risk and Values in Contemporary Britain* (WRI/University of Newcastle, 2000), co-authored with Rick Wylie.

Jonathan Levy is a lawyer and author of 'The Vatican Bank', a book chapter in *Everything You Know is Wrong: A Disinformation Guide to Secrets and Lies* (2002). He is also a graduate student of the University of Cincinnati's PhD Program in Political Science.

Karl Löfgren is Senior Lecturer in Political Science with the Division of IT, Organisation and Learning, School of Technology and Society, Malmö University, Sweden. His PhD thesis reviewed political parties' adoption and use of new information and communications technologies in Sweden and Denmark. He has published extensively on questions concerning e-democracy in representative political institutions in Sweden and Denmark, and is currently involved in a major research project on Swedish IT policy from a power and governance perspective.

Michael Margolis, Professor of Political Science at the University of Cincinnati, is co-author (with David Resnick) of *Politics as Usual: the Cyberspace 'Revolution'*. His scholarly and popular publications include books, chapters and articles on political parties, elections, public opinion, mass media and democratic theory. He has held visiting appointments in Scotland at the Universities of Strathclyde and Glasgow, and in Korea at Hankuk University of Foreign Studies (Seoul).

Cosmin Marian is a doctoral candidate in Sociology and Assistant Professor at the Faculty of Political Science and Public Administration, Babes-Bolyai University Cluj. His teaching and research interests are research methods in the social sciences. He is co-organiser of the National School of Social Statistics, and a member of the European Science Foundation's 'Citizenship, involvement, democracy' scientific network.

Irene Martín is a PhD candidate in Political Science at the Instituto Juan March in Madrid. Her primary research area is political culture in Spain and Modern Greece. She currently holds a research position at the Universidad Autónoma of Madrid. She is a member of an EU COST A14 Working Group examining the use of ICTs by political parties.

Rodica Mocan teaches graphic design at the Journalism Department of Babes-Bolyai University Cluj, with a special interest in new media and its application in education, culture and society. Her doctoral studies are covering the applications of new media in distance education and she is director of studies for the Journalism Open Distance Education programme. She organised the first live transmission over the Internet of a visual arts exhibition from Romania.

James Newell is Senior Lecturer in the School of English, Sociology, Politics and Contemporary History at the University of Salford. Author of *Parties and Democracy in Italy* (Ashgate, 2000), he has published numerous articles and book chapters on various aspects of Italian politics. He is a member of an EU COST A14 Working Group examining the uses of ICTs by political parties.

Paul Nixon is Senior Lecturer in European Politics at HEBO, Haagse Hogeschool, Den Haag, the Netherlands. He has published a number of works on a range of topics including electronic democracy, political parties and the Internet, and social policy and ICTs. He is a member of an EU COST A14 Working Group examining the uses of ICTs by new social movements and is presently co-editing a book on that topic.

Luis Ramiro is Associate Lecturer in the Department of Political Science, University of Murcia. He has published several articles and book chapters on Spanish party politics.

David Resnick was, until his death in 2002, Professor of Political Science and Director of the Center for the Study of Democratic Citizenship at the University of Cincinnati, was co-author (with Michael Margolis) of *Politics as Usual: the Cyberspace 'Revolution'*. In addition to his work on the Internet, he has published numerous scholarly articles and book chapters on the history of political theory and contemporary political philosophy. Before coming to the University of Cincinnati he taught at Cornell University.

Colin Smith is Lecturer in Management at the University of Huddersfield. He is currently completing a PhD that examines British parties' use of ICTs and has published a number of articles on the theme of e-democracy. He is also a member of an EU COST A14 Working Group examining the use of ICTs by political parties.

Seung-Yong Uhm has held senior posts in the Korean Civil Service, most recently in the office of the President. As deputy secretary for public affairs, he was responsible for the presidential website. Before that, as divisional director in the Korean Ministry of Information, he led the project to establish the leading portal site Korea.net. He is currently completing doctoral research at the University of Newcastle upon Tyne.

Bruno Villalba lectures in politics at the Centre de Recherches Administratives, Politiques et Sociales, Faculty of Law, University of Lille II. His research interests include environmental politics, political participation and new communication technologies and politics. He has published widely on French political parties, particularly on the Greens and the far right. He is also a member of an EU COST A14 Working Group examining the uses of ICTs by political parties.

Stephen Ward is Senior Lecturer in Politics at the European Studies Research Institute, University of Salford. His research interests include environmental politics and policy in the EU and the impact of the Internet on politics, particularly on participation and campaigning. He has published widely on both the Internet and politics and environmental policy. Currently, he is working (with Rachel Gibson) on a major research programme examining participation, political organisations and the impact of new ICTs funded by the ESRC's Democracy and Participation programme. He is also a member of an EU COST A14 Working Group examining the uses of ICTs by political parties.

Darren Wallis is Lecturer in Government at Nottingham Trent University. His main research interests relate to democratisation in Latin America, especially Mexico. His recent publications include 'Democratic transition and consolidation in Mexico' in J. Haynes (ed.), *Democracy and Political Change in the Third World* (Routledge, 2001) and articles ranging from electoral and party politics to indigenous movements in journals including the *Bulletin of Latin American Research, Journal of Public Affairs* and *Parliamentary Affairs.*

Acknowledgements

The origins of this edited collection can be found in meetings of the EU's COST (Co-operation in the field of Scientific and Technical Research) A14 Action – Government and Democracy in the Information Age (GaDIA) programme – in which the editors and many of the contributors have participated. The programme has allowed discussion and promotion of the study of the political and social impact of new information and communications technologies and the editors are grateful for the constructive comments of many working-group members.

Rachel Gibson and Stephen Ward would also like to acknowledge the support of Economic and Social Research Council (ESRC) and British Academy grants, which have allowed some welcome time to bring together this edited collection.

The publishers and editors would also like to thank Emerald Publishers for granting their permission to reprint some sections from 'Political parties' use of the web during the 2001 general election' by Julian Bowers-Brown and Barrie Gunter, originally published in the *Aslib Proceedings: new information perspectives*, Vol. 54 Number 3 (2002), in Chapter 5.

Finally, on a personal note, Steve would like to dedicate this book to Joseph, who was born during the latter stages of its preparation and has contributed by keeping his father relatively sane, if somewhat distracted, through the final drafts.

Stephen Ward
Paul Nixon
Rachel Gibson

Introduction

Stephen Ward, Rachel Gibson and Paul Nixon

Since the 1990s there has been much speculation about the role and health of political parties from both journalists and academics. The importance of parties as the primary link between citizens and the state and as a vehicle of representation and participation in the political arena has increasingly come under question. Almost at the same time, the emergence of new information and communications technologies (ICTs) and their potential impact on politics has furthered heightened this interest in the future of political parties. The Internet, in particular, has come to be seen as both saviour and executioner of political parties. The goal of this book, therefore, is to provide an assessment of how political parties are adapting to the rise of new ICTs, and what the consequences of that adaptation are for their future performance.[1] In particular, it concentrates on the role that the Internet, email and the World Wide Web (WWW) are playing in parties' relationships with voters and members and their use in electoral campaigning and internal party affairs. This brief introduction sets the general context for emergence of ICTs in the party arena and provides an overview of main themes and chapters contained in this collection.

Representative democracy and political parties: crisis and decline?

The literature of politics in western liberal democracies is currently littered with notions of widespread political change. Whilst some talk excitedly of a new era in politics, others bemoan a declining interest and engagement in democratic politics. Increasingly, the idea of representative democracy and party-centred democracy has been questioned from a variety of sources (academics, journalists, politicians). The symptoms of this supposed crisis of representative politics are commonly held to be:

- widespread decreasing levels of stable partisan attachment amongst voters for political parties; this arguably has led to increased electoral volatility and the rise of a range of new protest parties outside the traditional social democratic, christian democratic and conservative mainstream (Erik-Lane and Ersson, 1996);

- an alarming lack of knowledge and interest about the representative process and its traditional institutions and organisations such as parties and parliaments, particularly amongst younger citizens (Kaase and Newton, 1995);
- declining electoral turnout across a range of liberal democracies; arguably voters are becoming less likely to vote in national elections (Topf, 1995), whilst turnout in second-order elections (sub-national and supra-national) has become a minority interest;
- declining levels of trust in political representatives, parties and government institutions (Nye *et al.*, 1997; Putnam, 2000); voters have become increasingly cynical and distrustful of the claims and actions of politicians and parties – multiple surveys have indicated that parties and politicians are held in low esteem and are ranked with journalists in terms of truthfulness;
- declining collective action through the traditional representative vehicles of mass political participation, notably parties and old social-movement organisations such as trade unions (Seyd and Whiteley, 1992; Richardson, 1995; Jordan, 1998); surveys have indicated a considerable fall in members and also the general decline in levels of activism (Katz and Mair, 1994; Dalton and Wattenburg, 2000).

Explaining these symptoms is somewhat more problematic but a range of interrelated political and social causes (detailed below) has been put forward, not all of which support the notion of crisis.

- Detachment and dissatisfaction with politicians and government expressed through non voting or more general distrust stems from a belief that representative political institutions no longer work – they cannot deliver successful policies or they fail to address issues of real importance to voters and offer little choice to the voter. However, it is worth remembering that survey evidence also indicates that people have not necessarily lost trust in democratic values but rather in the traditional means by which they are delivered (Norris, 1999). Moreover, recently, others have indicated that a culture of contentment in liberal democracies is keeping more people away from polling booths (Geddes and Tonge, 2001). In short, for a significant proportion of the electorate in Western societies, needs are being met and there is little to provoke people into participation or voting.
- Lack of interest and knowledge of politics and the political process has been attributed to two phenomena in particular: first, the increasing range of alternative leisure activities available within society – put simply, there are more exciting things to do than participate in politics; second, a decline in serious coverage of politics in the media and

through the education system – the supposed tabloidisation of news coverage has arguably trivialised politics or treated it as another form of entertainment (Blumler and Gurevitch, 1995). Yet this has been disputed by others who point towards the increasing amount of specialist coverage via satellite and digital television and the Internet. Nevertheless, as the media has become more fragmented, political information is easier to avoid (Norris, 2000).

- Decline in social connectedness: an increasingly popular line of argument is the decline of social capital thesis (Putnam, 2001). Putnam argues that advanced capitalist societies are increasingly fragmented and individualised, with people being less likely to engage in common or social interaction. As social connectedness declines so do corresponding levels of trust and efficacy in the political system, which in turn undermines the fabric holding together civic society.
- Increasing individualism, freedom of choice and the rise of so-called consumer society has meant that citizens have become more demanding and less willing to allow others to make decisions on their behalf (Norris, 1999). Electorates have become used to being offered choices and products to match their individual preferences, but the political system has been slow to catch up. Hence, traditional participatory vehicles such as political parties operating across a range of issues and demanding significant input are no longer seen as efficient means by which to participate politically.

Democracy, parties and the Internet

Given the problems facing political parties and representative democracy outlined above, it is not surprising that some commentators, politicians and the parties themselves have increasingly looked for new methods of re-engaging the public and improving political communication. The arrival of the Internet and other new ICTs in the mid-1990s appeared to offer parties a range of new communication possibilities at just the right time.

New and old media compared

Part of the reason for this interest in new ICTs, such as the Internet, stems from their apparent difference from the old media. Abramson *et al.* (1988) identified several key differences between digital communication and the traditional electronic communication (television and radio). At one level these differences simply relate to the expansion of the existing capabilities of the electronic media: digital communication allows for a greater volume of information to be transmitted at a faster speed. However, the truly unique capacity of this medium relates to the user control and decentralisation of media ownership that it introduces to the communications process. In the traditional print and electronic media, while there is competition between individual producers of information, the consumer is essentially a passive recipient of news from a limited number of sources. The Internet, however, cedes information control to the individual consumer, who can actively search out the desired information and can edit and collate the relevant news sources. Further, and what is perhaps an even more revolutionary development, the Internet allows consumers themselves to become producers of news. Anyone with a little technical know-how and a little money can publish their own material on the Internet. Such features have also, therefore, introduced interactivity to media technology, allowing citizens to debate with politicians or to other groups of citizens from considerable distances, or to engage in written dialogue via computers.

Scenarios for change

The possibilities of new media communication quickly gave rise to a range of predictions about their impact on representative democracy and parties. These ranged from the radically optimistic to the dystopian, either sounding the death knell of unloved and unwanted parties or reinventing and reinvigorating the party organisation for the twenty-first century. Within this response, it is possible to identify at least five broad scenarios.

- Erosion and direct democracy: at one of end of the spectrum some commentators have suggested that the rise of new ICTs spells the end for traditional representative structures such as parties, as new ICTs provide increasing opportunities for citizens to input directly and individually into the policy-making process through electronic voting, referenda and e-discussion fora no longer under the control of parties (Morris, 1999).
- Accelerated pluralism: others have suggested that whilst full-scale erosion of parties is unlikely, so we are not about to return to the Athenian style direct democracy, the new-media era may well reduce the role of traditional representative organisations (Bimber, 1998). Conversely, however, the Internet may well provide a platform for many more single-issue networks and protest campaigns providing increased choice for citizen activity and increasing competition for parties.
- Participatory reinvigoration: towards the other end of the spectrum, some have argued that ICTs can be harnessed by political parties to re-engage the public and stimulate more participation through party structures (Depla and Tops, 1995). In particular, it has been argued that parties will use the interactive possibilities of technology to recruit more members and that the technology will allow members greater control over policy and party elites.

- Administrative and organisational modernisation: less radically, it has been suggested that parties may well harness some of the possibilities of the new ICTs but not necessarily the participatory ones (Gibson and Ward, 2000). Parties may simply use the information capacity and speed of the Internet to modernise and make more efficient their existing practices with limited impact on their participatory and representative functions.
- No change: finally, contrary to change hypotheses, some have simply suggested that the Internet is unlikely to have much impact on parties since it is not really about politics, but is dominated by the consumer interests of sex, sport and shopping (Davis, 1999; Margolis and Resnick, 2000). Consequently, the Internet will largely promote politics as usual.

Rationale and overview of the book

It is against the background of these broad, competing claims that this volume seeks to assess the impact of the new ICTs on political parties and the way in which parties are adapting such technologies for their own ends. Whilst bearing in mind the larger picture, it focuses more specifically on three themes, outlined in more detail in Chapter 1.

- Party competition and campaigning online: the use of the web for campaigning – does the arrival of new technology level the playing field by allowing smaller parties to bypass the traditional media and promote themselves via the WWW? Will it also alter the style of campaigning, further enhancing the alleged 'Americanisation' of electoral campaigning, for example?
- Internal party democracy: will the potential for interactivity via new ICTs promote greater internal democracy and more accountability of party elites, consequently reinvigorating participation within political parties? Or will political elites use their existing resource advantages to dominate use of the technology and consolidate their positions?
- The role of parties within democracies: what is the impact of technologies on the role of parties within democracies? Will it erode parties' traditional functions within the modern democracies, leading to a new style of party more akin to the American model, or, alternatively, will it allow parties to reinvent the traditional representative model of political parties?

Overall, we would argue that the book contributes a number of original elements to such debates. First, it draws together literatures from party change, political marketing, electoral campaigning and information society areas to form a broad theoretical approach. Second, the majority of studies of parties' Internet activities have, thus far, been North

American or North European in focus. This volume provides a broader geographical focus with chapters on Korea, Romania and the Mediterranean regions, where there has been limited analysis up to this point. Third, the majority of chapters include new, empirical research from the period 1998–2001. Although some would argue that it is too early to assess the relationship between new ICTs and political parties, many parties have operated websites for six or seven years now and we would argue that this volume provides an early benchmark against which to judge the future development of party strategies.

Chapter outlines

Chapter 1, by the editors, elaborates on the main themes/questions of the book (see above). It provides an overview of the current state of research into parties' interaction with new ICTs and links it to established work on political parties, notably, literatures on party organisational change, party campaign communication and democracy. The chapter looks at how far new ICTs might lead to new campaign styles and affect the shape of party systems, and at competition between parties and the use of new ICTs for internal democratic purposes.

The second chapter, by Karl Löfgren and Colin Smith, represents a theoretical and conceptual think-piece examining the role of technology in party development. This chapter discusses the theoretical triangle between parties, democracy and modern communication technologies with the point of departure in four ideal 'strategies' for parties' uptake and maintenance of new technologies. This is based in both new understandings of the relationship between democracy and modern communication technology, and classical models of parties and party organisations. This theoretical framework approach suggests that the relationship between the three entities is more complex than a simple dichotomy between the representative and participatory traditions of democracy. Moreover, it argues that the technology *per se* plays a limited role in most actual cases of political parties.

Chapters 3 and 4 focus on party competition online in the United States (US) and comparatively in the Mediterranean states (Greece, Spain, Italy and Portugal), drawing on web-content analysis, interviews and survey material. In particular, both chapters are interested in the equalisation versus normalisation debate; that is, whether new ICTs can level the campaign communication playing field for minor parties or whether they merely perpetuate the advantages of the major parties. The US-related chapter, by Margolis *et al.*, assesses evidence from 1996 to 2001, concentrating particularly on the presidential campaign of 2000. From their research, Margolis *et al.* remain sceptical of the democratic potential of the Internet in the US context.

Cunha *et al.*, in the Mediterranean-based chapter, examine the comparative use of ICTs in the 2000–2001 period in the more party-oriented democracies. In addition to the normalisation question, the comparative basis of the research enables the authors to examine whether common systemic political features inherent in Mediterranean political systems have produced a common approach to the adaptation of new ICTs.

Chapter 5, by Julian Bowers-Brown, analyses the use of the Internet by British political parties and is based on interviews and content analysis carried out around the UK 2001 general election. It compares actual and potential use of the Internet as a marketing tool and sets out to explain any gap between the two. Bowers-Brown argues that compared to the traditional transactional approach, a new relational paradigm provides a better basis for conceptualising the marketing of political parties. The WWW and email offer political actors a unique opportunity to put into practice a relational approach towards target audiences. If political parties are serious about adopting marketing perspectives for their purposes, the Internet should be used as a tool for building and maintaining relationships with voters.

Aside from its marketing potential, one of the central questions surrounding the potential impact of new-media technologies are whether they herald a new era of political participation. Notably, as we have indicated above, whether the Internet will erode or redefine the role of political parties, by introducing more direct or participatory forms of democracy. Chapter 6, by Bruno Villalba, examines such questions in relation to French political parties. Though initially French parties appeared slower to adapt than some of their Scandinavian and North European counterparts, since the late 1990s they have begun to use new communication and information technologies to try to build new relationships between themselves and their supporters. This relationship is analysed over a two-year period (1998–2000), which includes several elections (regional and European). The evidence presented here suggests that, thus far, parties, whilst acknowledging the increasing role of new ICTs, have failed to exploit potential participatory elements of technology.

The vast majority of party-Internet studies have concentrated on the national level. As a counterpoint, in Chapter 7, Rachel Gibson and Stephen Ward analyse the impact of new ICTs at the state and territory level in Australia. The Australian case also offers new and potentially significant systemic variation to test, since its level of net usage is higher than in many European countries and Australia has a hybrid political system of a decentralised federalism with a party-centred government. Examination of sub-national level activity allows for comparisons, not only between parties, but also between regions. Hence, the chapter seeks to build a greater theoretical understanding of variations in party online activity by assessing the impact of party philosophy, systemic political factors (electoral cycle, federalism) and technological factors (size of wired population).

Chapters 8 to 10 concentrate on the relationship between parties and the Internet in three democratising countries in different continents (Europe, Asia and Central America). Gabriel Badescu *et al.*'s chapter on Romania considers the development of democratisation in a former communist state, showing how the Internet is contributing to a stable and bi-directional flow of communication between citizens and political elites that is a necessary condition for democratic consolidation. The Internet has the potential to increase the quality and quantity of information exchanged between the public and elites. There is also an assessment of the use of the Internet within Romania, examining the 'supply' of information by the parties and political candidates. Attention is paid to the quality and quantity of information for each site, and how good the feedback is in each case.

Darren Wallis's study of Mexico (Chapter 9) presents an interesting case study of the impact of ICTs for at least two reasons. On the one hand, the proximity and influence of the US has meant that Mexico has absorbed ICTs more thoroughly than most other developing countries. At the same time, the introduction and use of ICTs as a tool of political communication – whether 'top-down' or 'interactive' – has occurred in an environment of democratisation of the party and electoral arenas. Democratisation produced institutional changes in the 1990s that facilitated the development and use of the net by parties and candidates. Once instituted, the net has in turn impacted on the democratisation process, and an analysis of this impact forms the main focus of the chapter. Using a variety of sources, such as party campaign pages, party documents, the press and a series of interviews, the focus is on the 2000 presidential campaign, which saw the first widespread use of the net for campaign purposes. The chapter considers the position of the web in relation to citizens' movements and groups, especially those that have a relationship to parties, and which played a key role in the transitional election of July 2000.

Rod Hague and Seung-Yong Uhm examine similar questions in relation to South Korea (Chapter 10). They focus specifically on comparing the online performance of political parties and Citizen Movement Groups (CMGs) and how this impacts on the wider concerns about the relationship between Korean civil society and political institutions. As with a number of the other chapters, the authors largely conclude that parties utilise the WWW for political marketing purposes and that the quality of online debate and interaction has been poor. However, they do note that for social movements the Internet is increasingly a useful tool for overcoming the problem of collective action.

Much media interest has been devoted to the so-called 'dark side' of the Internet; that is, its use by extremist parties and groups. In Chapter 11, Nigel Copsey examines the relationship between the extreme right and the Internet, focusing particularly on the British National Party's Internet strategy. The central questions considered in this chapter are why and in what ways has the extreme right increasingly targeted the Internet? What is its value for contemporary right-wing extremists? It also addresses the problem of control and whether these forms of activity can be effectively countered. The chapter begins by summarising the state of research already undertaken before tracing the origins and development of 'electronic fascism' from its earlier manifestations through to current technologies.

The final chapter, by the editors, draws together the debates from the various contributions, returning to the general themes and questions set out in this introduction and the opening chapter to provide an overall picture of the impact of new ICTs on party politics. It seeks to identify current trends in online political behaviour and the emerging patterns of party practice.

Note

1   By assessing the *impact* of new ICTs we are not intending to adopt a techno-logical determinist approach. Most of the chapters in this book stress the importance of social and political context and, as one would expect of social scientists, we favour a social shaping approach. What we are interested in, therefore, is the *relationship* between parties and ICTs.

References

Abramson, J., Arterton, C. and Orren, G. (1988) *The Electronic Commonwealth*, Cambridge, MA: Harvard University Press.

Bimber, B. (1998) 'The Internet and Political Transformation: Populism, Community and Accelerated Pluralism', *Polity*, XXXI, 1: 133–160.

Blumler, J. and Gurevitch, M. (1995) *The Crisis of Public Communication*, London: Routledge.

Dalton, R. and Wattenburg, M. (eds) (2000) *Parties Without Partisans: Political Change in Advanced Industrial Democracies*, Oxford: Oxford University Press.

Davis, R. (1999) *The Web of Politics*, Oxford: Oxford University Press.

Depla, P. and Tops, P. (1995) 'Political Parties in the Digital Era: The Techno-logical Challenge', in van de Donk, W.B.H.J., Snellen, I. and Tops, P.W. (eds), *Orwell in Athens: A Perspective on Informatization and Democracy*, Amsterdam: IOS Press, 155–177.

Erik-Lane, J. and Ersson, S. (1996) *European Politics*, London: Sage.

Geddes, A. and Tonge, J. (2001) 'Introduction', in Geddes, A. and Tonge, J. (eds), *Labour's Second Landslide: The British General Election of 2001*, Manchester: Manchester University Press, 1–8.

Gibson, R.K. and Ward, S.J. (2000) 'Conclusions: Modernising without Democratising?', in Gibson, R.K. and Ward, S.J. (eds), *Reinvigorating Democracy? British Politics and the Internet*, Aldershot: Ashgate, 205–212.

Jordan, G. (1998) 'Introduction – Politics Without Parties: A Growing Trend?', in Ridley, F. and Jordan, G. (eds), *Protest Politics: Cause Groups and Campaigns*, Oxford: Oxford University Press, 6–20.

Kaase, M. and Newton, K. (eds) (1995) *Beliefs in Government,* Oxford: Oxford University Press.

Katz, R. and Mair, P. (eds) (1994) *How Parties Organize: Change and Adaptation in Party Organisations in Western Democracies,* London: Sage.

Margolis, M. and Resnick, D. (2000) *Politics as Usual: The Cyberspace 'Revolution',* Thousand Oaks, California: Sage Publications.

Morris, D. (1999) *Vote.com,* Los Angeles: Renaissance Books.

Norris, P. (ed.) (1999) *Critical Citizens: Global Support for Democratic Governance,* Oxford: Oxford University Press.

Norris, P. (2000) *A Virtuous Circle,* Cambridge: Cambridge University Press.

Nye, J.S., Zelikow, P.D. and King, D.C. (1997) *Why People Don't Trust Government,* Cambridge, MA: Harvard University Press.

Putnam, R. (2001) *Bowling Alone,* New York: Simon & Schuster.

Richardson, J. (1995) 'Political Parties and the Challenge of Interest Groups', *West European Politics,* 18(1): 116–139.

Seyd, P. and Whiteley, P. (1992) *Labour's Grassroots: The Politics of Party Membership,* Oxford: Clarendon Press.

Topf, R. (1995) 'Electoral Participation', in Klingemann, H.D. and Fuchs, D. (eds), *Citizens and the State,* Oxford: Oxford University Press, 27–51.

1 Parties and the Internet

An overview

Stephen Ward, Rachel Gibson and Paul Nixon

Introduction

The task of this opening chapter is to introduce some of the main themes of the book by providing an overview of the current state of the literature and research on parties and the Internet. In doing so, our aim is to link Internet party research to the more general literature on political parties, covering themes such as party change, campaign communication and parties and democracy. Too often, Internet studies have been divorced from the pre-existing literature and have treated Internet usage as though it occurred in a vacuum. In particular, this chapter focuses on four key areas of parties' relations with the Internet:

- the growth of party Internet usage – why do parties go online and what are the political and technological factors explaining patterns of uptake?
- party campaigning and electioneering – is the Internet changing the style of politics and producing a new era of campaigning?
- party competition and party systems – how might the Internet affect electoral outcomes and the balance of power between parties? Is it likely to help new movements to challenge the status quo or existing players to bolster their power?
- Intra-party democracy and organisational change – what impact does the Internet have on the internal operation of parties? Will it produce more accountability of elites and increase participation? Or will it assist party bosses to bypass mid-level elites and party members altogether?

The growth and potential functions of websites: why parties go online

Although the level of Internet access is still patchy,[1] the growth of party websites has been rapid and global. From its origins in the 1994 US congressional elections, the Internet's use by parties has developed faster than any previous communication tool (Wring and Horrocks, 2000). By mid-2000, Norris (2001) found around 1,250 parties world-wide had moved online. In Europe and North America, there were often more than forty parties per country with websites, but even in developing countries there were often already twenty or more parties online. Thus, by 2000, in many countries, it was becoming more unusual for a party not to have a web presence. Whilst in many ways the patterns of party online activity matched intuitive expectations (more online in the rich established democracies), Norris also found that the level of technological development in societies was a better predicator of party uptake of the Internet than levels of democratisation.

Along with these macro-level factors, there are also potential benefits that encourage individual parties to create a web presence. The Internet is a multi-purpose tool and parties have developed a variety of functions for their sites. These can be summarised in three overlapping areas: administration; campaigning; participation and internal organisation. Of course, many party sites exploit all three.

- *The website as an administrative tool.* Websites can be used to provide considerable quantities of basic information for the public about a political party. Normally, party websites include information on organisational history, constitution or basic rules, policy documents, press and news stories, organisational information such as contact addresses, party structure, policy-making procedures. From a party perspective, the website can serve as a labour-saving device, reducing the number of telephone or postal enquiries. Parties are often inundated with requests for information from students, journalists and researchers and these can now be pointed towards the party website. In essence, the website acts as an archive or library resource.

- *The website as an active campaign tool.* Websites can also be developed more proactively as campaign communication tools, especially during election campaigns. Since many parties often claim that they do not receive coverage in the media, or that their message is distorted by news editors and journalists, via the Internet parties can become their own news producers and deliver the party's message unmediated to voters, thereby bypassing the traditional media (Nixon and Johansson, 1999a; Gibson and Ward, 2000a). Consequently, a website offers the chance for the party to set its own agenda. This is especially useful as journalists increasingly trawl the net looking for stories and regularly check party sites.[2] Not only can parties deliver a message directly to voters, but through the narrowcasting potential of the Internet, they can tailor their web pages and the information they send out to particular groups of voters or even individuals. Specific web pages can be provided for younger voters, women, environmentalists and so on, whilst cookies can be used to gather information on individual site visitors, so that parties can then deliver the material that best fits individual voters' concerns.

• *The website as a participatory and organisational tool.* Parties can also use the Internet to mobilise voters and encourage donations. Arguably, for those with access to the Internet it reduces the costs of participation by making it easier to join from the comfort of one's own home at the click of a button. However, ICTs have more potential than this. The interactive elements of the technology such as bulletin boards, chat rooms and email mean that it is now possible for parties to organise internal debates on a permanent, ongoing basis and hold electronic ballots on policies and positions within the party. Via the use of hypertext links the website also allows for organisational linkages and online networking between intra-party groups.

Although parties have developed many of these functions subsequent to their website creation, initially, most had rather more prosaic reasons for moving online. Indeed, at first, few had a clear strategy for using the web. Websites often emerged without political discussion from individuals within party headquarters, or members and volunteers (Löfgren, 2000; Gibson and Ward, 2000a). Cross-nationally, therefore, the two most common reasons for setting up a website are rather more mundane. First, the symbolic value of adopting new technology has been important. Parties have wanted to appear modern, relevant and up-to-date; not using the Internet might prove potentially embarrassing (Roper, 1999; Tops *et al.*, 2000). As one party webmaster commented, 'it [a website] is the mark of modernity'.[3] Similarly, peer pressure has been a considerable factor in party Internet use. Parties clearly copy each other. Newell (2001) found that in Italy:

> launching a site was clearly a kind of keeping up with the Jones's. That is parties launched sites simply because, as part of their more general communications strategy, it seemed essential to have a web presence as long as other parties had one.

In the US context, Selnow (1998) has referred to this as the 'me too' effect – everyone else has one so we want one too. Even though parties were uncertain of the tangible benefits, it seems that the risk of not having a website and so giving your opponents the edge was a greater stimulus to moving online. As Tops *et al.* (2000: 94) found, in the 1998 Dutch elections, the general consensus about having a website was 'if it does not do any good, it does not do any harm either'.

Party campaigning and elections: the Internet and the style of politics

Technological and communication developments, although not the only factors, clearly played an important role in shaping campaigning techniques over the twentieth century. One of the main areas where the Internet could have an impact is in the style of party campaigning. Although campaigning is commonly connected with electioneering, it has become an almost permanent feature of party activities (Bowler and Farrell, 1992). Here the literature on the development of campaign communication is useful in placing the growth of the Internet into a broader, long-term perspective. In order to understand the impact of the Internet we need to have some sense of the historical development of campaign techniques.

Trends in party campaigning and electoral style

In examining campaign communication in the post-war period, despite a plethora of differing labels, a relative consensus has developed around the 'professionalisation' or 'modernisation' of campaigning. Observers have identified a number of central trends in most liberal democracies since the 1960s (Bowler and Farrell, 1992; Kavanagh, 1995; Scammell, 1995, 1998; Wring, 1996; Farrell and Webb, 2000; Norris, 2000). These are outlined below.

- The increasing dominance of the media, particularly television, in the conduct of campaigns: television has become the major means of communication between politician and voter and parties/candidates have increasingly focused their campaigns around television performance and attempts to set the media's agenda.
- The increased use of political marketing techniques: as parties have tried to extend their appeal beyond their traditional sectional or class boundaries in the classic catch-all fashion, more importance has been placed on attempts to present and sell party/candidate policies to voters. Parties have therefore increasingly adopted techniques developed in the business sector, using soundbites and advertising slogans, as well as market testing their policy stances (products) through surveys.
- An influx of political consultants: in order to maximise marketing techniques, advisors from outside political parties have been brought in to assist with the conduct of campaigns. Parties have employed advertising agencies, media experts, journalists and opinion pollsters to advise on the presentation of policies and to gather feedback from voters.

The upshot of such developments can be seen in three areas.

- Party organisation: changes in campaigning have enhanced the idea of centralisation of control within parties and further undermined the notion of parties as vehicles of mass mobilisation. For example, television has arguably enhanced personality politics and focused on the role of political leaders. Election campaigning has become more standardised at a national level, leading to the downgrading of party activists and increased centralised control over local campaigns.
- The focus of campaigning: the style of campaigning has arguably moved away from substantive policy/issue focused towards a more personality-led focus. This in turn has led to increases in the levels of negative or attack advertising. Similarly, adopting marketing techniques and use of media for advertising have allegedly brought about a reduction in both the depth and length of campaign content, as the emphasis has turned to summarising the party/candidate message.
- Relationship between voter and party: as parties become less focused on mobilising their core voters or appealing to specific sectors of the public, increasingly, they have designed catch-all appeals to maximise their vote. Whilst to some extent this meant paying more attention to voter preferences, as the focus of the campaign moved to national television studios, there was a corresponding reduction in the levels of personal interaction between politicians and voters. Voters increasingly became passive spectators in the campaign process (Norris, 2000).

Such trends have also been caught up in a further debate concerning the notion of 'Americanisation' (Kavanagh, 1995; Negrine and Papathanassopoulos, 1996; Swanson and Mancini, 1996). It has been argued that collectively these features of 'professionalisation' have developed furthest and fastest in the USA and have subsequently been transferred or spread through most other democracies. Critics of the 'Americanisation' thesis, whilst not necessarily disagreeing with many of its features, have argued that, more accurately, such trends might be labelled as a facet of globalisation (Scammell, 1998). Moreover, they have also noted that distinct differences in electoral campaigning remain and that explanations for the changes in campaign styles are to be found in combinations of economic development, political culture, national party systems and electoral rules, which all shape campaigning styles.

Campaign styles and the potential of the Internet

One of the key questions about the emergence of new ICTs, such as the Internet, has been their potential impact on the trends outlined above. Their development in the 1990s, along with the fragmentation of the news media, has led some to argue that the modernisation process has developed a stage further into a new 'post-modern' era of campaigning

(Farrell and Webb, 2000; Norris, 2000). Here, campaigning is more or less permanent, with professional consultants assuming a central role in continuously interpreting and monitoring public opinion, attempting to manage the news output for politicians, and shaping and marketing policies in light of public preferences. Increasingly, in the post-modern era, voters are viewed as customers or clients and policies as products, with the product becoming less sacrosanct and more malleable as parties seek to reflect customer (voter) preferences (see Chapter 5). It has been argued that new ICTs will be a primary tool in providing the direct link in communicating citizen preferences to politicians. No longer will it be a case of candidates pushing their message onto the public, but through the interactive potential of new ICTs, citizens will have a greater ability to shape the campaign agenda and party strategies. Furthermore, precisely because the political communication environment of the 1990s became considerably more fragmented and also because of the potential for interactivity, the campaigns process has become even more complex for politicians to manage (Morris, 1999). Thus the impact of the Internet may bring new possibilities, but also signal a return to more traditional forms of campaigning, notably, in four areas in particular.

- Substantive information-based campaigning: the professionalisation of campaigning has pointed towards the development of marketing- and soundbite-led politics. It is possible to see the Internet not necessarily reversing this trend, but at least complementing or compensating it. Given the amount of information a website can store and its unmediated nature, it is possible for parties to provide voters with much more information about policy and organisation than through other media formats.
- Personalised campaigning: the development of catch-all parties appealing to large sections of the electorate via national media (television)-based campaigns has led to parties putting across a limited number of basic messages to all voters in an attempt to encapsulate their campaign. The Internet's narrowcasting possibilities and the ability of parties to identify and track their website users mean that there is considerable potential to target groups of voters, tailor messages to particular sections of the electorate and even personalise messages for individual voters through the use of cookies or email.
- Interactive campaigning: much prominence has been given to the allegedly revolutionary interactive nature of the new ICTs to transform campaigning. The Internet offers parties a low-cost and very direct way to seek the immediate feedback from voters on their policy preferences that is crucial to the modern marketing of politics. Party websites could clearly exploit this potential by incorporating online surveys, chat rooms, staging live dialogue sessions between voters and leading politicians and using email to create supporter discussion net-

works to mobilise and share campaign ideas. This would allow what Martin and Geiger (1999) refer to as a relational strategy, where the Internet is used to build and maintain relationships with a huge number of individuals at any one time and react instantaneously to voter preferences (see Chapter 5).

- Decentralised campaigning: in contrast to the centralising influences of the traditional media on campaign conduct, the Internet has been seen as a force for decentralisation. The comparative cheapness of the technology allows many more people to become publishers of information, creating the opportunity for candidates, local parties and individual members to produce their own sites, with the increased chance of fostering a platform for dissenting voices. Klotz has argued that in the US system:

> Web campaigning will likely further strengthen the trend toward individualised campaigns. Party affiliation of candidates is seldom featured prominently ... Through a website, each individual candidate enjoys a new capacity to communicate personal information and provide widely accessible, individualised issue platforms.
>
> (1997: 485)

In short, the sheer volume of information and turnover of sites may mean that it is more difficult for parties to exercise control over their campaigns.

Research evidence

There is a growing body of party-website research from an increasing range of countries that has examined the possibilities set out above, though many of these empirical studies have yet to be linked to the theoretical campaign communication literature. Support for the substantive campaign scenario can be found in the fact that the majority of website studies have suggested that parties and candidates in a wide range of countries have all supplied information-heavy sites with considerable policy and organisational detail (Birdsell and Muzzio, 1997; Margolis *et al.*, 1997, 1999; Gibson and Ward, 1998, 2000a and 2000b; Nixon and Johansson, 1999a and 1999b; Voerman, 1999; Newell, 2001). Yet, alternatively, others have suggested that party web use is increasingly geared towards the trivial, arguing that sites have become content-light electronic brochures or billboards, focusing instead on the use of audio-visual clips, graphics and gimmicks to attract and retain visitors (Stone, 1996).[4] A number of the US presidential and British party election sites have incorporated online games into their sites (Coleman, 2001), and Roper (1999) reports that one party in New Zealand offered prizes to website visitors.

In fact, it seems it is not simply a case of substance *or* trivia, but substance *and* trivia. Parties can provide both gimmicks and soundbites along with serious policy information. Whilst initially the Internet was very much a text-based medium, parties are beginning to experiment with audio-visual elements. It also seems that the behaviour of online browsers is beginning to influence website design. Browsers jump around pages and move in and out of sites quickly, looking for the information they require before moving on. When interviewed in 1999, several UK party webmasters commented that on average visitors spend between one and five minutes per visit and may browse no more than the homepage and one other page.[5] As a result, UK parties began to redesign their sites on the basis of less text, more white background space with banner headlines and soundbites. However, this does not necessarily indicate a trend towards trivialisation or a content-light approach. Perhaps the beauty of a website is that parties can offer both substance and glitz all in one site and the voter can choose how far, and where, to go.

One further element to the substance versus trivia debate is the prominence of negative advertising. Initially, it was feared that the lack of editorial control on the Internet might promote increases in personalised and negative campaigning. Whilst Klotz (1997) found such fears unfounded in the 1998 congressional elections, by 2000 Schneider found that the amount of negative advertising had increased, with some candidates setting up attack sites dedicated to lambasting their opponents. This may primarily be a US phenomenon.[6] Whilst mirror and spoof sites are becoming more popular elsewhere and some limited evidence of negative campaigning can be found in Australia and the UK,[7] in European multi-party systems negative campaigning has been largely absent so far (Carlson and Djupsund, 1999; Voerman, 1999). Voerman argues that, in the Dutch context, it makes little sense to attack parties who may end up being your governing partners after an election.

Parties have also certainly recognised, at least rhetorically, the potential of the net to narrowcast and personalise messages but have so far limited their use of it. As early as 1996, Bob Dole's US presidential campaign used cookies to gather information on, and deliver information to, voters (Rash, 1997). Certainly, parties and candidates have long since viewed the Internet as a potential means of targeting the youth vote (Centre for Policy Studies, 1998; Richards, 1999; Labour Coordinating Committee, 1997). Younger voters are often the most computer literate within societies but the least likely to turnout in elections. In the 1997 UK election, Labour's site was managed within the remit of the youth campaign team, whilst in 2001 it produced a separate site entitled 'RU UP 4 IT', aimed specifically at mobilising younger voters.[8] US presidential candidate Al Gore also ran a series of online forums for young voters in the 2000 campaign and one can also see some evidence of youth-focused targeting during the 1999 EU elections (Nixon and Johansson, 1999b).[9] However, though parties recognise the potential, they have been fairly cautious in their attempts to personalise their messages. There is still unease at the use of cookies to gather information on voters and also to send voters unsolicited email for fear of voter backlash. Moreover, the traditional media, particularly television, still dominate party communication and therefore parties are wary of confusing voters by producing too many targeted messages. In the medium term, the priority for parties is towards integrating their offline message into their online campaign. As one of the UK Conservative Party web managers explained in relation to election campaigns:

> consistency of message is everything: only if parties retain a laser like focus on their themes of the day can they hope to cut through all of that day's political activity and get their message across. Given that virtually everyone still gets their news from TV, radio or the print media, parties have to broadcast. They cannot yet narrowcast effectively – and, if they could, any message they sent would often cut across the majority of messages reaching a voter that day through the broadcast outlets. In short, if you are watching the Conservatives talk about health on TV, hearing about it on the radio and reading about it in the papers, it would be inappropriate to visit our website that day and be told what we think about defence.
>
> (Jackson, 2001: 26–27)

If parties have used narrowcasting cautiously, then they have been even more sparing in their use of interactivity, although they are increasingly using email and online question and answer sessions and interviews with leading party politicians. In particular, the Swedish parties have been early pioneers of this approach. In the 1998 elections, the Social Democrats hired staff to answer all emails personally and conducted over seventy live chats with leading politicians. Generally, however, most communication from websites is still one-way top-down, not two-way interactive (Gibson and Ward, 1998, 2000a, 2000b; Margolis *et al.*, 1997, 1999; Davis, 1999; Gibson *et al.*, 2000). Even where voters do get a chance to interact it is still on the parties' terms not the voters'. Survey evidence has indicated a distinct reluctance for parties too engage in open, two-way dialogue with voters on their own websites (Kamarck, 1999; Davis 1999; Stromer-Galley *et al.*, 2001). This should not come as a surprise. There are good reasons why parties have not engaged extensively in this type of activity. Opening up one's site to comment through bulletin boards or chat rooms is a risky business (see Chapter 10). Why allow one's opponents the opportunity of free access to advertise their party or abuse your party on your site? Moreover, the quality of open debating forums is relatively poor (Hill and Hughes, 1998; Streck, 1999; Nixon and Johansson, 1999b; Voerman and Ward, 2000), with a limited and self-selecting audience, the utility of any feedback for parties is relatively circumscribed. In short, currently, the risks of interactivity outweigh the gains.

Since in many countries the majority of candidates or local parties have still to move online it seems a little early to judge definitively the impact of the net (see below for figures). Whilst there has been more candidate activity in the USA, this experience may be comparatively unique since its party ties are much looser and political campaigning is more candidate-based. Whilst individual candidate sites are likely to become more common over time, thereby providing more information on candidates than has been previously available, there are good reasons for believing this is unlikely substantially to shift control to local parties or candidates in party-centred systems. First, national party headquarters have more access to resources and staff than do individual candidates or local parties who, for the most part, are reliant on volunteers to run their sites. Moreover, the use of new ICTs to appeal directly to voters from party elites would seem to further erode their reliance on local activists and party branches. The party message can be easily delivered via websites and email from central headquarters straight into voters' homes. Second, even where candidates have run online campaigns they have still been largely wedded to the party message, rather than to developing their own individual views. They are wary of journalists exposing candidates who are 'off-message' and in turn risking the wrath of party bosses (Earnshaw, 2001; Ward and Gibson, 2003).

Finally, much media attention has been devoted to online campaign fundraising particularly in the context of the US presidential campaigns. John McCain's 2000 presidential campaign attracted considerable column inches for its alleged success in raising money from new sources via the Internet and email. It was claimed that McCain raised US$3.7 million online but the figures are very difficult to verify and have been contested. Indeed, the focus on online fundraising as a major function of the net may be slightly misplaced. Compared with other means of fundraising these sums are still small. More to the point, despite the balleyhoo surrounding McCain's supposed success online, he still lost. Still, online fundraising is likely to be much more significant in the USA than in many other countries. Surveys of European parties find a much more circumspect approach to fundraising. In the UK, parties have raised money online and for some smaller parties, such as the SNP and Sinn Fein, raising funds from expatriates overseas has undoubtedly been made easier. However, in much of continental Europe, where state funding for parties exists, appeals for online donations are virtually non-existent (Voerman, 1999; Tops *et al.*, 2000; Gibson *et al.*, 2000).[10]

So far, parties have been circumspect in their online electioneering, using the Internet to do what parties have always done in elections. In the main, the web has been used as a supplementary communication tool aimed particularly at mobilising sympathisers or opinion-formers, such as journalists, rather than ordinary voters. Whilst initially little effort or importance was attached to party sites, the evidence from a range of recent elections suggests that parties are beginning to integrate it into their mainstream campaigns, sites are becoming more professional and increasing amounts of finance are being given over to new-media campaigning.

Party systems and inter-party competition: the impact of the Internet on outcomes

Whilst changes in campaign communication style are important, a potentially more intriguing question is the impact of the Internet on campaign outcomes and the balance of power between political parties. Does it make some parties more competitive than previously? Will it upset party systems uniformly, or more dramatically in democratising any one-party states?

Trends in inter-party competition

Globally, there has been a growth in the number of parties, not least as there has been an increasing shift towards multi-party democracies. The collapse of communism in Eastern Europe and the former Soviet Union has already led to increased levels of competition, with new parties forming, splintering and disappearing rapidly. Notwithstanding this overall trend towards democratisation, however, inter-party competition in Western democracies, according to the recent literature, is in decline. The convergence of parties of the left and the right on the 'catch-all' model during the 1950s and 1960s (Kirchheimer, 1966) meant that big battles between the political parties were put behind them, as both sides attempted to broaden their electorate and moved closer to the median voter à la Downs (1957). The new goal of parties was to govern effectively, rather than to secure the interests of rival social and economic sections within society as the mass-based party sought to do (Duverger, 1954; Michels, [1911] 1954).

The rise of the cartel party (Katz and Mair, 1994, 1995) in the decades following has seen a further reduction in the level of competition as the major political parties have become quasi agents of the state and have colluded to ensure their ongoing survival and success. This collusion has taken the form of state subventions to political parties, which are often tied towards previous electoral performance and privileged access to the increasingly state-regulated media. Indeed, in some instances, it is claimed, parties will protect the other members of the cartel by striking 'non-aggression' electoral pacts, or distributing some of the spoils of office to those out of power (Katz and Mair, 1995: 20).

As Katz and Mair point out, such decreasing access to political power poses 'barriers to the emergence of new groups [and means that] those on the margins may be neglected' (1995: 15). The collusion and

limitation of competition takes place between the larger and more established political parties, which leads to a situation where 'the state ...
becomes an institutionalised structure of support, sustaining insiders
while excluding outsiders' (ibid: 16).

The situation, however, is not frozen, as Katz and Mair are at pains to
point out. The party systems of democracies, since their formation, have
been through a process of adaptation and change. Each system has, in a
Marxist dialectical sense, sowed the seeds of its own decline and cartelisa-
tion is no exception. In shutting out 'real' opposition, the parties have
generated an anti-party, anti-establishment momentum in many countries
such as the USA, Austria, Belgium, Germany, the Netherlands and
Sweden, as typified by the Perot phenomenon and parties such as the
Freedom Party, the Flemish Block, the Republikaner and New Democracy,
which are growing in strength (see Chapter 11). By operating as a
cartel, by attempting to ensure that there are no clear 'winners' and
'losers' among the established alternatives and by exploiting their control
of the state to generate resources that can be shared out amongst themselves, the cartel parties are often unwittingly providing precisely the
ammunition with which new protesters can more effectively wage their
wars (ibid: 24).

Inter-party competition, party systems and the potential of the Internet

The impact of ICTs on the party competition and party systems has
already been contested. Broadly two schools of thought have emerged.
One predicts a potential opening up of party systems, increasing competition and, in particular, a levelling (or equalising) of the communication
playing field. Whereas, the other suggests the impact of the Internet is
likely to be limited, if not negligible, and may even strengthen the major
party players over time (see Chapters 3 and 4).

The equalisation thesis, pushed by cyber-enthusiasts, is based on the
ability of small or fringe parties to exploit the relatively low costs of the
medium, the lack of editorial control and supposedly non-hierarchical
nature of the Internet (Bonchek, 1995; Rash 1997; Corrado and Firestone,
1997). Thus, with relatively few skills and resources a minor party can have
just as sophisticated a site as a governing party and sit alongside it in cyberspace. Minor parties that previously received little or no coverage in the
traditional media now have a platform from which to reach a much larger
audience of voters. Thus Rash argues that 'if any force in American politics has levelled the playing field for the traditional major political parties
and groups with views somewhat outside the mainstream it is the presence
of the nets' (1997: 88). Although the equalisation thesis has been derived
from a liberal democratic, particularly a US, context, the idea of equalisation could have an even greater impact in one-party states. Here, cyber-
enthusiasts have argued that the Internet has the ability to undermine

undemocratic or authoritarian regimes, since they will find it extremely difficult to control information flows via the Internet. What is more, it is becoming easier for opponents of authoritarian regimes to organise and put information online anonymously. It is possible to set up sites outside nation-state boundaries that are then not subject to state censorship and can be accessed from inside an undemocratic country (see Chapter 9).

Naysayers have, however, challenged the basis of such claims, arguing that the Internet is not that different from, and indeed is reliant on, the traditional media. They have suggested that although the Internet may have once been a playground for all sorts of fringe movements, gradually the net is being commercialised and normalised, so that it is increasingly coming to resemble the offline world (Resnick, 1999). 'Normalisers' have noted that running increasingly sophisticated and design-conscious sites is not necessarily cheap. Hence, the more powerful mainstream parties with greater resources – both financial and staff – have the time and money to outperform fringe players (Lynch, 1996; Margolis *et al.*, 1997, 1999). Resnick argues that 'if we ask which political parties and candidates are likely to provide sophisticated web sites, the answer is clear: those who command the resources to hire the talent to produce them' (1999: 63). Furthermore, the net does not exist in a vacuum divorced from the tradi-tional media. Here the existing powerful party actors have a considerable advantage. They can advertise their sites in many more places and on many more occasions in the newspapers and on TV than can the minor parties. Nor is it simply the commercial or financial aspects of power that might undermine any democratising or equalising tendencies of the Inter-net. Governing parties, recognising the decentralist and democratic implications of the Internet for mass communication, could attempt to regulate or control access to the new media by their rivals. This could involve the introduction of government regulation of the amount of server space given to political parties by Internet service providers (ISPs). At the extreme, this could lead to certain parties being deemed anti-democratic and losing their right to publish information on the Inter-net.[11] In one-party states, close monitoring of online access and restriction of ISPs could reduce the potency of internal online dissent.

Research evidence

Whilst we are still in the formative stages of Internet usage, there is an increasing amount of research evidence emerging from North America and Europe in the form of website-content surveys and public-opinion data on Internet usage, both of which can provide some early pointers.

In support of the equalisation thesis, smaller fringe parties certainly tend to be the most enthusiastic about proclaiming the value of ICTs (see Chapters 3, 4 and 11). The US Natural Law Party has recently claimed that the Internet is 'the single most important element in growing a political party today'. A number of fringe parties, in both Europe and the USA, have also pointed to the practical benefits of the Internet in terms of mobilisation and organisation. As early as 1997, one far-right party in the UK also claimed that its website had been a significant tool for attracting finance, allowing it to stand more candidates in elections (Ward and Gibson, 1998). Hill and Hughes (1998) found that the Internet was more open to non-mainstream groups and points of view than the traditional media (1998: 180). Their sample of 100 US sites found around one-fifth from fringe organisations. Whilst many of these sites had a low profile, Hill and Hughes concluded that 'the fringes of politics absolutely cannot be ignored on the world wide web' (1998: 176).

However, the bulk of survey evidence tends to conclude that the major parties dominate cyberspace as they do the traditional media. They have more sites, their online profile is higher, the links into their sites are greater, they are updated more frequently and the overall levels of sophistication, such as use of multi-media elements, all tend to outstrip their fringe counterparts (Margolis *et al.*, 1997; 1999; Gibson *et al.*, 2000, 2002). Though in some systems the process of normalisation is not necessarily inexorable. In the UK, Gibson and Ward (1998; 2000a; 2000b) have found that there have been ebbs and flows in competition. In election periods, parliamentary parties, rather than just governing parties, do tend to outperform outsider parties by spending more resources on their sites. Whereas, in peacetime, when sites have often become dormant, fringe parties can narrow the gap. Furthermore, patterns are not necessarily uniform: some small parties can run relatively sophisticated online campaigns that rival those of the mainstream. For example, Green parties in a number of countries have produced fairly advanced sites (Gibson and Ward, 2000b, 2002; Voerman and Ward, 2000), suggesting that it is not simply size or resources that produce differences between parties, but incentives to use the technology may also account for key differences. For instance, Green parties' incentives for using the technology are higher since their traditional bastions of support (universities, teaching and public-sector professions) tend to be the very people with access to the technology.

Yet if the Internet is to have significant impact, it would not only have to equalise the communication playing field, but this would then have to alter the balance of support for parties. So far, the majority of the opinion-based research has been conducted in the USA. Nevertheless, there appears to be a growing consensus again favouring a limited-change thesis. The general picture that emerges from opinion-based research is as follows.

- The limited appeal of political party websites: relatively small numbers of people actively search out the party sites. Recent Eurobarometer data suggests that around 10 per cent of those with access to the Internet in EU countries have visited a party site in 2000 (Norris, 2003). In the 2000 US elections around 8 per cent visited candidate sites and similar percentage (7 per cent) was reported in the Danish general election of 1998.[12] Evidence from the 2001 UK elections suggested that party sites had even more limited appeal with only 2 per cent of the public bothering to access them (Crabtree, 2001).

- In general, the audience for party sites tends to be sympathisers, the politically committed or those with a developed interest in politics. In short, it is more likely to be those already active in politics (Norris, 2000, 2001).
- Party websites are not making much difference to voting patterns; they do not seem to change people's minds. Focus-group studies in the UK, Sweden and the Netherlands have found mixed reactions to the sites (Nixon and Johansson, 1999a; Crabtree, 2001). Poor-quality sites were clearly deemed a liability and many voters had high expectations drawn from their experiences of using private-sector business websites. Yet, in the British study, even where voters thought sites were useful, they were sanguine about the impact on their actual vote.
- Younger voters are more likely to use the web politically, perhaps not surprisingly given that they are the computer-literate generation. Hence, there may be some small hope for the cyber-enthusiasts here, since as numbers online grow and the generational shift takes place, online sources should become more important (Coleman, 2001). However, whether parties can attract these younger voters remains to be seen. For online political information, the public still tends to gravitate towards media sites such as CNN or the BBC, names that are familiar offline, rather than go direct to the parties.[13]

It is not just in liberal-democratic states that the equalisation thesis has come under scrutiny. The much-vaunted ability of the Internet to challenge one-party regimes has recently been challenged by empirical studies. Superficial media evidence suggested that the Internet played a significant role in undermining a number of regimes, including Mexico, Indonesia and Serbia, and has made life difficult for the Chinese and Cuban authorities (Hill and Sen, 2000; Williamson, 2000; Kalathil and Boas, 2001). Closer analysis reveals a more mixed picture. Certainly, the Internet has proved to be a useful tool for democratic campaigners. In countries such as Malaysia, Singapore and Indonesia the Internet, and email particularly, has proved a useful means of speeding up communication flows in periods of political crisis thereby accelerating demonstrations and oppositions (Ferdinand, 2001). Externally, it has also been useful in publicising issues for a global audience as with the Zapatista movement in Mexico (see Chapter 9). The Internet did not, however, create democratic opposition or overthrow regimes. It was useful but not crucial.

Nor is the Internet simply a tool for democratisers. It is worth remembering that authoritarian regimes are not helpless in the face of new communication tools. Increasingly, they are using censorship, regulation, and are also using the technology themselves to produce their own propaganda. Since such regimes often have best access to technology and to more resources than their opponents, at least internally they can have an initial advantage (Taubman, 1998). Rodan concluded from his study of Singapore that:

> against the liberal expectation of the Internet as a force for erosion of authoritarian states ... this study suggests a very different proposition must be taken seriously: such technology can also be harnessed by some states to consolidate a climate of fear and intimidation and create new opportunities to disseminate propaganda and information in their favor.
>
> (1998: 89)

The overall impact on competition online produces a fairly sober analysis. The Internet is not, as yet, capable of producing fundamental change to party systems, certainly not on its own. However, this does not necessarily mean that the Internet will have no impact. First, the Internet does seem to lower start-up costs for parties. Hence, it makes it easier to organise and sustain small parties. As Dalton and Wattenburg note:

> Small and new parties may also find it easier to organise than ever before. A small group of like minded individuals who in the past might have been too geographically dispersed to organise a party should find fewer obstacles in the world of the Internet which knows no geographic boundaries.
>
> (2000: 281)

Second, it does provide a presence for fringe actors, so that if offline opportunities or publicity allow, they have a platform. This may help produce unusual electoral results from time to time. The much-cited election of political outsider Jesse Ventura as Governor of Minnesota provides a clue. Ventura used the net to organise rapid supporter networks from scratch. However, the Internet alone did not sway the result. Ventura, having been a pro-wrestler, already had a high public profile and Minnesota was already a much more wired-up state than most others. Overall, ICTs alone do not level the playing field in established liberal democracies. For the most part, the main parties still hold the aces. Third, in newly democratised countries, however, the Internet may be able to make more of an impact, since party systems and the parties themselves are less well entrenched and more susceptible to technological change. Finally, the Internet and other ICTs can be useful in destabilising one-party regimes, but only in the context of a political/economic crisis and/or longer-term social change.

Participation and intra-party democracy: party organisation and the potential of the Internet

So far this chapter has dealt mainly with the party–voter relationship; however, it is plausible to suggest that Internet-based technology might have a greater impact internally within parties since, as we have noted, the political use of the Internet appeals more to those who are already active. Hence, there may be a more significant audience of users for party sites amongst members/activists than amongst the ordinary public. Use of ICTs for intra-party democracy purposes has attracted particular interest in the current climate of falling membership and reduced activism. As a result, some have seen the use of ICTs as a means of reinvigorating parties or re-engaging with party grassroots whilst others have seen increased application of ICTs as bringing further radical changes to the character of political parties and style of internal democracy.

Trends in the intra-party arena

Survey data from across Western Europe has indicated falling levels of membership (as a proportion of the electorate) and declining levels of party activism since the 1970s (Seyd and Whiteley, 1992; Katz and Mair, 1994; Scarrow, 1996; Dalton and Wattenburg, 2000). Most of the European models of party change in the post-war period (catch-all, electoral, professional and cartel models) have pointed towards a general weakening of collective forms of participation and significant changes in the role of grassroots supporters. The literature suggests that although party members may have gained more individual rights (votes and ballots), on a collective level, grassroots extra-parliamentary groups and mid-level party elites have been marginalised by party leaderships and parties have become more centralised. Such changes in intra-party behaviour have been stimulated by a variety of external and internal sources.

Social structural changes in post-war Western Europe, the lessening of clear class divisions, the emergence of class and partisan dealignment, meant that parties were no longer able to rely on in-depth recruitment and mobilisation from particular sections within society (Kirchheimer, 1966). Moreover, parties were no longer seen as the sole vehicle for participation in politics. The rise of interest groups and indeed other non-political leisure activities led to parties facing competition for support (Richardson, 1995). The erosion of strong societal-party ties meant that in order to win elections, parties needed to build wider but shallower coalitions of support. Parties responded by marginalising party members in favour of general cross-class appeals to the electorate as a whole, based around party effectiveness in office and the appeal of the party leadership rather than party ideology or policy.

As parties appealed in more general terms to the electorate and membership recruitment became less of a priority, parties became less reliant financially on individual members. As their memberships fell, parties increasingly looked elsewhere to fill the funding gap. Whilst some parties encouraged larger individual donations and support from organised interest groups, the cartel model of party change also notes the increasing reliance of major parties on state funding (Katz and Mair, 1995).

If societal changes provided a stimulus for party adaptation, then the rise of the mass electronic media provided the means by which to appeal directly to the electorate on a national basis. As we have noted above, the impact of the mass media on intra-party affairs has arguably resulted in reducing the importance of traditional types of campaign activity carried about by grassroots activists. The reduced emphasis on local campaigning has moved the focus of activity to central-party staff and national politicians. In short, campaigning has become a much more capital- rather than labour-intensive process (ibid; Wring, 1996; Farrell and Webb, 2000).

As the role of members has become more marginalised and party elites less reliant on the grassroots, so their role in intra-party affairs has altered. The traditional mass-party model, built on a large membership, viewed intra-party democracy as a collective, delegatory, bottom-up process, with a strong role for members, local parties and local elites. Both the catch-all and cartel models of party change have pointed to a different type of intra-party democracy based around a more individualised and atomised model of participation (Katz and Mair, 1995; Lipow and Seyd, 1996). The catch-all model viewed intra-party affairs as being largely a top-down process controlled by party elites. Party leaders were no longer simply accountable to activists, but to the wider membership and the electorate generally. Although their traditional role of mobilising, recruiting and campaigning for the party has become less central, individual party members could still be regarded as a resource by the leadership, particularly when they face challenges from extra-parliamentary groups or mid-level elites. Here, party elites may appeal directly to party members for support, bypassing local parties.

The cartel party model emphasises still further the role of individual members. They may be given more formal rights to participate through direct postal ballots on policy issues, leadership and candidate selection; however, this does not necessarily make leaders more accountable or the process more democratic: first, because the participative agenda and candidate choice is often restricted by party elites; second, it can be argued that atomised party members are unlikely to build a stable platform to challenge party leaders; and third, increasingly, the lines between formal party members and informal supporters are blurred, with parties encouraging donations, and participation from non-party members. Katz and

Mair have argued that mutual autonomy or stratarchy is beginning to exist, where local party officials may be discouraged from intervening in national party affairs but are given a relatively free hand in local affairs (1995: 20–21).

Intra-party change and the Internet

Though the Internet may not have matured as a means of political communication, it is possible to hypothesise on the likely impact of the new medium in the medium to long term. Once again, use of the new media in intra-party affairs could lead to differing scenarios. On the one hand, the advent of ICTs may support the weakening or atomising membership still further. Alternatively, it may also provide opportunities for the party members to extend their participation and even provide platforms for networking and dissent.

At one level, the Internet can be used for recruitment purposes to increase and maintain membership. From a rational-choice perspective, arguably, the Internet lowers the barriers (costs) to participation for individuals from more marginal and excluded groups. Political activity such as information gathering, joining organisations or directly contacting political institutions and organisations could become far easier and quicker (Bonchek, 1995). The arrival of set-top boxes and Internet TV could allow the house-bound, such as the elderly, single parents and the disabled, to participate more easily from their homes. It could also be employed to recruit new members from sections of the community that are less attracted through traditional media, and less likely to join political parties.

Even if we accepted that the Internet might enhance recruitment, whether it would strengthen the party grassroots is debatable (Tan, 1997). One could reasonably argue that any new members recruited via the Internet would have weak attachments to their local party. This is partly because the impersonal nature of the Internet would lessen face-to-face contact with other local activists/members, which is important in developing patterns of socialisation and collective action within local parties (Harmel and Tan, 1997). Additionally, if recruitment is controlled centrally through the national party site, it would again reduce links with the local party. Consequently, there is potential to create larger, but possibly more passive, memberships, with allegiances being thus concentrated at the national level (Seyd and Whiteley, 1992; Whiteley *et al.*, 1994).

A further potential impact of the Internet concerns levels of participation. Individual members could be encouraged to advance their views directly to party elites. The interactivity of the Internet, in the form of email, provides members with an additional and speedier mechanism to voice their opinions on party policy and organisation. The party could put large amounts of policy information/documents online and encourage feedback directly from members. Similarly, leading party figures could engage in debate and question sessions with ordinary members. Parties across Europe have already experimented with online discussion and online ballots and many now operate internal computer networks (Intranets), which are accessed via subscription by party members and staff, encouraging debate and exchanges of information (see Chapter 6). However, such possibilities tend to be largely based on a top-down, individualised model of party activity, which may not strengthen the position of the party grassroots to challenge elites.

Yet the Internet does offer some opportunities to increase collective participation also. Intra-party groups can develop their own independent patterns of participation and activity. Because of the decentralised nature of the Internet, intra-party groups, such as constituency parties, could publish their views to national and indeed global audiences without central party assistance/interference. Such autonomous websites could provide a platform for intra-party groups to network and in some areas act as fora for dissent and challenges to the official party line.

Research evidence

Research on internal party uses of ICTs is somewhat limited, but again some common patterns have emerged from studies. Obviously, for any of the scenarios outlined above to occur parties are required to be thoroughly wired up throughout the organisation, not simply at the national level. Evidence suggests that it is central headquarters and regional party offices, the party leadership and bureaucracy that are best placed and make the most use of the technology (Lynch, 1996; Smith, 1998, 2000). After all, they have more resources and full-time officials. Parliamentary parties and MPs follow but depend more on systemic features. In the federal, candidate-oriented, USA it has become the norm for representatives and senators to have sites. Around 90 per cent of senate candidates and 65 per cent of House candidates had websites in the 2000 congressional elections. In the more national-party-oriented UK many fewer MPs bother with sites. At the local level constituency and branch party activity is still very much a minority activity, although growing. A survey of UK constituency sites for the main Conservative and Labour parties found around 5–10 per cent online in 1998; by the general election of 2001 this figure had risen to somewhere around 20–25 per cent (Gibson and Ward, 1999; Ward and Gibson, 2003).

The impact of the web on increasing membership seems doubtful so far. Membership data has not shown any sustained rise since the arrival of the Internet in the mid-1990s and parties are often reluctant to provide exact figures of online recruitment. Interview and questionnaire data suggest, however, that the parties view the Internet as a reasonably beneficial recruiting tool, particularly during election campaigns (Gibson and Ward, 2000b, 2002; Gibson *et al.*, 2002). In the USA where parties/

candidates are regularly required to build and rebuild supporter networks the Internet may be a more useful tool simply because of its speed and efficiency and also because of the viral effect of email chains/pyramids. Interestingly, in the UK, the Labour Party has used its site prominently to recruit volunteers and supporters along with members. Hence, one can register support and help out in campaigns, but without having to commit to full membership, but neither does one then gain full membership rights (Margetts, 2001). Parties may come to rely on this sort of short-term, ad-hoc supporter as much as they do traditional members. Overall, it is quite possible that Internet and email recruitment are gradually replacing some existing methods of joining such as direct mail and letter writing, rather than significantly increasing party membership.

There is as yet limited evidence examining the impact of Computer Mediated Communication (CMC) on participation and internal discussion, though several studies have been conducted in European parties that have produced broadly similar findings (Gibson and Ward, 1999; Löfgren, 2000; Voerman and Ward, 2000; Pedersen, 2001). Pedersen found that application of new technology within the Danish parties did not significantly enhance participation rates. Although younger members were more likely to use them than other methods of participating, this was balanced by the fact that women were significantly less likely to. This follows the pattern of earlier experiments with teledemocracy in Canadian parties where the use of telephones for internal leadership ballots failed to increase turnout or extend participation (Cross, 1998). Studies also indicate that online party discussion fora tended to be dominated by small numbers of members or headquarters staff who were already active, and often knew each other offline anyway. Politicians and party elites rarely engage in electronic fora and therefore electronic channels have not been used as a means of holding elites accountable or as decision-making areas; mainly they are used for discussion and information purposes (Gibson and Ward, 1999). As Löfgren (2000) comments from another Danish study, internal online fora 'did not open up new communicative connections between members and the party elite. Rather it reinforced the connections between the members themselves.'

The impact on collective participation appears to be more mixed. What is noticeable is that it is becoming increasingly natural for intra-party groups or campaigns to move online. The 1997 UK Conservative Party leadership contest saw none of the main candidates with websites; just four years later, in the next leadership contest, all the candidates saw fit to run websites to support their campaigns. Equally, anti-leadership groupings in the UK Labour Party have used websites to publicise their campaigns to stand for the National Executive Committee.

The Internet has certainly allowed the expansion of one form of collective participation – virtual overseas branches. The US parties, the UK and Australian Labour parties have all seen growth of such organisations where expatriate members have networked online to create organisational structures managed via the Internet and email. It is now considerably easier for parties to operate outside of their normal geographic boundaries and for geographically dispersed members overseas to gather information and participate collectively in party affairs (Toulouse and Gross, 1998).

Clearly the use of ICTs within parties are still in a formative period and it is therefore unwise to make definitive predictions. However, the weight of evidence seems to indicate that use of web-based technology is unlikely to extend participation greatly, although it may deepen the quality of participation for those already active. It also seems likely that new technology is more likely to support current trend towards individualised modes of participation within parties and the bypassing of mid-level elites. Members are likely to be allowed more access to information and more voting rights but the format and the agenda of electronic consultation is still likely to be largely determined by the national party elite. As Gibson and Ward (1999: 364) note, therefore, 'simply providing online channels for participation in this manner is not the same as actually empowering members'. Nevertheless, we should not totally write off the contribution of electronic participation. It can allow for a more ongoing permanent debate and discussion and provide for more regular contact between activists than previously. In the long term electronic networks could provide more regular contact with the party, which may be useful for maintaining an activist and membership community, especially in geographical areas where parties have a limited physical presence. Furthermore, electronic debates and discussions are potentially more transparent than traditional face-to-face meetings. Even if one does not actually take part in discussion, it is still possible to have a window on internal debates.

Conclusions

One of the problems of analysing the effects of the Internet is the initial hype that surrounded its emergence. Not surprisingly, when radical changes have not occurred overnight, then it becomes tempting to declare the Internet as unimportant. However, we would argue that it is important to start from more realistic and scaled-down expectations that draw on historical precedents of technological adaptation and social shaping of technology. Change is already occurring; however, it is not the technology itself that brings this about (see Chapter 2). Our base point ought to be that parties are traditionally resilient organisations and will adopt and adapt to new technologies gradually as they have with radio, telephone, television and other computer software. So far, parties have used new information and communication technologies to do the things they traditionally do, only more quickly and efficiently. The Internet has been more swiftly integrated by parties than many previous technologies, but at this stage it is still a supplementary communication tool.

In this opening chapter we have tried to identify some of the main issues and early cross-national trends but, although the early history of the Internet has been US-dominated, we should be wary of assuming that the US model of Internet use will predominate globally. Individual party incentives, such as philosophy and resources, along with systemic political factors, such as electoral law, party system, political culture, will shape party use. The remaining chapters of this volume seek to explore some of the issues raised here in both national and cross-national contexts.

Notes

1 At the time of writing, Scandinavian and North American countries led the way (54 per cent have home access in Sweden, for example, followed by 48 per cent in the USA. However, the overall EU average was just 28 per cent and in some African states access is below 1 per cent (Eurostat 11/2001).
2 See, for example, the comments of George Jones, political editor of the *Daily Telegraph*, in the run up to the UK general election 2001, 'How will it be for you?', *Media Guardian*, 12 February 2001, 2–3.
3 Interview with webmaster of the European People's Party, 1 October 1999.
4 See also media reports on the Spanish and Canadian 2000 election campaigns. The main Spanish party sites, whilst being 'big on cool animation', were accused of blowing their budget on presentation rather than content ('The Campaign in Spain', *Slate*, 15 February 2000, http://slate.msn.com/netelection/entries/00-02-15_74973.asp). The Canadian sites were described as 'brochureware' ('Election Websites Reflect Canada's Quirks', *Techweb*, 25 November 2000, http://content.techweb.com/wire/story/TWB20001124S0002).
5 Interviews with UK party webmasters, 31 July–2 August 1999.
6 'Going Negative', *Slate*, 19 June 2000 (slate.msn.com/netelection/entries/00-06-19_84715.asp) provides details of three key 2000 Senate races – Pennsylvania, Michigan and Washington – where attack sites featured prominently.
7 For example, in the recent 2001 UK election the Welsh Liberal Democrats created an unofficial spoof Plaid Cymru (Welsh Nationalist party) site. In Australia, the Labor party site had prominent web pages entitled 'the Howard Project', attacking premier John Howard (Gibson and Ward, 2002).
8 The title is based on popular mobile-phone text-messaging language. The site intended to counter apathy amongst younger voters and included both serious policy alongside interviews with celebrities and competitions. However, the site was widely derided in the media as fake and patronising.
9 'Gore Targets Youth Vote', *Netpulse!* 4(18), 20 September 2000.
10 See also the report on the 2000 Spanish election 'The Campaign in Spain', *Slate*, 15 February 2000, *op cit.*
11 In Germany, Otto Schilly, SPD minister, has already threatened far-right groups with online restrictions. However, the extreme-right British National Party has legally forced the BBC to restore hypertext links to its site under a recently introduced human-rights legislation.
12 Pew Centre for People and the Press, 'Internet Election News Audience Seeks Convenience, Familiar Names', http://www.people-press.org/online00rpt.htm.
13 Ibid.

References

Birdsell, D.S. and Muzzio, D. (1997) 'Political uses of the World Wide Web in the 1996 US presidential campaign', paper presented to the History and Development of Political Communication on Television, International Conference, Amsterdam.

Bonchek, M.S. (1995) 'Grassroots in Cyberspace: Using Computer Networks to Facilitate Political Participation', paper presented to the 53rd Annual Meeting of the Midwest Political Science Association, 6 April, Chicago, http://www.ai.mit.edu/people/msb/pubs/grassroots.html.

Bowler, S. and Farrell, D. (eds) (1992) *Electoral Strategies and Political Marketing*, Basingstoke: Macmillan.

Carlson, T. and Djupsund, G. (1999) 'Old Wine in New Bottles? Candidates on the Internet in the 1999 Finnish Parliamentary Election Campaign', paper presented to the Nordic Conference of Mass Communication Research, 14–17 August, Kungalv, Sweden.

Centre for Policy Studies (1998) *Blue Skies Ahead*, London: Centre for Policy Studies.

Coleman, S. (ed.) (2001) *2001 Cyberspace Odyssey: The Internet in the UK election*, London: The Hansard Society.

Corrado A. and Firestone, C.M. (eds) (1997) *Elections in Cyberspace: Toward a New Era in American Politics*, Washington, DC: The Aspen Institute.

Crabtree, J. (2001) *Whatever Happened to the E-Lection: A survey of voter attitudes towards new technology during the 2001 Election*, London: The Industrial Society.

Cross, B. (1998) Teledemocracy: Canadian Political Parties Listening to their Constituents', in Alexander, C. and Pal, L. (eds), *Digital Democracy: Politics and Policy in the Wired World*, Toronto: Oxford University Press, 133–148.

Dalton, R. and Wattenberg, M. (eds) (2000), *Parties Without Partisans*, Oxford: Oxford University Press.

Davis, R. (1999) *The Web of Politics: the Internet's Impact on the American Political System*, Oxford: Oxford University Press.

Downs, A. (1957) *An Economic Theory of Democracy*, New York: Harper Row.

Duverger, M. (1954) *Political Parties: Their Organisation and Activities in the Modern State*, London: Methuen.

Earnshaw, B. (2001) 'Winning a seat in cyberspace: Candidates' web sites', in Coleman, S. (ed.), *2001 Cyberspace Odyssey: the Internet in the UK election*, London: The Hansard Society, 32–38.

Farrell, D. and Webb, P. (2000) 'Political Parties as Campaign Organisations', in Dalton, R. and Wattenberg, M. (eds), *Parties Without Partisans*, Oxford: Oxford University Press, 102–128.

Ferdinand, P. (2001) 'The Internet, Democratisation and the Communications Revolution', paper presented to the IDEA Conference, Stockholm, 27–28 June. Available at: www.idea.int/2001_forum/media/mrt_papers/peter-ferdinand.htm.

Gibson, R.K. and Ward, S.J. (1998) 'UK Political Parties and the Internet: Politics as Usual in the New Media?', *Harvard International Journal of Press Politics*, 3(3): 14–38.

Gibson, R.K. and Ward, S.J. (1999) 'Party Democracy Online: UK Parties and New ICTs', *Information Communication and Society*, 2(3): 340–367.

Gibson, R.K. and Ward, S.J. (2000a) 'New Media, Same Impact? British Party Activity in Cyberspace', in Gibson, R.K. and Ward, S.J. (eds), *Reinvigorating Government? British Politics and the Internet*, Aldershot: Ashgate, 106–129.

Gibson, R.K. and Ward, S.J. (2000b) 'An Outsider's Medium? The European Elections and UK Party Competition on the Internet', in Cowley, P. *et al.* (eds), *British Parties and Elections Review Vol. 10*, London: Frank Cass, 173–191.

Gibson, R.K. and Ward, S.J. (2000c) 'A Proposed Methodology for Studying the Function and Effectiveness of Party and Candidate Web Sites', *Social Science Computer Review*, 18(3): 301–319.

Gibson, R.K. and Ward, S.J. (2002) 'Virtual Campaigning: Australian Parties and the Internet', *Australian Journal of Political Science*, 35(1): 99–122.

Gibson, R.K., Newell, J.L. and Ward, S.J. (2000) 'New Parties, New Media: Italian Party Politics and the Internet', *South European Society and Politics*, 5(1): 123–142.

Gibson, R.K., Newell, J.L. and Ward, S.J. (2002) 'The New Technologies', in Newell, J.L. (ed.), *Berlusconi's Victory: The Italian General Election of 2001*, Manchester: Manchester University Press.

Harmel, R. and Tan, A. (1997) 'Changes in Party Structures and the Relationship of Parties and Democracy', paper presented at the Workshop on Change in the Relationship of Parties and Democracy, Texas A&M University, College Station, Texas.

Hill, J. and Hughes, K. (1998) *Cyberpolitics: Citizen Activism in the Age of the Internet*, Lanham: Rowman & Littlefield.

Hill, D.T and Sen, K. (2000) 'The Internet in Indonesia's New Democracy', *Democratization*, 7(1): 119–136.

Jackson, J. (2001) 'View from the Parties – the Conservatives', in Coleman, S. (ed.), *2001 Cyberspace Odyssey: The Internet in the UK election*, London: The Hansard Society, 26–28.

Kalathil, S. and Boas, T.C. (2001) 'The Internet and State Control in Authoritarian Regimes: China, Cuba and the Counterrevolution', Carnegie Endowment for World Peace, Working Paper No. 21.

Kamarck, E. (1999) 'Campaigning on the Internet in the Elections of 1998', in Kamarck, E. and Nye, J. (eds), *Democracy.Com? Governance in a Networked World*, New Hampshire: Hollis Publishing.

Katz, R. and Mair, P. (eds) (1994) *How Parties Organize: Change and Adaptation in Party Organisations in Western Democracies*, London: Sage.

Katz, R. and Mair, P. (1995) 'Changing Models of Party Organisation and Party Democracy: The Emergence of the Cartel Party', *Party Politics*, 1(1): 5–28.

Kavanagh, D. (1995) *Election Campaigning: The new marketing of politics*, Oxford: Blackwell.

Kirchheimer, O. (1966) 'The Transformation of West European Party Systems', in Lapalombara and Weiner (eds), *Political Parties and Party Development*, Princeton, NJ: Princeton University Press, 177–200.

Klotz, R. (1997) 'Positive Spin: Senate Campaigning on the Web', *PS: Political Science and Politics*, XXX(3): 482–486.

Labour Coordinating Committee (1997) *New Labour: A Stakeholders' Party*. The Interim Report of the Labour Coordinating Committee's Commission on Party Democracy.

Lipow, A. and Seyd, P. (1996) 'The Politics of Anti-Partyism', *Parliamentary Affairs*, 49(2): 273–284.

Löfgren, K. (2000) 'Danish Political Parties and New Technology: Interactive

Parties or New Shop Windows', in Hoff, J., Horrocks, I. and Tops, P. (eds), *Democratic Governance and New Technology*, London: Routledge, 57–70.

Lynch, P. (1996) 'Professionalization, New Technology and Change in a Small Party: The Case of the Scottish National Party', in Denver, D. *et al.*, *British Parties and Elections Yearbook 1996*, London: Frank Cass, 217–233.

Margetts, H. (2001) 'The Cyber Party', paper presented to the ECPR Joint Session Workshops, 6–11 April, University of Grenoble.

Margolis, M., Resnick, D. and Chin-chang Tu (1997) 'Campaigning on the Internet: Parties and Candidates on the World Wide Web in the 1996 Primary Season', *Harvard International Journal of Press Politics*, 2(1): 59–78.

Margolis, M., Resnick, D. and Wolfe, J. (1999) 'Party Competition on the Internet: Minor Versus Major Parties in the UK and USA', *Harvard International Journal of Press Politics*, 4(4): 24–47.

Martin, S. and Geiger, S. (1999) 'Building Relationships? The Marketing of Political Parties in Cyberspace', paper presented to the Academy of Marketing Special Interest Group, Political Marketing Conference, 15–16 September, Bournemouth.

Michels, R. [1911] (1954) *Political Parties: A Sociological Study of Oligarchical Tendencies of Modern Democracies*, New York: The Free Press.

Morris, D. (1999) *Vote.com*, Los Angeles: Renaissance.

Negrine, R. and Papathanassopoulos, S. (1996) 'The Americanization of Political Communication: A Critique', *Harvard International Journal of Press Politics*, 1(2): 45–62.

Newell, J. (2001) 'New Parties, New Media: Italian Political Parties and the Web', *Harvard International Journal of Press Politics*, 6(4): 60–87.

Nixon, P. and Johansson, H. (1999a) 'Transparency Through Technology: A Comparative Analysis of the Use of the Internet by Political Parties', in Hague, B. and Loader, B. (eds), *Digital Democracy: Discourse and Decision Making in the Information Age*, London: Routledge, 135–153.

Nixon, P. and Johansson, H. (1999b) 'Political Parties and the Internet in the European Parliament Elections', in Armitage, J. and Roberts, J. (eds), *Exploring Cyber Society, Conference Proceedings Volume 2*, Newcastle upon Tyne: University of Northumbria.

Norris, P. (2000) *A Virtuous Circle*, Cambridge: Cambridge University Press.

Norris, P. (2001) *The Digital Divide*, Cambridge: Cambridge University Press.

Norris, P. (2003) 'Preaching to the Converted? Pluralism, Participation and Party Websites', *Party Politics*, 9(1): 21–46.

Pedersen, K. (2001) 'Ballots and Technology in the Danish Parties: Enhanced Participation?', paper presented to the ECPR Joint Session Workshops, 6–11 April, University of Grenoble.

Rash, W. (1997) *Politics on the Nets: Wiring the Political Process*, New York: W. Freeman.

Resnick, D. (1999) 'The Normalization of Cyberspace', in Toulouse, C. and Luke, T. (eds), *The Politics of Cyberspace*, London: Routledge, 48–68.

Richards, P. (1999) *The Party's Over?*, London: The Fabian Society.

Richardson, J. (1995) 'Political Parties and the Challenge of Interest Groups', *West European Politics*, 18(1): 116–139.

Rodan, G. (1998) 'The Internet and Political Control in Singapore', *Political Science Quarterly*, 113(1): 63–89.

Roper, J. (1999) 'New Zealand political parties online: The World Wide Web as a tool for democratization or political marketing', in Toulouse, C. and Luke, T. (eds), *the Politics of Cyberspace*, London: Routledge, 69–83.

Scammell, M. (1995) *Designer Politics*, Basingstoke: Macmillan.

Scammell, M. (1998) 'The wisdom of the war room: US campaigning and Americanization', *Media, Culture and Society*, 20: 251–275.

Scarrow, S. (1996) *Parties and their Members*, Oxford: Oxford University Press.

Selnow, G. (1998) *Electronic Whistle Stops: The Impact of the Internet on American Politics*, Westport, CT: Praeger.

Seyd, P. and Whiteley, P. (1992) *Labour's Grass Roots*, Oxford: Oxford University Press.

Smith, C. (1998) 'Political parties in the Information Age: From Mass Party to Leadership Organisation?', in Snellen, I. and van de Donk, W. (eds), *Public Administration in the Information Age: A Handbook*, Amsterdam: IoS Press.

Smith C. (2000) 'British Political Parties: Continuity and Change in the Information Age', in Hoff, J., Horrocks, I. and Tops, P. (eds), *Democratic Governance and New Technology*, London: Routledge, 57–70.

Stone, B. (1996) 'Politic 1996', *Internet World*, November, 38–48.

Streck, J. (1999), 'Pulling the Plug on Electronic Town Meetings: Participatory Democracy and the Reality of Usenet', in Toulouse, C. and Luke, T. (eds), *The Politics of Cyberspace*, London: Routledge, 18–47.

Stromer-Galley, J., Foot, K., Schneider, S.M. and Larsen, E. (2001) 'How Citizens Used the Internet in Election 2000', in Coleman, S. (ed.), *Elections in the Information Age: Lessons from the US*, London: The Hansard Society, 21–26.

Swanson, D. and Mancini, P. (eds) (1996) *Politics, Media and Democracy*, Westport, CT: Praeger.

Tan, A. (1997) 'Party Change and Party Membership Decline', *Party Politics*, 3(3): 363–377.

Taubman, G. (1998) 'A Not So World Wide Web: the Internet, China and Challenges to Non Democratic Rule', *Political Communication*, 15(2): 255–272.

Tops, P., Voerman, G. and Boogers, M. (2000) 'Political Websites During the 1998 Parliamentary Elections in the Netherlands', in Hoff, J., Horrocks, I. and Tops, P. (eds), *Democratic Governance and New Technology*, London: Routledge, 87–100.

Toulouse, C. and Gross, J. (1998) 'The British Diaspora: Using the Internet as a Tool for Organising UK Citizens Living Abroad'. Paper presented to the American Political Science Association Annual Meetings, 1 September, Boston, MA.

Voerman, G. (1999) 'Distributing Electronic Folders: The Digital Electoral Campaign of 1998 in the Netherlands', Documentatie-centrum Nederlandse Politieke Partijen, University of Groningen.

Voerman, G. and Ward, S.J. (2000) 'New Media and New Politics: Green Parties, Intra-Party Democracy and the Internet (An Anglo-Dutch Comparison)', in Voerman, G. and Lucardie, P. (eds), *Jaerboek Documentatiecentrum Nederlandse Politieke Partijen 1999*, Groningen: University of Groningen, 192–215.

Ward, S.J. and Gibson, R.K. (1998) 'The First Internet Election? UK Political Parties and Campaigning in Cyberspace', in Crewe, I., Gosschalk, B. and Bartle, J. (eds), *Political Communications and the 1997 General Election*, Ilford: Frank Cass, 93–112.

Ward, S.J. and Gibson, R.K. (2003) 'Online and On Message? Candidate Websites

38   *Stephen Ward, Rachel Gibson and Paul Nixon*

at the 2001 General Election', *British Journal of Politics and International Relations*, 5(11): 1–18.

Whiteley, P., Seyd, P. and Richardson, J. (1994) *True Blues: The Politics of Conservative Party Membership*, Oxford: Oxford University Press.

Williamson, A. (2000) 'The Impact of the Net on the Politics of Cuba', *First Monday*, 5(8).

Wring, D. (1996) 'Political Marketing and Party Development in Britain', *European Journal of Marketing*, 30(10/11): 100–111.

Wring, D. and Horrocks, I. (2000) 'The Transformation of Political Parties?', in Axford, B. and Huggins, R. (eds), *New Media and Politics*, London: Sage, 191–209.

2 Political parties and democracy in the information age

Karl Löfgren and Colin Smith

Introduction

The development of new information and communications technologies (ICTs) has generally been accompanied by a recognition of their capabilities for the practice of democracy. In recent times, a debate has centred upon Internet-based technologies and the possibilities for 'electronic democracy'. While this debate first surfaced in the 1960s, in discussions of technological optimism (Etzioni, 1972; Toffler, 1980; Arterton, 1987), it has boomed since the late 1990s, as evidenced in a variety of academic books and articles in scientific journals.[1] The debate is also not purely academic; there have been many projects aimed at utilising the capabilities of ICTs that have, to a greater or lesser extent, been informed by the objective of 'strengthening' democracy. Examples of this can be found in 'experiments' with 'digital democracy', including the development of 'community networks' (as described in Tsagarousianou *et al.*, 1998); 'parliaments online' (as described in Coleman *et al.*, 1999); and different forms of 'open government' initiatives (Bellamy and Taylor, 1998).

Such projects, even those that are the outcome of grassroots initiatives, reflect in part the widespread international 'policy diffusion' of the rhetoric of the 'information society' (Karlsson, 1996). This rhetoric has featured heavily in responses to the purported 'democratic deficit' or 'crises of democracy' suffered by Western capitalist democracies (Barber, 1984; Budge, 1996). New technologies are widely – and often uncritically – credited as playing an essential role in restructuring and redefining established political systems. New ICTs, given their unique properties – more equal access to political processes, interactivity and decentralisation (Abramson *et al.*, 1988) – are judged able to counteract trends towards political 'sclerosis' and 'reinvigorate', or even 'reinvent' democracy as we know it.

In this literature's search for new 'virtual' institutions and organisations political parties have been notable by their absence. This is perhaps because parties were considered to have played out their role in the polity. As Western democracies have moved from the more traditional mode of steering – 'government' – to less hierarchical forms of governing or 'governance' (Rhodes, 1997; Stoker, 1998; Pierre, 2000), parliamentary structures, such as parties, are not seen as occupying a central position. The fact remains, however, that political parties are not yet anachronisms within liberal political systems (Budge, 1996). There is growing evidence to suggest that parties have been increasingly innovative in their uses of the new ICTs. Besides the more speculative 'cyber democratic literature' (which still prevails), a new generation of empirical research in the field of parties and ICTs has emerged (Norris, 2001; Hoff *et al.*, 2000; Gibson and Ward, 2000; and Margolis and Resnick, 2000). This body of work represents an attempt to ground more thoroughly our understanding of the practice of new technologies within parties in traditional political-science concepts and empirical study.

This chapter seeks to move one step forward in the development of more encompassing frameworks for the study of political parties and new ICTs. Our aim is to theorise about the relationships, or couplings, between the three central elements at the heart of this book; political parties, democracy and ICTs. The chapter does not focus on the technology *per se*, which, as mentioned above, very often takes centre stage, but on the discourses and strategies for the implementation and utilisation of new technology. In contrast to much of what is written on electronic democracy, we do not perceive democracy as a static variable or as a perspective embedded in participatory tradition that has generally been disinterested in the role of political parties (because of their hierarchical organisation structure and their chief position within the representative system). Our theoretical approach is by nature eclectic, as there is a lack of cohesive and cumulative research traditions within this field. Nevertheless, our own and others' empirical studies will be used to illustrate our discussion, and to exemplify our theoretical arguments. The nexus for the discussion is political parties' role as a *linkage* between people and government, which is conceived as one of the primary *functions* of the party within a democratic polity by most party theorists. By discussing the parties' understanding and conception of this linkage, as manifested both in their strategies and their actual application of ICTs, we abstract different forms of 'democratic' ICT strategies. These strategies act as basic standards for assessing the democratic aspects of ICTs in the parties' external and internal communication. Our use of these democratic strategies is not prescriptive, and we do not at this point set out to argue that the adoption of one strategy is necessarily preferable over another. However, these strategies clearly relate to personal preferences on empowering voters and/or members through the utilisation of new ICTs.

Democratic linkage

The democratic coupling of political leadership and the public (in general) represents a classical issue within political science.[2] However, in recent years there has been a growing recognition of the pivotal role of relatively autonomous elites within democracy (Etzioni-Halevy, 1993). While initially interpreted along egalitarian lines, whereby there is free circulation between the public and elites, more recently accounts have focused on the horizontal connections created over policy, in particular economic issues, which are increasingly detached from politics on a nation-state level. This 'elite desertion' of the disadvantaged has promoted greater socio-economic inequality and distracts from the quality of democracy (Etzioni-Halevy, 1999: 242).

On top of political fatigue and increased cynicism amongst the public, this growing disconnection undermines the political climate of tolerance for diversity of opinion, for disagreement and controversy (Etzioni-Halevy, 1999: 246). Applied to political parties it reveals a two-tier framework for analysis with party members acting as 'sub-elites' and the general electorate forming 'the public'. Rather than using the term 'coupling' to denote this relationship, however, the party literature most often uses the term 'linkage' – a broad term within the tradition of political liberalism that centres on the intermediaries or political mechanisms connecting the voters to their leaders, such as elections, opinion polls, mass media and various forms of political associations, which naturally include the political party. The literature on political parties provides a variety of meanings for 'functional linkage', and there is no real consensus over how to define the term.[3] In envisaging the party as facilitating democratic linkage between people and the governors, however, the electronic media, given their interactive and decentralised structure, will clearly play an important role.

Following Lawson (1988: 14–16), it is possible to identify four different forms of linkage of relevance to political parties: *participatory*, where the party facilitates direct citizen involvement in government activities; *electoral*, or *representative*, where the party can be controlled by the citizenry through elections; *clientistic* linkage, where the party is a channel for the exchange of votes for favours and or services; and, finally, *directive* linkage, where the party is an agent on behalf of the government to control citizens' behaviour, via coercive and educational methods. Among these, the latter two have little in common with Western liberal democratic systems. The clientistic linkage bears resemblance to non-democratic and corrupt political systems in which the elite 'buy' votes from the citizens (mainly known from the ancient republic of Rome – '*panem et circenses*'). Lawson connects 'directive linkage' to the 'communist parties' in the former Eastern bloc. However, this sort of linkage actually corresponds better with the linkage that *ideally* exists between the state and the citizens in the African post-colonialist 'mass-parties' (for example, in Tanzania or

Kenya). History has, however, clearly shown that this label in most cases has been a 'cover up' for more or less totalitarian regimes where the real 'linkage function' has been based upon tribal or ethnic affiliations. The linkage function of the former communist parties in the Eastern bloc is in this context much more complicated.

The first two forms of linkage are directly relevant to our discussion here. Both exist in modern party systems, but are usually subdivided into linkages for members (participatory) and linkages for voters (representative). Participatory linkage is coupled with the classical understanding of the 'mass party', in which members convene to deliberate and decide on the parties' policies through active participation in its structures. Representative linkage, however, has actually been predominant in contemporary Western liberal democracies with their elected assemblies. The vast majority of parties have also, at least initially, nominated the vast majority of elected office holders within liberal democracies. Even though participatory linkage is commonly believed to be in conflict with representative linkage, the two often operate concurrently in the practice of everyday party politics.

Whether one type of linkage is 'democratically' superior is clearly a contestable issue relating back to the classical debate between participatory and representative forms of democracy. Placing this debate in the study of political party development specifically, we can see that there are those such as Michels (1954) who argue for strong internal democracy in the party organisation as the basic foundation for a strong democratic polity. Democracy within the internal party organisation, it is argued, fosters *democratic education* of the citizens, a sense of *responsibility* in relation to the polity as a whole, and the overall *legitimacy* of the parties as the possibilities for *participation* are widened and the *articulation of interests* increased. On the other side, there are those who argue against internal democracy within parties as it is seen to decrease the *effectiveness* of the party to act in the wider political environment, since it reduces the level of inter-party competition, a crucial element of representative democracy (Schumpeter, 1943). The decline in competition undermines the chain of parliamentary command and threatens the pluralism of society since the building of public opinion is left to particular interest associations and the mass media, rather than the active and aggregative forces of parties.

Not only is this dichotomy a normative debate on democracy; it also more or less represents two different analytical distinctions – 'the cadre party' and 'the mass party' (Duverger, 1990) – of the actual organisational structure of parties. Here the cadre party represents a model mainly focusing on exclusive selection of candidates, within the caucus, for elections without a permanent membership organisation and symbolises the 'representative' model of democracy. In contrast, the mass party symbolises an emancipating membership organisation, which signals a more 'participatory' model. Although ideal models, there exists some correspondence between these normative and analytical distinctions.

Our perspective maintains the dichotomy of representative vs. participatory forms of party democracy as the point of departure for the discussion, but expands it to provide a broader framework for capturing the dominant strategies and ideologies of parties in adopting the capabilities offered by ICTs. This is premised on the results of our own work and that of others, which demonstrates that party adaptation to the new ICTs is a multidimensional phenomena.

Party strategies on ICTs

Given that we seek to draw conclusions about the contemporary practice of democracy from parties' use of new ICTs, we begin very broadly with discussion of democratic models, strategies and discourses in the information age (Hoff *et al.*, 2000; Bellamy, 2000). Even though the conception of linkage is a good point of departure for an analysis of parties and democracy, it easily ends up in a debate around this classical dichotomy between participatory and representative forms of democracy. For example, an earlier attempt to introduce these opposed strands with respect to the parties and new ICTs was presented by Depla and Tops (1995), who perceived two new party forms facilitated by new communications technologies: First, the *modern cadre party*, where the new technologies foster new forms of political participation through functional discussion forums;[4] second, the *professional electoral association*, where political parties are organised around a single political leader, and where the new technology is used to strengthen the temporary campaign association set up for promoting the leadership of the party. Whereas the former party model can be perceived as a 'reinvention' of the participatory mass party, the latter bears much resemblance to the 'cartel party', that is, the modern form of the elitist-driven representative party (Katz and Mair, 1995).

In addition to the two classical conceptions of democratic party strategies – emancipatory mass party and the elitist cartel party – we envisage two emergent models of European party democracy with the advent of new ICTs; a consumerist conception that represents a continuation of the cartel party and the grassroots conception that is a more new and distinctive form of party. While most established political parties in Western Europe can be identified as being in one of the first two categories, the consumerist and cyberdemocratic models seem to find stronger echoes in new parties and fringe groups.

In using the term 'strategy' to discuss party adaptation to the new ICTs, we are seeking to avoid an overly deterministic approach whereby the introduction of ICTs within political parties is seen as leading to certain outcomes. The relationship between the technological and organisational framework of a party is complex and interactive (Orlikowski, 1992). Instead, we adopt a more institutionalist account of political change whereby organisational development follows a slower, less determinate and more endogenous course (March and Olsen, 1989). 'Institutions', understood as (party) traditions, norms and habits, play a significant role in the way new technology is adopted and used. Concurrently, the parties' adaptation of new ICTs mirrors the changing character of political parties in contemporary liberal democracies and the structural changes of political parties' linkage functions.

We envisage these strategies to embody a broad discursive conception of citizenship and democratic governance.[5] The parties themselves articulate the relation between their democratic self-image and ICTs in such ways that it produces meaning and identity. Before elucidating the strategies in more detail, it is also important to state that we perceive these strategies as 'logics of appropriateness' (March and Olsen, 1989: 23–24). There are no European parties, for example, following a pure 'demo-elitist' strategy, or a 'grassroots strategy', instead, they embody elements from a variety of constructed strategies.

Finally, in defining these strategies or logics of appropriateness we acknowledge the importance of locating them in the traditions, history and norms that are embodied within a party. Thus, a party already rooted in a participatory tradition will be more likely to follow an ICT strategy that is supportive of a more interactive approach than one following a more representative logic. Table 2.1 outlines the key characteristics of the four ICT strategies adopted by each of our party types.

The mass-party strategy

The classic conception of the mass party is associated with social democratic parties of Western Europe. The mass party adopts a representative approach to democracy at the systemic level whereby elected politicians are perceived as the delegates of well-defined interests and are primarily accountable to those interests, rather than the electorate at large. Party members, through local branches, are included in all the different stages of the political process and are 'emancipated' through their direct participation in the party. Democratic legitimacy, therefore, depends on the popular and direct involvement of individuals in the formulation of party policies, which in turn demands extensive membership organisations to provide avenues for input to the policy-making process (Katz and Mair, 1995: 6–7). Ideally, the parliamentary group is subordinated and confined to decisions taken by the membership organisation.

Given these characteristics of the mass party, we should expect its new ICT strategy to focus on the membership organisation and intra-organisational debate. Electronic fora that widen members' input to the policy process, both in terms of parliamentary politics and the

Table 2.1 Typology of democratic ICT strategies in political parties

	'Mass-party strategy'	'Cartel party strategy'	'The Consumerist strategy'	'The Grassroots strategy'
Central type of Linkage (representative style)	Representative (Delegacy)	Representative (Party as agent of state)	Representative ('Consumer–Producer' relationships)	Participatory/Communitarian
Central Forms of ICT-mediated Participation	Electronic conferences, Manifestations (political websites) Personal contact with politicians	Manifestations (political websites), Establishing contacts	Manifestations, Opinion polling, Soliciting for financial campaign support	Membership of virtual organisations, Electronic voting, Electronic meetings,
Dominant Procedural Norm(s)	Development of adaptive political systems, Development of public debates	Development of adaptive political system	Development of (individual) rights	Development of virtual identities (independent of social cues), Development of public debates
Political Nexus	Public debate	Expert, elite discourse	Political service declarations, Voter preferences	Deliberative electronic discussions, Consensus
Rights and Roles of members	Exclusive rights, Decisional involvement (e.g. nominations)	Selective incentives for members, Mutual autonomy between elite and members	No members, Temporary supporters	Sympathisers, Open and loose memberships
Role of voters	Potential members	Potential voters	Consumers with predefined preferences	Same as above
View on Citizenship	Emancipatory	Pluralist, Liberal	New liberal	Communitarian
Direction of Information-flow	Bi-directional (biased)	Uni-directional (top-down)	Bi-directional	Multi-directional
Role of ICTs	Complementary to other forms of political communication	Campaigning	Campaigning, Intercepting public opinion	ICTs replace membership organisation

intra-organisational processes, would therefore be key applications. These systems would allow for mobilisation of the members when needed and swift dissemination of information from the leadership to the local branches. Given that this takes place in an environment of inter-party competition, the manifestation of party politics via websites would also occur. Indeed, the websites would act as 'shop-windows' for the party's politics to attract new members. The appearance, however, is designed to attract those groups and interests that the party already represents.

As we have already suggested, there is of course no such thing as a 'pure' mass-party strategy with respect to the use of new ICTs. However, traits of this strategy can be found in some of the classical social demo-cratic parties, for example the Danish Social Democratic Party (SP) as described by Löfgren (2000). The SP has made a clear distinction between services for the members and services for the voters and citizens. In rela-tion to its members, the SP joined a Bulletin Board System run by the Danish Federation of Trade Unions (LO) named 'net.Dialog' in 1996 (originally set up in 1994), which also operates as an Intranet between the different 'associations' within the labour movement. All members of the SP, the trade unions with affiliated associations, and subscribers to the daily social democratic newspaper *Aktuelt,* can join the 'net.Dialog' confer-ence service. Whilst the members, in principle, are provided with different new channels for influencing policy-making, the website operates as a 'service function' and manifestation for the non-members, without the same possibilities to affect the policy-making processes.

Similar examples can also be found in British parties, where Labour, the Liberal Democrats and the SNP have well-established conferencing systems ostensibly designed to open up new channels of participation for their memberships. Yet there are dilemmas inherent in assessing the actual uses of such systems, dilemmas that become apparent during times of intense campaigning activity for parties, such as during general elec-tions. At such times, the use of conferencing systems to support a top-down dissemination of strategic campaigning information contradicts assumptions that such systems are a pure manifestation of a classical mass-party model/strategy (Smith, 1998).

The cartel party strategy

The Cartel Party, coined by Katz and Mair (1995), is envisaged as a succes-sor to other models of party, the mass party among them. What charac-terises this model, and the ICT strategy that supports it, is the 'disengagement' of the membership organisation from the party, as the mass media takes over responsibility for maintaining contacts between the political elites and voters/citizens. Furthermore, the political parties' lead-erships are less dependent on both the financial and voluntary labour support from members because of public funding and increased employment of professional party workers. The party, as such, has become a part of the state, and the party elite identifies itself with the other agents of the public administration, rather than with its members. Moreover, the distinction between members and non-members (voters) is blurred, and the (few remaining) members are conceived as individuals granted some selective incentives, rather than as an organised collective. The party elite is no longer accountable to its members, but rather to the electorate as a whole. Conversely, the electorate at large has become more important to the party as it can no longer rely on the support of pre-defined groups and interests at the elections. Campaigning that is professional and well targeted becomes steadily more important as a result of increased competition in the electoral 'market place', and requires more financial resources as a result.

Given these traits, the new ICT strategy associated with the cartel-party model is one that is therefore mainly concerned with the campaigning and narrowcasting facilities of the new technology. One of the main applications, therefore, will be party websites with a particular focus on the 'leader' rather than the party as a whole. If interactivity is utilised, its outcomes are controlled by the party bureaucracy and the party leadership and used largely to monitor public opinion. Even though the websites fulfil the function of bypassing traditional mass media, this strategy is strongly attached to its symbolic rationality of modern mass media with its focus on individuals (rather than collectives) and conflict (rather than consensus). Members can be provided with some selective fora for argument and debate and easier access to the information systems but face largely similar channels of communication to voters. In addition, the local branches are provided with support to build their own websites, but within centrally authorised templates and rules.

It is possible to argue that this is the dominant strategy for contemporary parties in Europe today. Several empirical studies on political parties have shown that elements of this strategy are embodied in the actual utilisation of modern ICTs. This is illustrated in some of the studies on the 1997 UK general election (Ward and Gibson, 1998; Smith, 1998, 2000). Scandinavian examples, which approximate this logic, are also identifiable in the Swedish Moderate Party and in the Danish Liberal Party (Löfgren, 2001). Common for them all is the identification of a top-down control of democratic expression in the parties as visualised on the (major) British parties' websites, and the focus on downward dissemination of information for a broader public than just the narrow circle of traditional sympathisers and members. What is also apparent is that manifestations of this strategy go beyond the use of the web by parties. Evidence can also be found in the use of dedicated 'internal' communications networks by parties to transmit campaigning information around their organisations, and advanced database technologies to identify critical groups of voters and target specific messages to these groups in an attempt to win their support (Smith, 1998).

The consumerist strategy

Although currently only existing in embryonic form, we suggest that the consumerist strategy is likely to become increasingly evident. Representing an extreme form of the cartel party, its strategy is derived from a utilitarian and rational conception of democracy that assumes satisfaction and protection of individual interests from the key goal of government (Bellamy and Taylor, 1998). 'Citizenship' in this context is restricted to a notion of voters as stakeholders in public services who give their approval or disapproval to policy decisions through a market mechanism. Political participation is reduced, therefore, largely to 'exiting' the 'public supermarket'. Membership in political parties, in a participatory sense, no longer offers an influential channel for actively 'making a difference'. A consumerist party has no permanent members, according to this logic, only temporary campaign workers. In relation to the cartel-party strategy, the consumerist party tries even more to anticipate and discern the public opinion, and to identify the voter's preferences.

Following the cartel party, the new ICT strategy of a consumerist party is multidimensional. In addition to websites, advanced database systems for opinion polling and targeting messages more effectively are of great importance for success in campaigning. Encouraging membership organisation and participation, however, does not form a focus of new ICT application. Means are offered in the inter-election period for individuals to express their discontent about the level of service being provided via the websites and such data is stored for marketing purposes. However, beyond this most people have very limited options to initiate input into the system either as individuals or collectively.

While typically not seen in the European context, there is some evidence to suggest that such a strategy may be creeping into the activities of North American parties and candidates. The Canadian 'Reform Party' conducted a telephone referendum for registered voters (in North Vancouver) over proposed changes to the juvenile crime Act (Young Offenders Act – YOA). Individuals could cast their vote on the legislation via a pay-phone number. This 'pay-per-vote' situation clearly forced voters into making a strategic assessment of the importance of registering their opinion (Barney and Laycock, 1995).

Another example of this strategy, although not always facilitated by a party, is the emergence of decision support systems for electoral choice, such as the Dutch 'StemWijzer' for the 1994 general election in the Netherlands (Edwards, 1998). By working through a number of questions (multiple choice) on, for example, a website, the voters' preferences are matched to the political candidates.

The 'grassroots' strategy

This party ICT strategy bears a strong resemblance to the leftist forms of 'cyber-democracy' as described by, for example, Hagen (1997). The permanent and formal membership organisation is eliminated and replaced by more informal relationships between members. Thus, in sharp contrast to the consumerist strategy, the grassroots strategy is based upon the participatory ethos of new popular movements such as environmentalists and peace activists. Seeking office is of less importance for the party than developing extra-parliamentary activities and participation. The organisational structure is horizontal and decision-making takes place through consensual deliberation in which all 'participants' are equal both in terms of votes and involvement in the discussion. Crucial to this form of party strategy is the development of democratic identities among supporters whereby they become politically empowered. In that sense, the grassroots strategy differs from the traditional mass party because it no longer places the emphasis on representation of interests but on representation of identities.

New ICTs are of prime importance to this party strategy since they facilitate a new public sphere in which deliberation and the creation of new identities is conceivable. As with the Internet, the organisation has no real 'centre' but exists as a loose network. The relevant actors assemble in 'cyberspace' and encounter each other as equals in a virtual world. The scope for prejudice is significantly reduced as visual social cues are concealed and replaced by new self-produced identities. New technologies serve as a tool for internal communication within the network and also as a 'political weapon' in the shape of direct email opportunities for public exposure of 'scandals within the system' on websites, and circulation of electronic petitions.

As with the consumerist strategy this is an emergent form of party behaviour and is still hard to identify with empirical examples. A possible example is the German party *Die Digitalen*, which competed in the 1999 city election of Berlin. Die Digitalen operates solely on the Internet with an 'open policy' programme whereby the policy formulation is open to all 'members', who are wholly in charge of organising and co-ordinating its development. Of course, greater influence accrues to activists who are more regularly involved in the process. Examples can also be found in the Swedish Leftist Party, and their hearings – via the Internet – of party policy to the electorate in general (Löfgren, 2001). Crossing to the other side of the ideological spectrum, many extreme-right parties (and 'hate groups') make use of new ICTs in a grassroots manner. Internal co-ordination and deliberation are facilitated via electronic communication by many of these organisations and the focus on building of identity is just as imperative. Even among other parties, such as the Swedish Liberal Party, there is evidence of a widespread understanding of the need for less geographically defined memberships that allow 'citizens' to maintain a direct connection with party elites. Such arrangements could clearly be facilitated most efficiently through electronic communication. (Löfgren, 2001)

Conclusions

The triangle of relationships between modern communications technologies, political parties and democracy is complex in nature wherein the technology *per se* plays a subordinate role. The argument we have presented here is that the new ICT strategies evident in political parties in Western liberal democracies today represent various mixes of democratic approaches in which the representative and participatory linkage functions of the party are assigned differing levels of importance. While technological change allows for innovation, it cannot be divorced from overall party strategy nor can it be understood by observing the technical part of a party's uptake of new technology. Thus, while new technologies certainly enable parties to rethink the democratic linkage in unprecedented ways, these are based on prior ideological, cultural and administrative references and beyond that are reflective of broader institutional views on citizenship, power and popular influence.

Notes

1   See Hoff *et al.* (2000); also van de Donk and Tops (1995) for reviews and discussions of the literature.
2   Naturally, elitist thinking is by no means new considering the classical works over time on elites such as Mosca, Pareto, Michels, Weber and Schumpeter.
3   For a critical discussion and review, see Widfeldt (1997).
4   Similar trains of thought in the shape of 'party-based direct democracy' can be found in Budge (1996).
5   We will not here embark upon an elaboration of how to define 'discourse'; a concept with a variety of definitions. In our context it refers to a 'structured totality resulting from an articulatory practice' where an articulatory practice is defined as 'any practice establishing a relation among elements such that their identity is modified as a result of practice' (Laclau and Mouffe, 1985: 105, quoted from Hoff, *et al.*, 2000: 26).

References

Abramson, J.B., Arterton, F.C. and Orren, G.R. (1988) *The Electronic Commonwealth: The Impact of New Technologies upon Democratic Politics*, NY: Basic Books.

Arterton, F.C. (1987) *Teledemocracy: Can Technology Protect Democracy?*, Newbury Park, CA: Sage Publications.

Barber, B. (1984) *Strong Democracy: Participatory Democracy for a New Age*, Berkeley, CA: University of California Press.

Barney, D. and Laycock, D. (1995) 'The Recline of Party: Armchair Democracy and the Reform Party of Canada', paper presented for the British Columbia Political Studies Association Conference, Simon Fraser University, Burnaby, British Columbia, 5–6 May 1995.

Bellamy, C. (2000) 'Modelling Electronic Democracy', in Hoff, J., Horrocks, I. and Tops, P. (eds), *Democratic Governance and New Technology*, London: Routledge, 33–54.

Bellamy, C. and Taylor, J.A. (1998) *Governing in the Information Age*, Buckingham: Open University Press.

Budge, I. (1996) *The New Challenge of Direct Democracy*, Cambridge: Polity Press.

Coleman, S., Taylor, J. and van de Donk, W. (eds) (1999) *Parliament in the Age of the Internet*, Oxford: Oxford University Press.

Depla, P.F.G. and Tops, P. (1995) 'Political Parties in the Digital Era. The Technological Challenge', in van de Donk, W.B.H.J., Snellen, I.Th.M. and Tops, P.W., *Orwell in Athens – A Perspective on Informatization and Democracy*, the Netherlands: IOS Press.

Duverger, M. (1990) 'Political Parties', in Mair P. (ed.), *The West European Party System*, Oxford: Oxford University Press.

Edwards, A. (1998) 'Towards an Informed Citizenry? Information and Communication Technologies and Electoral Choice', in Snellen, I. and van de Donk, W. (eds), *Handbook on Public Administration in the Information Age*, the Netherlands: IOS Press.

Etzioni, A. (1972) 'Minerva: An Electronic Townhall', *Policy Sciences*, 3: 457–474.

Etzioni-Halevy, E. (1993) *The Elite Connection*, Oxford: Polity Press.

Etzioni-Halevy, E. (1999) 'Élites, Inequality and the Quality of Democracy in Ultramodern Society', *International Review of Sociology – Revue Internationale de Sociologie*, 9(2): 239–250.

Gibson, R.K. and Ward, S.J. (eds) (2000) *Reinvigorating Democracy? British Politics and the Internet*, Aldershot: Ashgate.

Hagen, M. (1997) 'Electroniche Demokratie: Computernetzwerke und Politische Teorie in den USA', *Medien and Politik*, 9, Hamburg: Lit Verlag.

Hoff, J., Horrocks, I. and Tops, P. (eds) (2000) *Democratic Governance and New Technology: Technologically Mediated Innovations in Political Practices in Western Europe*, London: Routledge.

Karlsson, M. (1996) 'Surfing the Wave of National IT Initiatives – Sweden and International Policy Diffusion', *Information Infrastructure and Policy*, 5: 191–204.

Katz, R.S. and Mair, P. (1995) 'Changing Models of Party Organisation and Party Democracy – The Emergence of the Cartel Party', *Party Politics*, 1(1): 5–28.

Laclau, E. and Mouffe, C. (1985) *Hegemony and Socialist Strategies – Towards a Radical Democratic Politics*, London: Verso.

Lawson, K. (1988) 'When Linkage Fails', in Lawson, K. and Merkl, P. (eds), *When Parties Fail: Emerging Alternative Organisations*, Princeton: Princeton University Press.

Löfgren, K. (2000) 'Danish Political Parties and New Technology: Interactive Parties or New Shop Windows', in Hoff, J., Horrocks, I. and Tops, P. (eds), in *Democratic Governance and New Technology: Technologically Mediated Innovations in Political Practices in Western Europe*, London: Routledge, 57–70.

Löfgren, K. (2001) *Political Parties and Democracy in the Information Age – The Cases of Denmark and Sweden*, Copenhagen: Politiske Studier.

March, J.G. and Olsen, J.P. (1989) *Rediscovering Institutions – The Organisational Basis of Politics*, NY: Free Press.

Margolis, M. and Resnick, D. (2000) *Politics as Usual: The Cyberspace 'Revolution'*, London: Sage Publications.

Michels, R. (1954) *Political Parties: A Sociological Study of the Oligarcical Tendencies of Modern Democracy*, Glencoe: Free Press.

Norris, P. (2001) *Digital Divide? Civic Engagement, Information Poverty and the Internet in Democratic Societies*, NY: Cambridge University Press.

Orlikowski, W. (1992) 'The Duality of Technology: Rethinking the Concept of Technology in Organisations', in *Organisation Science*, 3(3): 398–427.

Pierre, J. (ed.) (2000) *Debating Governance*, Oxford: Oxford University Press.

Rhodes, R.A.W. (1997) *Understanding Governance: Policy Networks, Governance, Reflexivity and Accountability*, Suffolk: Oxford University Press.

Schumpeter, J. (1943) *Capitalism, Socialism and Democracy*, London: Allen and Unwin.

Smith, C. (1998) 'Political Parties in the Information Age: From Mass Party to Leadership Organisation?', in Snellen, I. and van de Donk, W. (eds), *Handbook on Public Administration in the Information Age*, the Netherlands: IOS Press.

Smith, C. (2000) 'British Political Parties: Continuity and Change in the Information Age', in Hoff, J., Horrocks, I. and Tops, P. (eds), *Democratic Governance and New Technology: Technologically Mediated Innovations in Political Practices in Western Europe*, London: Routledge, 71–86.

Stoker, G. (1998) 'Governance as Theory: Five Propositions', *International Social Science Journal*, 155: 17–28.

Toffler, A. (1980) *The Third Wave*, London: Pan.

Tsagarousianou, R., Tambini, D. and Bryan, C. (eds) (1998) *Cyberdemocracy: Technology, Cities and Civic Networks*, London: Routledge.

van de Donk, W.B.H.J. and Tops, P.W. (1995) 'Orwell or Athens? – Informatization and the Future of Democracy', in van de Donk, W.B.H.J., Snellen, I.Th.M. and Tops, P.W. (eds), *Orwell in Athens – A Perspective on Informatization and Democracy*, the Netherlands: IOS Press.

Ward, S.J. and Gibson, R.K. (1998) 'The First Internet Election? UK Political Parties and Campaigning in Cyberspace', in Crewe, I., Gosschalk, B. and Bartle, J. (eds), *Political Communications and the 1997 General Election*, Ilford: Frank Cass, 93–112.

Widfeldt, A. (1997) 'Linking Parties with People? Party Membership in Sweden 1960–1994', Göteborg studies in Politics 46, Kungälv.

3 Major parties dominate, minor parties struggle

US elections and the Internet

Michael Margolis, David Resnick and Jonathan Levy

Introduction: cyber-democracy unrealized

The hype promised a radical renewal of American democracy. The Internet would remake our social and political world. Interaction among citizens in cyberspace would enrich public opinion and increase participation in democratic politics. In contrast to the established mass media, computer-mediated communication would afford ordinary citizens opportunities to become their own publishers. Political activists – "netizens" if you will – would employ email, newsgroups, and websites to reduce the costs of forming new political groups and building new coalitions. Indeed, cyber-democrats such as Howard Rheingold, Rhonda and Michael Hauben, and Andrew Shapiro heralded the Internet's promise for realizing heretofore-utopian dreams of informed engagement in political and civic affairs. At the very least, the reduced costs of organizing would foster viable new parties and interests to challenge the dominance of the Democrats, Republicans, and established political-interest groups (Hauben and Hauben, 1998; Rheingold, 1995; Shapiro, 1999).

We began our studies of the Internet's impact on democratic politics in the early 1990s. As citizens we hoped to see unprecedented levels of intelligent democratic participation, but as political scientists we needed to temper our hopes by careful empirical investigation. We concentrated much of our research on parties and elections online. While some radical thinkers saw in the Internet a way of replacing political representation by new forms of electronic direct democracy, we were convinced that complex, advanced industrial societies would need political parties in the indefinite future.

Political parties are the core intermediary structures that link citizens and their government. Political participation in free elections is a necessary condition for realizing democracy in contemporary mass polities, and party competition is the mode by which we conduct democratic elections. Political parties have shown an ability to aggregate the myriad interests that typify modern pluralistic polities. The Internet provides a new public space – an electronic agora – in which citizens can connect with one another. Surely, the Internet presents opportunities for political parties, especially those outside the mainstream, to place their messages before the public, to raise funds, to recruit new members, and to enhance citizens' participation in democratic politics in general.

The openness of cyberspace seemed to present a way to liberate politics from many of the constraints, pressures, conventions and procedures that had made it fall short of the promise of true democracy. The practice of democracy online would have the potential to renew and deepen practice of democracy in the real world. Now we are sceptical that these hopes will ever be fulfilled. Far from reaching out to revolutionize the politics of the real world, political activity in cyberspace has tended to reflect and reinforce the familiar behavioral patterns of that world.

Political parties, media, and the Internet

Until 1995, before the extraordinary popularity of the World Wide Web, minor parties in the United States did have a jump on the Democrats and Republicans in utilizing cyberspace to facilitate organization, mobilization, and communication among members and supporters (Mann, 1995). By 1996, however, the Democratic and Republican parties and the established political-interest groups that support them had become the dominant partisan organizations online. Since 1996 we have periodically browsed the first-level US political party list on Yahoo! For this entire period the number of websites listed for the Democratic and Republican parties – national, state, local, and affiliated organizations – has consistently exceeded the combined total of websites listed for all other American parties and their affiliates (Margolis, Resnick, and Wolfe, 1999; Yahoo! 1996–2002). Since 1998 we have also been able to measure the traffic to the parties' national websites.

As shown in Table 3.1, the top-level Democratic and Republican parties websites and those of their presidential candidates draw more visitors than do those of the minor parties. Moreover, excepting the Libertarian Party, they have far more links to bring in visitors from other websites. While only the Republican Party's traffic ranked in the top 25,000 in 1998, the websites of the major parties and of their presidential candidates ranked in the top 10,000 during the fall 2000 election campaign. In contrast, the Libertarian Party's site was the only minor-party website that broke into the top 100,000. Indeed, the Libertarian Party's number of links in – though not those of its presidential candidate – is the one case in which a minor party's numbers matched or exceeded those of the major parties. Otherwise, the number of links to the Democratic and Republican parties and candidate websites are from one-and-a-half to as many as thirty times greater than those to their minor-party rivals.

Even though they hardly matched the top 10,000 ranking for the web-

Table 3.1 Web presence of political parties and presidential candidates' party

Website criteria	Democrat	Republican	Libertarian	Green	Reform	Natural Law
Party Rank Oct. 1998	Below 100,000	Top 25,000	Below 100,000	Below 100,000	Below 100,000	Below 100,000
Links in for Party Oct. 1998	3,179	3,089	2,444	83	133	429
Party Rank Oct. 2000	Top 10,000	Top 10,000	Top 100,000	Below 100,000	Below 100,000	Below 100,000
Candidate rank Oct. 2000	Top 10,000	Top 10,000	Top 100,000	Top 100,000	Top 100,000	Below 100,000
Party rank March 2001	18,436	12,813	22,130	121,785	138,364	99,795
Links in for candidates Oct. 2000	5,602	7,768	787	887	3,294	255
Links in for party Oct. 2000	6,334	7,729	9,242	2,791	2,340*	2,025

Source: Alexa, October 18, 2000 and March 5, 2001, www.alexa.org.
Numerical rankings were provided in addition to categorical rankings in the 2001 releases of Alexa.

Party Sites ranked:
www.democrats.org
http://gorelieberman.com
www.rnc.org
www.lp.org
www.greenparties.org**
www.reformparty.org
www.natural-law.org

Candidate Sites ranked:
http://www.algore2000.com
http://www.georgewbush.com
harrybrowne2000.org
http://votenader.com
gopatgo2000.org
hagelin.org, forum.hagelin.org, forums.hagelin.org

Notes
*Reform links in are for March 5, 2001. They were unavailable in October when the party had a dispute with Pat Buchanan over the official nomination.
**Green "links in" were to the Association of State Green Parties (ASGP). The National Green Party USA (www.greenparty.org) had only 77 links. As of February 18, 2002, the ASGP site had become the "Green Party of the US" (www.greenpartyus.org). Links in were not yet available from Alexa. (www.greenparties.org) had become the worldwide site with 785 links in. Meanwhile the "Green Party USA" claimed: "Recent events have shown some confusion among Greens and the public about which party is 'the' Green Party in the United States. G/GPUSA has been filing FEC reports as a national political party for years, and was the only national Green Party filing with the FEC during Election 2000. A splinter group from several state parties formed another Green Party in July of 2001, calling itself GPUS. Their name was chosen over GPUSA objections, as it was certain to cause confusion." The Green Party USA had 1022 links in as of February 18, 2002. See www.greenparty.org/bulletin_010502.html.

sites of both Al Gore and George Bush, minor-party candidates' websites were more popular than their parties' sites in 2000. Harry Browne (Libertarian), Ralph Nader (Green), and Pat Buchanan (Reform) all ranked in the top 100,000 for visitor traffic. While the candidates' official campaign sites became dormant after the presidential election, the pattern of visitors to party websites repeated itself for most parties in the spring of 2001. Once again, the Libertarian Party was an exception. In comparison to the

Democratic and Republican national sites the Libertarian Party's website traffic improved between October 2000 and March 2001.[1]

The data summarized in Table 3.2 tell a similar story: the major parties and their presidential candidates received far greater coverage in the print and television news media than did the minor parties and their candidates. Indeed, for every Lexis-Nexis and Evening TV News category except Ross Perot in 1996, the average ratio of major to minor party coverage is greater than the ratio found for online Usenet newsgroups. The Libertarian Party, notwithstanding the relative prominence of its Internet presence noted in Table 3.1, is particularly unsuccessful in garnering coverage in mainstream media. For every offline category measured, it gets even less notice than do the Green and the Reform parties. For stories broadcast on the evening network television news, Americans' most popular source of information about national public affairs, the Libertarian Party beats out the Natural Law Party 1–0 in 2000. For 1996 and 1998 the two parties are tied with no prime-time evening-news stories at all. Surprisingly, the party's relatively poor coverage extends to the number of messages posted to Usenet newsgroups as well. The Green Party receives better coverage than the Libertarians in all media each year, even outdoing the Democrats and Republicans on Usenet newsgroups in 2000.[2]

Table 3.2 News items mentioning American parties

Database	Democrat	Republican	Libertarian	Green	Reform	Natural Law
Lexis-Nexis 1996[a]	917	1,091	63	57	193	113
Lexis-Nexis 1998[b]	935	1,342	29	57	112	37
Lexis-Nexis 2000[c]	978	1,020	76	272	113	40
Evening TV News 1996[d]	80	101	0	10	86	0
Evening TV News 1998[e]	52	28	0	3	9	0
Evening TV News 2000[f]	77	79	1	33	35	0
Google Usenet Grps. '96[g]	11,070	8,540	7,738	9,090	5,100	1,510
Google Usenet Grps. '98[h]	14,030	17,250	7,120	10,910	4,040	1,680
Google Usenet Grps. '00[i]	53,950	79,900	11,250	95,200	8,760	2,090

Notes
a   Oct. 2–Nov. 5. Search paradigms: Democrat!, Green, Reform within the same sentence as Party AND story also contains: (America! OR USA OR United States); Republican and Natural Law within same sentence as Party; (http://web.lexis-nexis.com/universe).
b   Oct. 1–Nov. 3. Same search as a.
c   Oct. 4–Nov. 7. Same search as a.
d   Jan. 1–Dec. 31. Search paradigm: Name AND party; (http://tvnews/vanderbilt.edu).
e   Jan. 1–Dec. 31. Same search as d.
f   Jan. 1–Dec. 31. Same search as d.
g   Oct. 2–Nov. 5. Google Usenet groups database (http://groups.google.com/). Search paradigms: Republican Party or GOP (in English only); Democratic Party or Democrat Party; Libertarian Party or Libertarians; Green Party or Greens and not "Golf"; Reform Party; Natural Law Party.
h   Oct. 1–Nov 3. Same search as g.
i   Oct. 4–Nov. 7. Same search as g.

That minor political parties' uses of the net have not had much impact on political outcomes should not surprise us. Political science has demonstrated time and again that except when cataclysmic events like war, social upheaval, or economic depression impinge on their daily lives, most Americans do not participate in politics, and most neither know nor care very much about it. For instance, a survey conducted by the Pew Internet and American Life Project (October 10–November 26, 2000) found that only 33 percent of Internet users – approximately 18 percent of the adult population – sought election news online during the 2000 election campaign and its aftermath. Forty-three percent of the users, that is, about 8 percent of the population, claimed "online election news affect[ed] their vote choice." While these figures represented increases over 1996, trends are difficult to project. People under 30 were more likely to use the Internet than were those over 50, but the two groups hardly differed from one another (34 versus 30 percent) in seeking election news online. Overall, the longer people had been online, the more likely they were to have sought election news online (Pew, 2000). In the absence of data from systematic cohort or panel surveys over time, we cannot determine whether information-seeking reflects conditioning, that is, more online experience leads to more political interest, or a digital divide, that is, longtime users were more affluent to begin with and already had above-average interest in politics. Suffice it to say that the percentage of Internet users who reported having sought news online remained about the same between March 2000 and March 2001: 61 and 58 percent respectively (Pew, 2002: 24).

Researchers have noted the difficulty of mobilizing citizens to challenge the electoral domination of the two major parties and the interest groups that support them, especially when social and economic conditions remain relatively benign. The Pew study respondents who sought election news listed websites for CNN (59 percent), Yahoo!/MSN (57 percent), MSNBC (52 percent), Broadcast TV Networks (45 percent), and National Newspapers (33 percent) as their top five sources. The websites of Special Interest Groups (16 percent) and of the House, Senate, or White House (16 percent), which tied for ninth and tenth place, were the only non-media sites listed. None of the websites of minor political parties or candidates is listed, an indication that fewer than three percent of the general public cited them as sources for election news (Pew, 2000: 6). These data suggest that Internet users received essentially the same coverage of election news that was found offline. Why should we expect access to political news and information on the Internet to change old habits?[3]

Party competition online: a level playing field?

Literature on party change indicates there is routine competition among mainstream political parties. The dominance of the Democratic and

Republican parties in the American political system has emasculated parties of the left and right and meant that ideological battles between parties have eroded as both sides have attempted to broaden their support by appealing to the putative "median voter." A further reduction in the level of competition has resulted from the major parties having become quasi-agents of the state, colluding with the state to preserve election rules that ensure their continued survival and success (Katz and Mair, 1995; Lowi, 1999). Recently, however, their dominance has produced a backlash. In shutting out opposition and limiting ideological debate, mainstream parties in the USA (and elsewhere) have generated anti-establishment, anti-party challenges manifested in such phenomena as the Greens, the populist right, and Ross Perot's candidacies (see Chapter 1).

As was noted in Chapter 1, the advent of the Internet, seen initially as a democratic force, led to expectations that information and communications technologies (ICTs) might disproportionately benefit fringe and minor parties thus assisting the growth of anti-establishment parties (Corrado and Firestone, 1997; Rash, 1997; Morris, 1999). The lack of editorial control and relative low cost of creating a website meant that minor political movements could establish a platform for their views more easily than in the mainstream media and could reach a considerably larger audience. In short, the Internet could help level the electoral playing field. Yet a number of authors have pointed to the "normalizing" of party competition in cyberspace, whereby the offline advantages of major parties over minor parties are simply replicated on the web (Margolis *et al.*, 1997, 1999; Resnick, 1999; Sadow, 1999; Margolis and Resnick, 2000). While websites clearly offer smaller parties a much cheaper means of reaching vast new audiences, the major parties' monopoly of other media and their bigger advertising budgets provide them with far greater leverage in guiding voters to their sites. More significantly perhaps, as web technology has advanced, the need for full-time highly skilled webmasters and/or paid professionals to manage a site has become more important, further disadvantaging the smaller parties.

Despite this general tendency, Gibson and her colleagues have shown that some minor parties in the UK and Italy – much like the Libertarians in the USA – have succeeded in resisting aspects of normalization, particularly with regard to the sophisticated design of their websites (Gibson and Ward, 2000b; Gibson *et al.*, 2000). Moreover, ebbs and flows in competition have been identified: during election campaigns the major parties outperform their minor counterparts, spending considerably more resources on their websites, but between election campaigns fringe parties sometimes match them (Gibson and Ward, 2000a, 2000b). Thus, while the web has not opened the party system for non-traditional choices, it has weakened the barriers in some cases.

Minor vs. major parties

In addition to surveying the online presence of the major and minor parties for their listings in major indices on the web and their links to other sites, we adapted Gibson and Ward's coding scheme to characterize the functionality and design of the websites of parties and candidates (Gibson and Ward, 2000c). The scheme allows us to summarize information on a range of functions, such as information provision, voter participation, campaigning for electoral support, resource generation (that is, money and members), and networking with other like-minded organizations. We also examined design elements, such as the glitziness of the site in terms of multimedia use, its ease of navigation, and its freshness. We selected the websites of the parties whose candidates for the presidency appeared on the Ohio ballot in November 2000. Using the Gibson–Ward coding scheme also allowed us to make comparisons between US and UK parties (see Gibson *et al.*, 2003). We supplemented these observations with data from questionnaires or telephone interviews conducted with state and national party officials regarding the purpose and success of online election campaigns.

At the outset we should remind ourselves that candidates' personal organizations rather than national political parties generally dominate US presidential election campaigns (Keefe, 1998: 319). This led to some circumstances that would hardly be possible in party-centered polities such as the UK. For instance, even though the Natural Law Party actually had an active website during the fall 2000 campaign (see Table 3.1, p. 55), the Alexa Wayback Archive excludes it. The archive includes three websites for the party's presidential candidate, John Hagelin, but none for the party itself (archive0.alexa.com/collections/e2k/full_list.html#gps). Reflecting a similar order of importance, Pat Buchanan's site flourished throughout the campaign while the official Reform Party site became "Temporarily Unavailable" on September 16, shortly after Buchanan won his legal dispute with the party's executive committee and officially laid claim to the party's presidential nomination and to its US$12.6 million share of the presidential campaign fund.[4]

The data on the parties' sites shown in Tables 3.3a and 3.3b indicate that the US national parties provided considerable background information – organizational history, party platforms, policy statements, and the like. All scored near the top of the 16-point scale. The situation is reversed for participation, particularly with regard to solicitation of feedback by email. US parties' scores averaged 5.7 out of 16. Only the Reform Party scored in the top half of this scale.

The Democratic and Republican websites placed less emphasis on resource generation than did the minor US parties. Whereas the Democratic and Republican parties' scores vary from 5 to 9, the minor US parties (excepting the Reform Party, which previously had relied upon

Table 3.3a US parties: functions of websites

	Information provision	Resource generation	Participation	Networking		Campaign
				Internal	External	
National parties						
Democrat	14	5	6	5	6	8
Republican	15	9	3	5	7	8
Libertarian	14	13	7	5	2	7
Green	13	7	5	4	10	4
Reform	13	3	10	5	4	4
Natural Law	13	12	3	5	0	5
Mean score	13.7	8.2	5.7	4.8	4.8	6.0
Range	0–16	0–13	0–n	0–6	0–15	0–10

Table 3.3b US parties: website style and delivery

	Glitz/ Multimedia	Access in principle**	Navigation	Freshness
National parties				
Democrat	6	2	3	6
Republican	6	3	2	6
Libertarian	6	1	4	6
Green	5	0	2	5
Reform	3	0	3	6
Natural Law*	4	0	3	5
Mean score	5	1	2.8	5.7
Range	0–6	0–5	0–n	0–6

Source: Alexa Wayback Machine, Archive of Election 2000, for all candidates and parties except the Natural Law Party.
Commissioned by the Library of Congress, this collection contains 800 gigabytes of data that reproduce 833 election-related websites daily from August 1, 2000 to January 21, 2001 (archive0.alexa.com/collections/e2k/full_list.html). Coverage is incomplete. Some websites of minor parties, such as Natural Law (natural-law.org), are excluded, and some websites, such as the Green Party's (greenparties.org) or Pat Buchanan's (gopatgo2000.org) are included for only part of the period.

Notes
*Source: Natural Law Party website, August 7, 2001.
**All home pages were slow to load using a 56 kbs modem.

Ross Perot's largess) scored in the top half of the scale. The Libertarian and Natural Law parties scored at or near the maximum. Notwithstanding the national party organizations' relatively weak control over how presidential campaigns are run, party websites still provided various types of campaign support for their candidates. These included information on obtaining absentee ballots, joining mailing lists, downloading campaign materials, and becoming online volunteers. The Democrats, Republicans and Libertarians were especially active, averaging over seven of ten types of campaign activities. All the parties frequently updated their websites but the Reform and Natural Law websites displayed below-average levels of glitz.[5]

As we expected, presidential candidates used their websites (see Tables 3.4a and 3.4b) first and foremost as personal promotional tools, not as vehicles to win support for their party as a whole. The virtual absence of the candidates' parties from their websites, however, was somewhat surprising. Except for visitors to Harry Browne's website, which proudly declared him to be the Libertarian candidate for president, the naive visitor would be hard-pressed to discover which party each candidate stood for.

Neither Al Gore nor George W. Bush displayed Democratic or Republican symbols on his homepage, nor did their parties' names appear except in the text of news releases. Internal links were not to websites of the state party organizations. Instead, most went to the Gore and Bush state-campaign organizations, or else to otherwise non-partisan

Table 3.4a US national candidates: functions of websites

	Information provision	Resource generation	Participation	Networking		Campaign
				Internal	External	
National sites						
Al Gore	14	5	6	5	1	5
G.W. Bush	12	4	3	4	1	4
Harry Browne	12	4	7	1	1	5
Ralph Nader	10	3	1	1	2	7
Pat Buchanan	8	3	4	1	0	5
John Hagelin	8	1	1	1	2	2
Mean score	10.3	3.5	3.7	2.2	1.2	4.7
Range	0–16	0–13	$0-n$	0–6	0–15	0–10

Table 3.4b US national candidates: website style and delivery

	Glitz/ Multimedia	Access in principle*	Navigation	Freshness
National sites				
Al Gore	6	2	4	6
G.W. Bush	4	2	1	6
Harry Browne	4	1	1	6
Ralph Nader	2	0	3	6
Pat Buchanan	3	0	2	6
John Hagelin	4	0	0	6
Mean score	3.8	0.8	1.8	6
Range	0–6	0–5	$0-n$	0–6

Source: same as Table 3.3a and 3.3b.

Note
*All homepages were slow to load using a 56 kbs modem.

groups of voters, such as students, Latinos, African-Americans, veterans, young professionals, or senior citizens for Gore or Bush, who happened to support the candidate but not necessarily the rest of his party's ticket. Despite his successful court battle against the party regulars' endorsement of John Hagelin to secure the Reform Party's official nomination and its US$12.6 million in presidential campaign funds, Pat Buchanan made no mention of the Reform Party on his home page. Ralph Nader's website stated that he endorsed the Green Party's platform, but it did not state that Nader was running as the Green Party's official nominee. Partisanship on John Hagelin's website was used only to guide voters to the candidate. Visitors were instructed to click on a map to determine the proper way to cast their ballot for Hagelin in their respective home states.

The candidates' campaign sites provided substantial information about their personal organizations, but somewhat less than the party sites provided about their political organizations. The sites also provided a good deal of information about the candidates' campaigns, but, again, somewhat less than did the party sites. None of the candidates engaged heavily in resource generation: the mean score was only 3.5 and the highest score (5, for Gore) was below the mean for the parties. The Gore and Bush websites focused mainly on providing information that reinforced voters' presidential predispositions or tried to win over the presidential choice of swing voters. Not only were the Gore and Bush home pages devoid of a Democratic or Republican logo or link, they also contained no pleas for support of any candidates running for Senator or Representative on their party's ticket. Finally, the candidate sites were even less inviting than the party sites regarding voters' participation in organizational affairs.

Except for becoming members of an email list, those who wanted to volunteer to work for the campaign were directed to the URL of the candidates' campaign organization in their home states. Campaign souvenirs and merchandise were not promoted heavily, nor were there dues paying campaign memberships comparable to traditional party memberships. As Gore and Bush had accepted full funding from the presidential campaign fund for their fall campaigns, they could collect money only "for legal and accounting services to ensure compliance with federal law," not for running the campaign itself. Donations of "soft money" go directly to political party organizations, ostensibly for party-building activities or for campaign activities that are run independently of the candidates' organizations. Large donations of this type were not solicited on either the candidate or the national party websites.

Neither the parties nor the candidates placed much emphasis on facilitating website access for visitors with special needs. None of the US parties or candidates made provision for the physically handicapped. Only the

Democratic and Republican websites and the Gore, Bush, and Browne candidate websites offered Spanish translation; and only the Libertarian Party website clearly displayed a text-only option, a convenience for those with low-speed Internet connections.

Website questionnaire and interview data

In the US federal system, state and local party organizations co-ordinate their efforts with candidate organizations and otherwise participate in aspects of presidential campaigns independently of the national parties. We used email questionnaires and telephone surveys directed to knowledgeable state and national party officials to complement our observations about the US parties' national party websites. Responses on thirty different party websites (thirteen Democratic, eleven Republican, and six minor) were collected between February and June 2001. Four minor-party and two Republican officials responded by email. The remaining twenty-four responses were obtained by telephone.[6]

Even though our sample was limited, some clear patterns emerged. Minor-party officials saw their websites as more critical to their election campaigns than did major-party officials. All but one of the minor-party respondents ranked fundraising via the website as important or very important. The same number also saw their party's website as important or very important for recruiting volunteers, and two-thirds saw it as similarly important for voter feedback. In contrast, all but two Democrats and four Republicans said fundraising via the Internet was "not important." (These four Republicans answered "don't know.") Moreover, only five Republicans and five Democrats saw their websites as important or very important sources of volunteers.

The results do suggest that our observations regarding the ability of national websites to impart general information and to campaign directly can be extended to state parties as well. All but one website reported using personal email to voters, and two-thirds reported using targeted email to groups. A majority of respondents ranked two specific uses -informing the electorate and communicating with activists – as important or very important website functions. While this pattern generally held for all parties, the minor-party respondents chose "very important" more often than did the major-party respondents, and the Democratic respondents thought that these website activities were less important than did the Republicans. Somewhat surprisingly, six out of ten Republicans responding to the question ranked feedback as important or very important, but only four out of thirteen Democrats ranked it so highly.

When it came to comparing the importance of online activities with offline activities, however, the major and minor parties differed greatly. Three minor-party officials ranked online campaigning first or second when compared to commercial advertisements, candidate appearances, personal communication, and campaign paraphernalia. Seven Democrats and four Republicans gave online campaigning the lowest ranking. Only one Democrat ranked it as high as second. All six minor-party respondents said that online campaigning significantly affected their candidates' election results. Only one Democrat and two Republican respondents rendered similar judgments. Below are some statements from respondents that illustrate these differences.

> Since we received no television network coverage, the website was extremely important ... The Libertarian Party has a lot of geeks and nerds as members. We were the first to be active on the Internet in 1996. We thought we would stay number one on the web, but obviously Bush and Gore can outspend us with $67 million in campaign funds ... The Internet does level the playing field a bit however. For example, in August 2000 our site traffic was equal to or greater than the Bush or Gore campaign sites.
>
> (Browne for President)

> Our budget was low, so Internet was effective for us. We were happy with our site.
>
> (Nader, 2000)

> We feel it definitely boosted our campaign efforts.
>
> (Hagelin for President)

> The website was not as useful as expected in raising money. Traditional donors like a personal touch and want to communicate with a person. Traditional supporters may be anti-tech.
>
> (Colorado Democratic Party)

> The website had little impact on voters. There is not much hope in the future for web campaigning either. People are dazed by too much media exposure, it's just too easy to dump the website and move on. Websites are not effective campaign tools.
>
> (Washington Democratic Party)

> The Internet is the new frontier. Technology is always changing. Perhaps 20 percent of voters will use Internet in two years from now requiring a shifting of priorities ... Even if two percent of population uses Internet for news that cannot be ignored.
>
> (Ohio Democratic Party)

> We advised candidates not to spend too much time on their websites, maybe only a half hour [daily].
>
> (Vermont Democratic Party)

It was like preaching to the choir, as we were not really reaching anyone except the already converted.

(Maine Republican Party)

The Internet is not a priority.

(North Dakota Republican Party)

We take online campaigning as a valuable tool that will be used much more in the next campaign.

(Minnesota Republican Party)

In sum, minor-party respondents rated campaigning via the Internet as more important than did their major-party counterparts. Even though the major parties overshadowed minor parties on the web, minor parties still had a relatively greater presence in cyberspace than they had in the mass media. The major-party respondents saw Internet campaigning more as a demonstration of their technical prowess than as an effective way to elect their candidates. This demonstration had little payoff today, but it might be rewarded in the future. Although nearly everyone agreed that the Internet was becoming an important campaign medium, they made little effort to measure the performance of their websites. Only seven Democrats, two Republicans, and three minor-party officials reported using surveys, polls, focus groups, or other systematic feedback to measure their websites' effectiveness.

Conclusion: cyberspace reflects the real world

The most popular political-party websites – indeed, political websites in general – attract less traffic than the most popular commercial sites. This pattern of commercial dominance is not surprising. In cyberspace, as in the real world, most people's interest in government and politics pales in comparison to their interest in business, commerce, sports, entertainment, and family or personal matters. Notwithstanding the acclaimed importance of public-policy decisions, communication about government and politics comprises only a small proportion of the traffic on the Internet.[7] By and large, the business of the Internet – and especially of the web – is business.

Cyberspace is now maintained by private corporations and populated mostly with consumers of information, products, and services (GVU Surveys; Khare, 1995; Sandberg, 1995). Concerns about democratic politics play only a small part in the hype about the Internet in the popular press. A Lexis-Nexis Universe search of articles in major newspapers from May 1994 through April 1998 averaged well over 1,000 articles every month that mentioned "Internet," or "World Wide Web," or "Information Superhighway (or Highway)." But only 398 of these – fewer than 1 percent

– also contained words with the roots "politic" or "democra" within 100 words of the aforementioned terms. The party officials and webmasters whom we interviewed generally emphasized using the Internet for communicating information to the faithful and for organizing them more effectively. They did not show much concern for developing more democratic procedures to conduct party business. In the tradition of Western capitalism the Information Highway is here mainly to advertise and sell products and services, not to improve the democratic quality of American politics and civic life (Caruso, 1996).

The data on American parties' presence on the web and in the mass media tend to show major-party dominance rather than a trend toward the equalization of competition among major and minor parties. The situation is more ambiguous in party-centered polities where candidates do not campaign with as much independence from their parties. Nonetheless, the expectation of inherent equalization is unrealistic, given the tide of marketing that has swept the Internet. As the World Wide Web drew more people into Cyberspace, the established parties took notice of the new medium, if only to protect their privileged political position in the real world. Once again: except in extraordinary circumstances, most Americans neither know nor care very much about political issues or campaigns. Voters tend to support established parties and interests, therefore, simply because they are more familiar with them than with their alternatives.

Notwithstanding the confidence of our minor-party officials that their efforts in cyberspace would be rewarded in the future, we find few signs that the trend toward normalization is likely to change. In the great tradition of our discipline, however, we remind our readers of the incompleteness of the findings, we note the tentativeness of our conclusions, and we call for further study of the Internet's impact on parties and elections over time.

Appendix: survey procedures

Surveys began in mid-February 2001 and continued through the first week of June 2001.

1. National parties and presidential candidates

A. The Gore and Buchanan campaigns disbanded their web operations before the survey began in February and proved unreachable using email. The Bush campaign emails and phone calls went unanswered. The Bush campaign phone line appeared inoperative.
B. The Nader campaign was reachable only by email. Email messages bounced, however, as their mailbox was over capacity, indicating email was not being checked on a regular basis. Likewise, email to the Democratic Senatorial Campaign Committee bounced.

C. The Republican and Democratic national parties, senatorial and congressional campaign committees were each contacted a minimum of three times by telephone and a maximum of seven times by telephone as well as by email.
D. Other national parties were contacted once by email and a minimum of three times by telephone.
E. Contact problems included repeated voicemails unanswered, and individuals not in the office or in meetings. On two occasions permission for survey had to be obtained from higher-ups who could not be reached (for example, RNC).
F. Several websites offered forms but no direct email address as a means of contact.

2. State parties

An effort was made to contact all state GOP and Democratic parties by telephone. Many state parties did not list telephone numbers on their websites. One state GOP party declared its website was "controlled from Washington, DC." Larger state parties proved as difficult to penetrate as national parties despite several callbacks and messages. Approximately 20 percent of state parties did not have live operators, only voicemail systems, thus making contact difficult.

Notes

1 Whether or not this relative improvement occurs regularly in odd-numbered years when no federal elections occur will require further investigation. Data from questionnaires and interviews with party officials and webmasters suggests that minor-party officials attach more importance to their websites than do officials of the major parties. They may give them more attention than major-party officials and devote relatively more resources to them in non-election years.
2 The pattern of coverage displayed in the tables repeats what we found for web presence and news coverage for British political parties in 1998 (Margolis, Resnick and Wolfe, 1999: tables 1 and 3). While minor parties and candidates had a more prominent presence on the web than they did in traditional mass media, that presence was still small in comparison to the web presence of the major parties. Moreover, as the Libertarian case illustrated, there was little evidence that prominence on the web routinely gained notice or produced results in the real world. Successes such as Jesse Ventura's 1998 gubernatorial campaign in Minnesota appear to be exceptions, but they may reflect the candidate's celebrity rather than the power of political uses of the net. Indeed, most party leaders, candidates and campaign managers report using the Internet for top-down communication, organization, and – to a lesser extent – fundraising among supporters. They rely on more traditional means for winning over undecided voters or influencing public opinion (Davis, 1999: chapter 4; Kamarck, 1999; and interviews).
3 Nor do Internet users seem eager to post comments on websites, an opportunity that the browser companion program, "Third Voice," provided. Introduced

with some fanfare in the late 1990s, Third Voice initially stirred controversy, but it failed to sustain much interest and went out of business early in 2001. (See Margolis and Resnick, 1999.)

4   As archived by Alexa, the site remained unavailable through President Bush's inauguration on January 20, 2001.

5   We did not score US minor parties that lacked a national presence. Past observations suggest that these parties would have lower scores (Margolis *et al.*, 1997 and 1999).

6   Data on minor parties included responses from officials about candidate campaign sites of Harry Browne, Ralph Nader, and John Hagelin, the Constitution (anti-tax) party's national website, and the Libertarians' Indiana and national websites. Republican responses included eight state parties, the Republican National Committee, the National Republican Congressional Committee, and the Republicans Abroad. All thirteen Democratic responses covered state party websites. See this chapter's appendix for the survey procedures. The questionnaire is available from the authors upon request.

7   For links to relevant URLs, see Georgia Tech's Graphics, Visualization & Usability Center's website (http://www.gvu.gatech.edu/user_surveys/others/).

References

Caruso, D. (1996) "The Net Nobody Knows," *Utne Reader*, 75 (May–June): 41–49.

Corrado, A. and Firestone, C.M. (eds) (1997) *Elections in Cyberspace: Toward a New Era in American Politics*, Washington, DC: The Aspen Institute.

Davis, R. (1999) *The Web of Politics: The Internet's Impact on the American Political System*, Oxford: Oxford University Press.

Gibson, R.K., Margolis, M., Resnick, D. and Ward, S.J. (2003) "Election Campaigning On The WWW In The US And UK: A Comparative Analysis," *Party Politics*, 9(1): 47–76.

Gibson, R.K., Newell, J.L. and Ward, S.J. (2000) "New Parties, New Media: Italian Party Politics and the Internet," *South European Society and Politics*, 5(1): 123–142.

Gibson, R.K. and Ward, S.J. (2000a) "New Media, Same Impact? British Party Activity in Cyberspace," in Gibson, R.K. and Ward, S.J. (eds), *Reinvigorating Government? British Politics and the Internet*, Aldershot: Ashgate.

Gibson, R.K. and Ward, S.J. (2000b) "An Outsider's Medium? The European Elections and UK Party Competition on the Internet," in Cowley, P. *et al.* (eds), *British Parties and Elections Review Vol. 10*, London: Frank Cass.

Gibson, R.K. and Ward, S.J. (2000c) "A Proposed Methodology for Studying the Function and Effectiveness of Party and Candidate Web Sites," *Social Science Computer Review*, 18(3): 301–319.

GVU Surveys (http://www.cc.gatech.edu/gvu/user_surveys). For links to additional sources on Internet surveys, see http://www.gvu.gatech.edu/user_surveys/others/.

Hauben, M. and Hauben, R. (1998) *Netizens: On the History and Impact of Usenet and the Internet*, Los Alamitos, CA: IEEE Computer Science Press.

Kamarck, E.C. (1999) "Campaigning on the Internet in the Off-Year Elections of 1998," http://ksgwww.harvard.edu/visions/kamarck.htm.

Katz, R. and Mair, P. (1995) "Changing Models of Party Organisation and Party Democracy: The Emergence of the Cartel Party," *Party Politics*, 1(11): 5–28.

Keefe, W.J. (1998) *Parties, Politics and Public Policy in America*, Washington, DC: CQ Press.

Khare, R. (1995) "Demographic Status Report," http://www.w3.org/pub/WWW/Demographics/StatusReport.htmld/index.html.

Lowi, T.J. (1999) "Toward a Responsible Three-Party System: Plan or Obituary?," in Green, J.C. and Shea, D.M. *The State of the Parties: The Changing Role of American Parties*, 3rd edn, Lanham, MD: Rowman & Littlefield, Inc., 171–189.

Mann, B. (1995) *The Politics of the Net*, Indianapolis: Que.

Margolis, M. and Resnick, D. (1999). "Third Voice: Vox Populi Vox Dei?," *First Monday*, 4(10): October 11, 1999. Available at: http://www.firstmonday.dk/issues/issue4_10/margolis/index.html.

Margolis, M. and Resnick, D. (2000) *Politics as Usual: the Cyberspace Revolution*, London: Sage.

Margolis, M., Resnick, D. and Chin-Chang Tu. (1997) "Campaigning on the Internet: Parties and Candidates on the World Wide Web in the 1996 Primary Season," *Harvard International Journal of Press Politics*, 2(1): 59–78.

Margolis, M., Resnick, D. and Wolfe, J. (1999) "Party Competition on the Internet: Minor Versus Major Parties in the UK and USA," *Harvard International Journal of Press Politics*, 4(4): 24–47.

Morris, D. (1999) *Vote.com, How Big Money Lobbyists and the Media are Losing their Influence and the Internet is Giving Power to the People*, Los Angeles: Renaissance Books.

Pew (2000) "Internet Election News Audience Seeks Convenience, Familiar Names," Washington, DC: Pew Internet & American Life Project. Available at: http://www.pewintermet.org/.

Pew (2002) "Getting Serious Online," Washington, DC: Pew Internet & American Life Project. Available at: http://www.pewintermet.org/.

Rash, W. (1997) *Politics on the Nets: Wiring the Political Process*, New York: W. Freeman.

Resnick, D. (1999) "The Normalization of Cyberspace," in Toulouse, C. and Luke, T. (eds), *The Politics of Cyberspace*, London: Routledge, 48–68.

Rheingold, H. (1995) *The Virtual Community: Finding Connection in a Computerised World*, London: Minerva.

Sadow, J. with James, K. (1999) "Virtual Billboards? Candidate Web Sites and Campaigning in 1998," paper presented to the American Political Science Association annual meeting, Atlanta, Georgia.

Sandberg, J. (1995) "Rush to Claim Turf on Internet Ends Tradition of Free Domain Names," *Wall Street Journal*, (9/14): B2.

Shapiro, A. (1999) *The Control Revolution: How the Internet is Putting Individuals in Charge and Changing the World We Know*, New York: Public Affairs (A Century Foundation Book).

Yahoo! (1996–2002). Available at: http://dir.yahoo.com/Government/U_S_Government/Politics/Parties/.

[This chapter is dedicated to the memory of David Resnick.]

4 Southern European parties and party systems, and the new ICTs

Carlos Cunha, Irene Martín, James Newell and Luis Ramiro

Introduction

There can be little doubt that, by virtue of the Internet's distinctive characteristics, parties' engagement with it carries the potential for an enhancement of the quality of democracy. Whether that potential is, or is likely to be, realised in the future is something that depends on the choices of parties themselves – where such choices will in turn be a function of their strategic implications given the systemic and cultural contexts within which the parties find themselves. This being the case, it would seem highly unlikely that what has so far been discovered about the impact of the net on parties and party competition in some democracies will be found to be replicated in exactly the same form in all democracies. For example, we might reasonably expect (though a case could also be made for the opposite view) that in party systems that are highly competitive in the Sartorian (1976) sense, parties will be more active in exploiting the technology in an attempt to enhance citizen political involvement than are parties in less competitive systems where, by definition, victories are on larger margins and the distribution of the strength among parties is uneven. Somewhat more straightforwardly, we might reasonably expect that in systems where the proportion of ordinary citizens online is higher, parties would be more active in exploiting the technology for campaigning than in systems where the proportion is lower. This, then, is our point of departure: while much has been written about the advent of the Internet for the quality of democracy, we need to examine polities whose party system and other characteristics differ from those of the democracies – mainly America and the northern European polities – that have hitherto been used to explore the political implications of the net. Only then will we avoid the potential trap of technological determinism. Only then will we move closer to a fuller understanding of the conditions under which the net may have an impact upon political parties in a broader sense.

In this chapter we explore how parties in Portugal, Italy, Spain and Greece are engaging with the technology, because the southern European

countries' common denominators have so often been regarded as justifying their placement in a category apart from the northern European and
Anglo-American democracies.[1] For example, there has long been a temp-
tation in sociological writing to identify a 'Mediterranean culture',[2] the
most salient features of which are often disparagingly described as clien-
telism; a relative absence of fairness and equality in administrative procedures; an absence of trust and mutual respect between citizens and the
state – and so forth. Such features are in turn often attributed to the
broad historical commonalties of these countries, in particular the failed
emergence in the age of state- and nation-building of a strong bourgeoisie
able rigorously to apply the distinctive bourgeois values of law and order,
responsibility and competition, and thus able to subordinate, in the
general interest, alternative power centres whose influence was such as to
undermine the authority of the state.

That such broad, macro-historical influences might be expected to find
reflection in the way in which the countries' parties engage with Internet
technology at the beginning of the twenty-first century seems, on the face
of it, to be unlikely. But there are other reasons to anticipate finding a distinctively southern European pattern in this respect. Most obviously, until
recently, these countries have (with the important exception of Italy)
tended to lag behind northern Europe in terms of their rates of economic
development, and this may in part explain the well-known tendency for
rates of 'take-up' of the new technologies to be somewhat lower here.[3]
Second, the parties and party systems of southern Europe are often
thought of as displaying distinctive properties (Pridham and Lewis, 1994;
Morlino, 1995 and 1998). In particular, while it has been possible to consider the four countries as 'consolidated democracies' since the mid-1980s
(Gunther, Diamandouros and Puhle, 1995; Linz and Stepan, 1996), nevertheless, they lack the long traditions of democratic rule that have allowed
political parties in other parts of western Europe gradually to develop
more or less stable relations with their potential voters. The implications
of this are particularly apparent in the cases of Portugal, Spain and
Greece.

When Portugal, Spain and Greece underwent 'democratic transitions'
in the 1970s, political parties played a very prominent part in the political
changes (Morlino, 1995 and 1998), and this gave them a significant socialisation role in terms of the inculcation among citizens of the norms and
habits of 'democracy'. At the same time, newly legalised political parties
found that advanced communications technologies were already well
developed, and this had important implications both for the way in which
the parties would try to reach voters and for the organisational styles they
would adopt. On the one hand, television-based communication was a
facilitating condition allowing parties to convey their message efficiently
and effectively to a range of social groups and regions that had hitherto
been excluded from the political process. But, on the other hand, new

technologies bore with them the risk that they would lead to a trivialisation of politics – turning it into another form of mass entertainment – and thus that citizens would become alienated from the political process. In other countries, the technologies had already played a part in bringing about the spread of the 'catch-all' party model with its corresponding detachment of voters from parties. In southern Europe, parties' attempts to marshal technological resources in the service of similar strategies may have had negative consequences for the quality of these countries' democracies as well (Diamandouros, 1997). This can be seen in the highly ambivalent attitudes of citizens towards political parties in southern Europe (Torcal, Gunther and Montero, 2002). What all this suggests, then, is that we already have grounds for believing that there may be distinctive implications of the interaction between politics and communications technologies in southern Europe, implications that are not replicated in exactly the same form elsewhere. Consequently, our aim in this chapter is to try to establish, in a tentative and exploratory fashion, whether there is anything distinctive about the way in which southern European parties are engaging with the new, web-based technology; and, if so, to suggest how it might be explained.

The remainder of this chapter is divided into four sections. In the first of these we take the 'equalisation' and 'normalisation' hypotheses described by the editors in the introductory chapter and assess its relative merits in the four countries here considered.

In the second section we consider the extent to which parties are making efforts to exploit the interactive potential of the web to enhance the quantity and quality of citizens' political participation, allowing them to be the producers as well as the consumers of political communications. Most of the empirical studies conducted so far outside southern Europe conclude that parties have yet to exploit the full interactive potential of the technology, with the majority of sites offering not much more than one-way communication via email. On the one hand, it seems reasonable to expect this finding to be replicated in the four countries examined here as well: parties are by and large 'vote-maximising' entities, and it is unreasonable to expect them to engage in dialogue with citizens via interactive web features that thereby make them vulnerable to the attacks of journalists and opponents. On the other hand, we might expect such a tendency not to be completely uniform; previous research on the Italian case (Gibson, Newell and Ward, 2000; Newell, 2001), for example, suggested that the reluctance of parties to exploit the interactive potential of the web was less true of parties with well-developed extra-parliamentary organisations than it was of what Donovan (2002) calls 'quasi-parties'.[4]

In the third section we tackle the issue of the Internet's impact on the body politic head-on by looking at usage of the new technology from the 'bottom up'. That is, the quantity and quality of what the parties do online, explored in the previous two sections, will provide *some* evidence about the implications of the technology for the quality of democracy; but ultimately, answers to this question will depend crucially on how many people are online, the kinds of people who are online, and what they use the Internet for. As is often observed, one of the crucial features of the Internet arguing for a muted impact of the new technology is the fact that it is reliant, in the main, on voters actively searching out sites. 'Websites do not allow parties to push their message onto unsuspecting voters as television or radio do' (Ward and Gibson, 2002). A now-large number of studies have confirmed that smaller proportions of the publics of the southern European countries are online than of the publics of northern European countries and America.[5] However, this leaves open the possibility that, in terms of political significance, who is online and what they do online compensate for, or even outweigh, the small numbers.

In the fourth and final section we draw some conclusions about whether there is any indication that the style of party Internet usage is different in the southern European countries than in the rest of Europe or the wider world, and about the cultural and institutional contrasts that might account for differences between the four countries considered here.

Equalisation versus normalisation

In an attempt to assess the relative merits of 'equalisation' versus 'normalisation' empirically, this research makes use of two main sources of data: a series of interviews carried out with party webmasters in the four countries in 2000 and 2001,[6] and an index devised by Gibson and Ward (1998) to measure the extent to which parties exploit the web for the purposes of campaigning and electioneering. Gibson and Ward have devised indices for a number of the purposes for which parties employ sites (for example, networking, resource generation, information provision and participation); and, of course, there is a sense in which most of what parties do with the web can be regarded as related to the former purpose. Campaigning and electioneering, and their associated index, are distinguished from the others merely because they refer to parties' direct efforts to win over voters through their sites. Other activities such as resource generation and recruitment are here regarded as indirect efforts, as means to the achievement of successful campaigning and electioneering, and are thus not considered.

The index of website-campaign effectiveness used to measure the extent to which parties exploit the web for the purposes of campaigning and electioneering (hereafter referred to as the index of 'campaign effectiveness') is composed of four sub-indices: design sophistication, accessibility, freshness and targeting. The first of these is designed to measure the visual appeal and dynamism of a site on the assumption that an eye-catching and entertaining site will recruit more voters than a plain and static one. Access is designed to measure ease of access and navigation around the site on the rather obvious assumption that the material presented can only have a real impact if the visitor can get at it easily. So access measures the presence of features designed to assist the visitor's surfing. Freshness is designed to measure how current or stale a party's site is on the supposition that only up-to-date sites will succeed in retaining visitor interest. Targeting is designed to measure the degree to which the party uses its site to tailor its messages to specific groups of voters on the postulation that the more it customises its product in this way, the more effective it will be. In effect, it measures the degree to which the party is exploiting the narrowcasting capabilities of the new media to sell itself.

Each of the four indices was used to study the sites of eight Greek parties in November 2001; fourteen Spanish parties in November–December 2001; fourteen Portuguese parties, party alliances and political associations in February 2002 during the extraordinary (early) legislative electoral campaign,[7] and fifteen Italian parties in February 2002. In each country, the parties were chosen for analysis in such a way as to cover the full range of the ideological spectrum from left to right and, so far as possible, to include all the parties with parliamentary representation. Details of the scoring system used in the application of each of the indices, together with the names and web addresses of the parties analysed, can be found in the Appendices to this chapter.

Table 4.1 shows the sets of scores that were obtained by each party when its site was analysed using the four sub-indices described above. For each party, its share of the seats obtained at the general election immediately preceding the date on which the analysis was undertaken is also shown. Normalisation versus equalisation can be assessed by calculating the correlation, r, between seat share – designed to stand as an indicator of party size – and the parties' overall scores.[8] Doing this gives remarkably similar correlations of 0.44 for Portugal, 0.40 for Italy, 0.40 for Spain and 0.35 for Greece. On this data, then, party size does seem to make a difference – though its influence could hardly be said to be considerable. A correlation of 0.35, for example, suggests that less than one-eighth of the variation in the sophistication of parties' sites as we are measuring it can be accounted for by size alone. Not surprisingly, therefore, a number of significant exceptions to the relationship between size and site sophistication can be identified in Table 4.1. In Greece, for example, while the largest party (PASOK) is also the party that scores most highly on our indices, the parties that occupy second and third places in terms of our measure (I Fileleftheri and Synaspismos) are just a fraction of the size of PASOK.[9] Similarly, in Italy, while the three largest parties – the Left Democrats, *Forza Italia* and the National Alliance – are also among the top scorers in terms of website sophistication, three of the smallest parties – Communist Refoundation, the Greens and Pannella's Radicals – have sites whose sophistication at least matches those of the former parties. It is worth pointing out that the three small parties just mentioned are all 'new politics' parties, the social characteristics of whose members and sympathisers (that is, younger rather than older; better rather than less-well educated) are also more likely to typify web users. Given, too, that it is precisely these kinds of parties that are likely to lack exposure in the traditional media, not surprisingly, we find that they are at least as assiduous in exploiting the technology as their larger rivals, thereby enabling them to take advantage of the potential the technology gives them to circumvent the traditional media altogether and to appeal to voters directly.

The case of Portugal is particularly interesting from this point of view. Here, the party that, in terms of our indices, exploits the Internet most assiduously is the small, orthodox Portuguese Communist Party (PCP). This is a party that, because it is perceived as 'anti-system', has been consistently marginalised by the other principal players in the party system even when, as in 1995, its support could have been accepted by the largest party, the Socialists, to avoid having to govern as a minority. Presumably, the Communists' efforts to exploit a technology that allows the traditional media to be bypassed reflects, at least to some degree, the efforts of the party to overcome its isolation and the constant attempts of its rivals to cast doubt upon its 'democratic credentials' (Bosco, 2000). For example, it would seem significant in this connection that the PCP was one of the first parties in Portugal to launch a site (preceded only by the larger Social Democrat Party and the Socialist Party) and that its site is recognised by webmasters of the larger parties as among the best in terms of content. The PCP's information official had no hesitation when asked what the single most imperative aim of his party was in engaging with the new technology: it was 'to get the message to the public and party positions to Internet users'.

In Spain, the effect of size is weakened by the nationalist parties' extensive use of the Internet. The bigger nationalist parties (CDC, PNV and UDC) especially have been very keen on using the Internet to expand their identity-based message. In this sense, it is quite significant that it is EA (a small Basque centre-left nationalist party) that has the highest score.[10]

Further light can be cast on how 'pro-' versus 'anti-system' ('left' versus 'right') factors may mediate the technology's impact by considering all four countries together. In doing so, we sought to express the influence of ideology on website sophistication in rough and ready terms by calculating the mean campaign-effectiveness score for the sites of parties of the 'left' and comparing this with the mean score for the sites of parties of the 'right'. In the case of Greece, this means comparing the mean for KKE through DIKKI in Table 4.1, with the mean for KEP through POLAN; in the case of Portugal, the mean for PSR through PS, with the mean for PSD through PP; in the case of Italy, the mean for RC through *Pannella*, with

Table 4.1 Southern European party websites' campaign effectiveness

Party name	Design sophistication	Accessibility	Freshness	Targeting	Total score	No. of links in	Share of parl. seats (%)
Greece							
KKE	1	3	0	3	7	146	3.7
Synaspismos	2	3	10	2	17	124	2.0
PASOK	4	3	10	3	20	312	52.7
DIKKI	1	3	5	0	9	60	0
KEP	4	1	10	0	15	3	0
ND	1	3	5	2	11	91	41.7
I Fileleftheri	3	3	10	2	18	39	0
POLAN	0	1	-5	1	-3	24	0
Portugal							
PSR	1	1	-5	1	-2	n/a	0
PCTP-MRPP	3	3	0	0	6	8	0
BE	2	2	3	1	8	62	–
AS	0	1	-5	0	-4	n/a	–
UDP	1	1	-5	0	-3	6	0
PH	1	0	1	0	2	n/a	0
PCP	3	3	9	1	16	162	6.5
PS	2	2	5	3	12	126	48.7
PSD	3	1	2	1	7	93	38.3
MPT	2	2	n/a	n/a	n/a	16	0
PL	2	2	-5	0	-1	19	–
PP	2	3	1	1	7	67	6.5
*Italy**							
RC	5	3	9	5	22	545	5.6
Dem. Sin	5	2	10	5	22	1,380	23.5
Cunitari	3	2	-5	0	0	65	1.3

Party							
Lab	3	2	6	1	12	17	1.0
Verdi	5	2	10	3	20	241	2.4
Pannella	5	2	10	1	18	170	0
PPI	4	1	8	4	17	162	9.7
Dini	2	2	0	0	4	148	1.6
UV	3	1	5	0	9	45	0.2
PRI	3	2	8	0	13	36	0.3
CCD	5	2	6	1	14	135	3.0
CDU	2	2	5	0	9	68	1.7
FI	6	3	10	3	22	321	18.7
Liberali	3	2	8	0	13	n/a	0.6
Lega	4	3	9	5	21	471	9.4
All. Naz	4	3	10	1	18	391	14.8
Fiamma	2	2	2	1	7	91	0
Spain							
Batasuna	5	3	10	2	20	22	0
IU	5	3	9	5	22	319	2.3
IC-Verds	3	2	10	3	18	62	0.3
Chunta	4	3	0	2	9	52	0.3
BNG	3	3	4	2	12	161	0.9
ERC	5	2	10	2	19	170	0.3
EA	5	3	10	3	21	5	0.3
PSOE	4	2	9	4	19	367	35.7
CC	5	1	0	3	9	100	1.1
PA	3	2	10	3	18	45	0.3
CDC/UDC =CiU	5 4	2 2	10 5	4 4	21 15	239 n/a	4.3
PNV	4	4	7	1	16	174	2.0
PP	5	4	10	4	23	467	52.3

Note
*Percentages do not sum to 100 because 40 of the 630 seats (6.3%) are held by other parties not included here.

the mean for PPI through *Fiamma,* and in the case of Spain, the mean for Batasuna through PSOE with the mean for CC through PP. The calculation results in a mean for the Greek 'left' parties of 13; for the Greek 'right' parties of 10. The mean for the Portuguese 'left' parties is 8; the mean for the Portuguese 'right' parties, 5. Meanwhile, the mean for the Spanish 'left' parties is 18; the mean for the Spanish 'right' parties, 17. Finally, the mean for the Italian 'left' parties is 16; the mean for the Italian 'right' parties is 13. Thus we find some modest support for the view that one of the effects of the new technology may be to strengthen, at least in the medium of cyberspace, the more change-oriented parties in their competition with the more conservative parties.[11]

If, however, the technology is to have a real impact on party competition, then the accessibility of parties' sites is clearly of key importance. Smaller and/or more change-oriented parties may have sites whose sophistication matches that of the sites of their larger and/or more conservative rivals; but if the sites are difficult to locate, then any potential benefit is lost: one of the claims of the normalisation hypothesis, it will be remembered, is precisely that the larger, better-resourced parties' sites will be easier to access than those of the smaller parties. As mentioned, part of this will have to do with the larger parties' domination of the traditional media through which they will be able to advertise their web presence more successfully than the smaller parties. But what about in the medium of cyberspace itself? It may, or may not, be the case that larger parties are more successful in publicising their sites across the web. In order to assess this, we counted the number of links or back-pointers into parties' sites using Google (www.google.com).[12] The results – shown in Table 4.1 in terms of the correlation, r, between party size measured in terms of numbers of parliamentary seats and numbers of links to the sites – suggest that size does have an impact. Thus, while the r for Spain and Greece is 0.83 and 0.74 respectively, that for Portugal is also 0.74, while that for Italy is 0.60. Clearly, these correlations are not to be dismissed. However, when similar correlations were calculated using data deriving from an analysis of Portuguese and Italian parties' sites carried out in 1999 and 2000, respectively, the result was an r for Portugal of 0.53, an r for Italy of 0.80. The significance of this is that, if normalisation is a process whereby the larger parties come to dominate in cyberspace through time, then it is noticeable that when these figures are compared with those deriving from the more recent analyses of the Spanish and Greek party sites, it emerges that the two countries whose parties' sites were analysed most recently are not, however, the countries whose correlations are highest.

But the issue continues to be of concern to smaller parties. The Portuguese Humanist Party's webmaster[13] emphasised, 'Portals are increasingly filtering what the public has access to. Access via portals is beginning to dominate and control what people view'. Here again, small parties encounter obstacles in their access to the web because of their economic limitations. An example of this is the recent cutbacks in spending by the Greek Synaspismos that affected its subscription to the Athens news-office website that had a link to the party site. In fact, the party webmasters fear that even though a few years ago the Internet provided small parties with an opportunity to have as much visibility on the web as large parties, these private firms' portals are increasingly playing an important role regarding that visibility, and the small parties will be slowly left out because of budgetary constraints.

If then, as the evidence seems to be suggesting, the implications of the web for party competition are non-negligible, an added incentive to the smaller parties to try to exploit the technology in order to steal a march on their larger rivals is arguably provided by the electoral systems used in the countries under examination. The Greek Parliament is elected by a system of reinforced proportional representation in fifty-one multi-member constituencies and five single-member constituencies. The Portuguese Assembly of the Republic is also elected by proportional representation in multi-member constituencies. The Spanish Congress of Deputies is elected by proportional representation in each province. Although three-quarters of the members of the Italian Parliament are elected by the single-member, simple plurality system, this has allowed smaller parties to survive and prosper. This is because it was introduced in 1993 at a time of considerable party-system turmoil, and because it forces parties close together on the ideological spectrum to form electoral alliances in order to avoid the risk of opponent parties taking seats at their joint expense. It has thus given smaller parties considerable negotiating power in the formation of electoral alliances. In all four countries, then, arrangements for the conduct of elections are such as to make smaller parties' hopes of being able to transform a growth in electoral support into the exercise of real political influence not unrealistic – as the distribution of parliamentary seats shown in Table 4.1 suggests. The spur to small-party activism can therefore only be more keenly felt in such systems than in such consolidated two-party systems as Britain or the United States where, for a small party, the transformation into political influence of a growth in electoral support is much less likely to take place. Consequently, it could be argued that smaller parties in the former countries have an additional incentive not felt by smaller parties in the latter countries to exploit campaigning tools of all kinds – including, of course, the Internet.[14]

What we are inclined to suggest, therefore, is that even if some kind of generalised normalisation process were to be considered the most likely consequence of the web's development in liberal democracies, our southern European data suggest that in no sense will this be an unqualified process: institutional and party-system features, as well as ideology, will count at least as much as sheer size when it comes to what the parties are able and willing to do with the technology so that, given the right circumstances, the technology's potential to act as a 'party-competition leveller' is likely to remain very much a real one.

Participation and interactivity

In order to measure the degree to which parties in our four countries were exploiting the interactive features of the technology in an attempt to enhance the quantity and quality of citizen political participation, we again made use of the party webmaster interviews and the Gibson and Ward (1998) coding scheme mentioned above. In the present case, we deployed the coding scheme's 'participation' index. This is divided into three sub-indices: (a) openness; (b) feedback; and (c) debate. The first two indices deal with the promotion, by elites, of mass participation: openness simply measures how many opportunities party sites offer to contact key figures/units within the party; feedback taps further into that by measuring the nature of the input that is sought in terms of how substantive, specific and structured it is; the final index, debate, measures the extent to which the websites promote citizens' engagement and interaction with one another: mass-based 'real-time' debate and discussion. As before, details of the scoring system used in the application of each of the sub-indices can be found in Appendix 1.

Participation is a function that southern European parties often de-emphasise in the design of their sites. Thus, though the highest attainable score on this index was 12, fewer than half the parties examined in each of the four countries managed to score more than 5 (see Table 4.2). And of the parties that scored less than 5, many of them made hardly any provision for participation at all (that is, they scored less than 3 out of a possible maximum of 13). Overall, the Italian and Spanish parties (with average scores of 5.2 and 5.1 respectively) appeared to place much more emphasis on the participation function in the design of their sites than did the parties of either of the other two countries.[15]

The absence of party effort in the area of participation was an interesting finding for several reasons. First, one of the most well-publicised positions that has been taken up in the speculative literature on the likely impact of the new ICTs on democratic processes emphasises their offer of a potentially enhanced role for ordinary citizens in the formulation of public policy by virtue of their making it easier for such citizens to engage in debate both with each other and with political leaders.[16] Second, it has been suggested that parties might actually want to encourage such enhanced involvement as a means of reducing the gap that has opened up between themselves and citizens in recent years. In other words, political parties, worried by a loss of authority in their exercise of political power, might see in the potential offered by the new ICTs a means of re-invigorating their relationship with voters (Bentivegna, 1999: 11–12). Third, as measured by trends in party membership and voter turnout, it seems likely

Table 4.2 Southern European party websites' participation

Party name	Openness	Feedback	Debate	Total score	Share of parl. seats (%)
Greece					
KKE	1	1	0	2	3.7
Synaspismos	5	2	0	7	2.0
PASOK	4	2	1	7	52.7
DIKKI	2	1	0	3	0
KEP	1	1	0	2	0
ND	2	1	0	3	41.7
I Fileleftheri	3	2	1	6	0
POLAN	1	1	0	2	0
Portugal					
PSR	1	1	0	2	0
PCTP-MRPP	1	0	0	1	0
BE	1	0	0	1	–
AS	1	0	0	1	–
UDP	1	0	0	1	0
PH	1	0	0	1	0
PCP	4	1	1	6	6.5
PS	1	0	0	1	48.7
PSD	2	0	0	2	38.3
MPT					0
PL	1	0	0	1	–
PP	1	2	0	3	6.5
*Italy**					
RC	6	0	0	6	5.6
Dem. Sin	5	2	1	8	23.5
Cunitari	4	0	0	4	1.3
Lab	4	2	1	7	1.0
Verdi	4	0	1	5	2.4
Pannella	1	2	1	4	0
PPI	3	2	0	5	9.7
Dini	0	1	0	1	1.6
UV	1	0	0	1	0.2
PRI	3	1	0	4	0.3
CCD	3	3	1	7	3.0
CDU	2	0	0	2	1.7
FI	1	2	1	4	18.7
Liberali	1	2	1	4	0.6
Lega	4	1	1	6	9.4
All. Naz	5	2	1	8	14.8
Fiamma	2	0	0	2	0
Spain					
Batasuna	0	0	0	0	0
IU	4	2	1	7	2.3
IC-Verds	4	1	0	5	0.3
Chunta	4	0	0	4	0.3
BNG	3	1	0	4	0.9
ERC	2	0	0	2	0.3
EA	0	3	2	5	0.3
PSOE	5	2	2	9	35.7
CC	4	2	0	6	1.1
PA	3	1	0	4	0.3
CDC/UDC = CiU	2 4	2 3	3 2	7 9	4.3
PNV	2	0	0	2	2.0
PP	3	3	2	8	52.3

Note
*Percentages do not sum to 100 because 40 of the 630 seats (6.3%) are held by other parties not included here.

that the southern European countries examined here have experienced this growth in public disaffection towards parties to at least the degree that is typical of other democratic systems (and probably more so for Italy bearing in mind the political scandals and party-system upheavals that took place in the middle of the 1990s and whose effects have not yet fully worked themselves out). For all these reasons, one might have expected these countries to be particularly sensitive to the participatory potential of the new media. Instead our data appear to give credence to the hypothesis mentioned earlier; namely, that because engaging citizens in interaction exposes them to the attacks of rivals, southern European parties display the same reluctance to promote it as do the parties of liberal democracies generally. For example, the Portuguese Social Democrat Party web-master[17] proclaimed that most of the contributions to his party's discussion fora were 'not presented in a responsible manner. Often they are wisecracks or have a malicious intent'. Likewise, the spokesperson for Communist Refoundation in Italy explained how his party's website had once made available a discussion forum that had been left unmoderated because of the party's fear of being accused of censorship. However, the forum fell prey to narrow groups of individuals who used it merely to exchange insults with one another, and so the party had had to close it down. Synaspismos in Greece had had a similar experience. The shortage of human resources available to moderate its forum led the party web-masters finally to do without it. The Fileleftheroi, on the other hand, control their various discussion fora through the hired services of an external private company.[18]

The extent to which parties design their websites for the purposes of promoting visitor participation appears to be little influenced by size. As before, we calculated the correlation, r, between our index scores on the one hand, and party size measured in terms of seat share on the other. The results were correlations of -0.01 for Italy, $+0.24$ for Greece and $+0.38$ for Portugal – with Spain scoring the highest at $+0.55$. Such relatively low scores suggest looking more closely at what the smaller parties are doing.

We suggest that the significance of these low correlations can best be brought out by two important differences in the way in which small, as compared to large, parties appear to approach the new medium. First, one cannot overemphasise the impact that human resources in smaller parties can have when dedicated members voluntarily invest extraordinary amounts of time for their perceived partisan cause. This invaluable time commitment can lead small partisan sites to be innovative not only at the participatory level but at other levels as well. By contrast, in larger parties – with their lower levels of volunteerism than smaller parties – the allocation of limited resources curtails the budgets provided for Internet innovation. Webmasters and other Information Technology officers in Portugal, for example, all discussed the technophiles' struggles to convince older leaders, more set in their ways, of the advantages and opportunities available on the web. In many cases it was the impetus of upcoming elections, especially very close contests, that finally appropriated increased funds and distributed them to the new medium.

Second, smaller parties, while having more limited monetary resources, clearly embrace the levelling aspects of the Internet. While all officials/webmasters emphasise the importance of the web in spreading an unfiltered message to the public and media, the smaller parties are more likely to experiment with chat rooms and other more fully participatory characteristics because they are less entrenched in the system and have less at risk in plunging into the innovative aspects of the medium. However, all parties have to tackle the mediation/monitoring of the debate fora/chat-rooms, and this, in the absence of the volunteer labour more common in smaller parties, requires expensive, paid technicians.[19]

One would have expected that leftist parties, whose ideological profiles are more in tune with the underlying philosophy of the web (especially its libertarian character), would give greater relative emphasis than the more conservative parties to those functions with the more profound implications for the quality of democracy, such as participation. This appeared to be the case for Italy and Greece where, calculating mean scores for parties grouped into 'left' and 'right' categories as described in the previous section, we found the mean participation scores for the two groups to be 5 and 3 for Greece[20] and 8 and 3 for Italy. The much smaller difference in Portugal (3 for the 'left' parties; 2 for the 'right' parties) together with the absence of the expected findings in Spain (where, if anything, parties of the 'right' do more in terms of participation than parties of the 'left') may well be best explained by what the Portuguese Communist Party official had to say about the Internet and participation. The Internet is merely an additional communication device. The Communists consciously do not emphasise interactivity because human, face-to-face interaction is essential and cannot be replaced by machines.[21] The Greek Synaspismos also referred to this aspect when discussing the possibility of becoming a member via the party web page; they clearly did not like the idea of not meeting personally those interested in becoming members. In fact, this appeared to be an important perspective voiced by officials of left-of-centre parties in general. The class struggle is not virtual; therefore continued, face-to-face interaction with the public is essential. The web's greatest use is in its facilitation of the process.[22]

Therefore, while many parties have chosen to embrace the medium, they appear to do so only in ways that resonate with, rather than contradict, their own ideological outlooks. Thus, participation has clearly increased in the internal life of parties. All parties have found the new medium ever-more useful in internal communication/participation via email, bulletin boards, and even interactive and online conferencing. For example, the Portuguese Socialist Party webmaster[23] emphasised that the

Internet was especially good for sending information to candidates and leaders regarding party policy, and for correcting 'erroneous information which might be circulating in the media'. On the other hand, when it comes to external communication, one would expect a movement of the anarchistic variety to be more likely to embrace truly participatory developments than more traditional parties whether of the left or the right.

Parties on the left are especially concerned that the medium, which favours the wealthy in terms of access, must be opened up to the poor. The Portuguese Socialist Party (PS) and the Spanish PSOE, IC-V and CDC, for example, want to insure that every party member is eventually provided with a free email account via the party site. The PS also wants computers placed at all council levels, now that all district offices are connected. Because there is still considerable lag (especially in the provinces) in providing public access via local institutions, one potentially very important way in which parties could attempt to enhance the involvement of citizens in their internal activities is if they created centres allowing members (or even non-member/public) access to the Internet. While web access would allow surfers to attain diverse information, and not necessarily of a partisan nature, the mere presence of the web-seeking public in party centres would increase their exposure to the party 'message' (whether through initial exposure to the party home page as a portal or through traditional methods such as posters and manipulation of the physical environment surrounding them).

An unusual emphasis that southern European parties place on the web surfaces for emigrant representation. Greek, Spanish and Portuguese parties have separate pages and data banks for citizens living abroad, or have noted that the web, including email, is an effective method of informing emigrants of the political situation in the homeland and of opening up lines of communication with distant voters as elections approach. The Portuguese Earth Party Movement's webmaster[24] emphasised the small party's connection to overseas members via the medium. This is likely to become truer of Italy as well, now that Parliament has passed the legislation necessary to give effect to a recent constitutional change giving the vote to Italians resident abroad. This may assume greater significance for all four countries if cross-national mobility levels rise in the EU.

The 'bottom-up' perspective

This leaves us, finally, with the task of examining whether the parties' engagement with the web finds any echoes in terms of how southern European mass publics engage with the technology. That is, are parties' web-based activities in any sense matched by a willingness of ordinary citizens to interact with the technology for party-political purposes? Or are we forced to accept, as has hitherto been the conclusion for most, if not all, other democracies, that parties' web-based messages are falling largely on deaf ears?

From the most recent comparative data we find confirmation of the well-known differences regarding the share of the population that has access to the Internet in these countries. The lowest percentages in the European Union for both access and usage of the Internet from home are to be found in the four southern European countries; and even though the proportions are growing rapidly in most of them, the differences, as compared to the average for the rest of the EU, are still quite significant (see Table 4.3).[25] We find the same pattern even when considering usage and access to the Internet in general (which includes access from other places such as offices, schools, universities, cybercafés and friends' homes).

However, looking just at the distance between the technologically poorer countries of the EU and the rest in order to draw conclusions about a 'party-digital divide' runs the risk of falling into the trap of 'technological determinism', for general differences regarding access to, and usage of, the Internet may or may not be reflected in differences in usage of the Internet with regard to political parties. Put another way, the observed technological differences may or may not be mirrored in any correspond-ing *political*-technological differences.

When we focus on use of the Internet for such specific purposes as visit-ing the websites of political parties, the first aspect that catches our eye is that the share of the population that uses the new technologies for this purpose is very low in every country. For example, in the spring of 2000, an average of 27 per cent of the EU population that was aged 15 or over (excluding the four southern European countries) had Internet access at home. However, only 13 per cent of those who had access from home and used it[26] (that is, only 3.4 per cent of the population aged 15 or over) had visited the website of a political party in the previous three months. But the second remarkable fact is that the divide between the southern coun-tries of the EU and the rest seems to fade when talking about Internet use related to party politics. Greece, Italy, Portugal and Spain do not seem to cluster together as they do when looking at use of the Internet in general. What we find are two different subgroups within the region. On the one hand, Spain and Portugal are still amongst the countries with the lowest percentages of political Internet use (only France has a lower percentage). On the other hand, we find Italy, and especially Greece, occupying higher rankings.

We can draw two conclusions from these findings: first, that it is undeniable that the technological differences – as well as the party-political differences considered in earlier sections of this chapter – justify considering these four countries as a group with characteristics of its own when analysed in the broader West European context. Second, however, our findings suggest a new hypothesis concerning political usage of the

Table 4.3 General and political usage of the Internet in the EU and in Southern Europe, 2000–2001

	Eurobarometer 53 April/May 2000					Flash Eurobarometer 103 June 2001		
	Internet at home (%)	Use of internet at home (% of those who have it at home)	Have visited the website of a political party in the last 3 months (% of those who have it and use it at home)	Have visited the website of a political party from home in the last 3 months (% of the population)*	Discuss politics frequently (%)	Internet at home (%)	Use of internet (%)	Use from home** (%)
France	13	82	3	0.3	9	26	41	22
Spain	**10**	**77**	**9**	**0.7**	**7**	**23**	**37**	**19**
Portugal	**8**	**89**	**11**	**0.8**	**7**	**23**	**30**	**19**
Germany	14	83	8	0.9	11	38	52	35
United Kingdom	24	90	7	1.5	9	46	55	41
Ireland	18	79	11	1.6	12	46	56	39
Italy	**19**	**74**	**12**	**1.7**	**15**	**33**	**35**	**24**
Greece	**12**	**80**	**23**	**2.2**	**22**	**12**	**21**	**9**
Belgium	20	76	17	2.6	8	35	46	29
Luxemburg	27	66	15	2.7	18	44	47	36
Austria	17	96	18	2.9	16	46	55	40
Netherlands	46	92	8	3.4	6	58	64	52
Finland	28	80	19	4.2	12	48	63	44
Sweden	48	90	14	6.0	14	64	69	55
Denmark	45	91	21	8.6	18	59	68	51
Av. rest EU*	**27**	**84**	**13**	**3.4**	**14**	**45**	**56**	**38**

Source: Eurobarometer 53 (April/May 2000) (European Commission). The data on political discussion are the results of analysis using the Eurobarometer 53 dataset (Melich, 2001). Flash Eurobarometer 103 (June 2001) is available at: www.europa.eu.int/information_society/eeurope/benchmarking/index_en.htm. The sample in the first case was around 1,000 people except for Luxemburg (600). UK (1,000 in GB and 300 in Northern Ireland) and Germany (1,000 in the East and 1,000 in the West). The sample in the second case was around 2,000 for every country except for Germany, where it was around 4,000 of the population aged 15 or older.

Notes

*Own calculations from previous columns. The countries are ordered according to the percentages in this column.

**These percentages, and those showing the proportions having access to the Internet from home, are almost certainly very strongly influenced by the variation from one country to another, in the costs of accessing the Internet. Data on Internet access prices can be consulted at: http://www.sourceoecd.org/data/cm/00000382/sti_indic_average_price.jpg.

***This is the average for all EU countries excluding the four southern European countries.

Internet and, more specifically, of party websites. The differences between the two subgroups identified above suggest that this kind of usage may be affected by factors other than those common to the southern European countries as a group. One of these may have to do with political culture or the political attitudes of citizens prior to the introduction of these new means of political communication. The parallelism between the percentages of those accessing party websites on the one hand, and political involvement measured by the frequency of political discussion on the other, points in this direction.

The other possible factor is a purely political one having to do with the organisational characteristics of the political parties. That is, the differences between the two subgroups may in part be explicable in terms of pre-existing differences in the ways in which the parties of the southern European democracies seek to relate to voters and citizens. In fact, our findings would seem to support Morlino's (1998) claim that Italian and Greek parties generally have more stable, 'institutionalised' relations with their followers than do the Spanish and Portuguese parties. Although this conclusion seems to suggest that the parties' engagement with the new technology is likely to consolidate already-existing differences between the four countries, it also suggests that the potential for parties actively to exploit the Internet will be greater in those countries in which the peculiarities of both political parties and the political culture facilitate communication between parties and citizens and, therefore, their digital interaction.

Conclusions

What we have found in analysing parties' engagement with web technology in the four southern European countries are, as might be expected, some similarities as well as differences when compared to the situation in other liberal democracies. The first concerns the pessimistic prediction, drawn from American and northern European research, that the advent of the technology will lead inexorably to a replication in cyberspace of the large-party domination already characteristic of the traditional media. Our southern European data fails unequivocally to confirm this suggestion and in doing so leaves open the possibility that, depending on the specific party system and institutional contexts within which party use of the technology is embedded, 'party-competition leveling' may well remain a distinct possibility.

Second, in terms of participation, while the possibility of some distinctively southern European patterns seems present in our data (for example, in relation to the potential to engage overseas voters), overall, the nature of party web activity appears to differ very little from that of parties in other liberal democracies. That is, in Europe, as elsewhere, one is very hard pressed to find evidence of parties' making any real efforts to use the technology to alter citizens' traditionally passive political role. True, the parties appeared interested in a *degree* of interactivity, for in this way the technology can provide them with feedback or 'signals about what to do' (as the Italian CCD spokesperson put it). Significantly, however, the feedback sought almost always relates to positions that the parties have themselves pre-defined. What it is not about is enhancing the role of citizens in the formulation of party positions through the provision of *visitor*-initiated and -controlled forms of interaction. Thus, beyond the provision of bulletin boards, few parties provide opportunities for online discussion such as opportunities for real-time debate or online discussion with leaders.

What we did find was that the parties were increasingly using the new medium for internal communication. It is conceivable, therefore, that internal participation has been enhanced by ICTs. This may have significant implications as far as the 'democracy-enhancing' potential of parties' web activity is concerned if, as seems possible, it contributes to reinvigorating declining party organisations. For, a healthy democracy is one in which citizens are not only free to choose, but in doing so are free from the elite manipulation that can easily take place when they are isolated from one another. In other words, effective accountability of governments to the governed requires not only numbers, but also organisation. Political parties are, therefore, central to the functioning of democracy, and this means that their reinvigoration may well amount to a significant empowerment of ordinary citizens. We recommend deepening the level of analysis further to a micro-level examination of internal participation/democratisation to analyse the impact ICTs may be having on party functioning.

Third, while Spain and Portugal are amongst the countries at the low end of political Internet use, Italy and Greece have higher rankings than the United Kingdom and Germany. This is especially interesting because some studies show Greece lagging behind Portugal in web use. So one needs to look not only at how many people are connecting, but also at what they are connecting to. Political culture provides an additional facet for future study of ICT impact on society.

All in all, therefore, our analysis suggests both that there are some distinctively 'southern European' features of the political implications of the new technology and that there may be some important differences among the countries themselves. Obviously, the quantity and the nature of the data we have had available for analysis mean that our conclusions can be no more than highly tentative. What we *can* assert confidently is that analysis of the southern European nations reinforces the point that whether democracy is enhanced by ICTs will be crucially conditioned by the social and political contexts in which they are deployed.

Appendix 1: coding scheme for party websites

Campaign effectiveness

Design sophistication (0–6)

Parties were given one point for the presence of each of: graphics; frames; moving/flashing icons; sound; video; games.

Accessibility (0–5)

One point was given for the presence of each of: text-only option; site search engine; no extra software necessary to access entire site; home-page icon link on lower-level pages; foreign-language translation.

'Freshness' (minus 5–plus 10)

This is a two-fold index measuring freshness of home-page and frequency with which press-releases and other current-affairs items are updated:

1   home page clearly out of date (stale) = minus 5; home page not clearly out of date but not clearly current = 0; clearly current (fresh) = plus 5;
2   daily updating of press releases/current-affairs items = 5; 2–3 day updates = 4; <2–3 day updates but >weekly updating = 3; <weekly but >monthly updates = 2; <monthly but >six-monthly updates = 1; <six-monthly updates = 0.

The reason for this two-fold measure is that parties may be placing their latest news on the site, but if overall it appears stale, then visitors will lose interest. This overall impression is likely to be gained from the home page as this will be the first view the visitor has of the site. If this is clearly stale, then visitors are unlikely to search for up-to-date news elsewhere on the site.

Targeting (0–6)

One point was given for the presence of pages aimed at: geographically based groups; economic or professional groups (for example, unions, doctors, lawyers, graduates); identity-based groups (for example, women, lesbians, gays); young people; issue-based groups. An additional point was given if the site incorporated a cookie.

Participation

Openness (0–6, additive)

One point was given for each of the following direct email contacts: webmaster; leader; party organisation; MP/MEPs; local regional offices; international offices. Parties without MP/MEPs were scored from 0 to 5.

Feedback (0–4, ordinal)

One point was given for a general invitation to submit views/comments via an email contact; two points were given for an invitation to contribute more specific input on particular policies or substantive areas of concern; three points were given for a close-ended questionnaire/opinion poll and four points were given for regular opportunities for online debates with leaders and politicians.

Debate (0–3, ordinal)

One point was given for a guestbook/comment sheet within the website; two points were given for access to a bulletin board via the site; three points were given for access to chat rooms and online discussion.

Appendix 2: party web addresses

Web addresses of Italian parties

AN	Alleanza Nazionale	National Alliance	http://www.alleanza-nazionale.it
CCD	Centro Cristiano Democratico	Christian Democratic Centre	http://www.ccd.it
CDU	Cristiani Democratici Uniti	Christian Democratic Union	http://www.cdu.it
CI	Partito dei Comunisti Italiani	Party of Italian Communists	http://www.comunisti-italiani.it
Dem.	Democratici	Democrats	http://www.democraticiperlulivo.it
DS	Democratici di Sinistra	Left Democrats	http://www.dsonline.it
Fiamma	Movimento Sociale-Fiamma Tricolore	Social Movement-Tricoloured Flame	http://www.msifiammatric.it
FI	Forza Italia	Come on Italy!	http://www.forza-italia.it
Lega	Lega Nord	Northern League	http://www.leganord.it
PPI	Partito Popolare Italiano	Italian People's Party	http://www.popolari.it
Radicali	Radicali	Radicals	http://www.radicali.it
RC	Rifondazione Comunista	Communist Refoundation	http://www.rifondazione.it
RI	Rinnovamento Italiano	Italian Renewal	http://www.rinnovamento.it
SDI	Socialist Democratici Italiani	Italian Democratic Socialists	http://www.socialisti.org
UDEUR	Unione Democratici per l'Europa	Democratic Union for Europe	http://www.udeur.it
Verdi	Federazione dei Verdi	Green Party	http://www.verdi.it

Web addresses of Greek parties

DIKKI	Dimokratiko Kinoniko Kinima	Democratic Social Movement	http://www.dikki.gr
I Fileleftheri	I Fileleftheri	Liberals	http://www.liberals.gr
KEP	Kinima Eleftheron Politon	Free Citizens Movement	http://www.eleftheripolites.gr

KKE	*Kommunistiko Komma Elladas*	Communist Party of Greece	http://www.kke.gr
ND	*Nea Dimocratia*	New Democracy	http://www.nd.gr
PASOK	*Panellinio Sosialistiko Kinima*	Pan-Hellenic Socialist Movement	http://www.pasok.gr
POLAN	*Politiki Anixi*	Political Spring	http://www.politikianixi.gr/html/index.htm
Synaspismos	*Sinaspismos tis Aristeras ke tis Proodou*	Left and Progress Coalition	http://www.syn.gr

Web addresses of Portuguese parties

AS	*Alternativa Socialista*	Socialist Alternative	http://www.terravista.pt/Meiapraia/1219
BE	*Bloco de Esquerda*	Left Alliance	http://www.bloco.org
MPT	*Movimento o Partido da Terra*	Earth Party Movement	http://www.mpt.pt
PCP	*Partido Comunista Português*	Portuguese Communist Party	http://www.pcp.pt
PCTP-MRPP	*Partido Comunista dos Trabalhadores Portugueses*	Portuguese Workers' Communist Party	http://www.pctpmrpp.org
PEV	*Partido Ecologista – Os Verdes*	Ecologist Party – The Greens	http://www.osverdes.pt
PH	*Partido Humanista*	Humanist Party	http://www.movimentohumanista.com/ph
PL	*Partido Liberal*	Liberal Party	http://www.cidadevirtual.pt/liberal
PNR	*Partido Nacional Renovador*	National Renovator Party	http://www.partidonacional.org
PP	*Partido Popular*	Peoples Party	http://www.partido-popular.pt
PS	*Partido Socialista*	Socialist Party	http://www.ps.pt
PSD	*Partido Social Democrata*	Social Democrat Party	http://www.psd.pt
PSR	*Partido Socialista Revolucionário*	Revolutionary Socialists	http://www.terravista.pt/ancora/3206/
UDP	*União Popular Democrática*	Popular Democratic Union	http://www.udp.pt

Web addresses of Spanish parties

Batasuna – EH*	*Batasuna/Euskal Herritarrok*	Unity/Basque People	www.batasuna.org www.euskal-herritarrok.org
BNG	*Bloque Nacionalista Galego*	Galician Nationalist Block	www.bng-galiza.org
CC	*Coalición Canaria*	Canarian Coalition	www.coalicioncanaria.es
CDC	*Convergència Democràtica de Catalunya*	Democratic Convergence of Catalonia	www.convergencia.org
Chunta	*Chunta Aragonesista*	Aragonese Council	www.chunta.com
EA	*Eusko Alkartasuna*	Basque Solidarity	www.euskoalkartasuna.org
ERC	*Esquerra Republicana de Catalunya*	Republican Left of Catalonia	www.esquerra.org
IC-V	*Iniciativa per Catalunya-Verds*	Initiative for Catalonia-Greens	www.ic-v.org
IU	*Izquierda Unida*	United Left	www.izquierda-unida.es
PA	*Partido Andalucista*	Andalusian Party	www.p-andalucista.org
PNV	*Partido Nacionalista Vasco*	Basque Nationalist Party	www.eaj-pnv.com
PP	*Partido Popular*	Popular Party	www.pp.es
PSOE	*Partido Socialista Obrero Español*	Spanish Socialist Workers Party	www.psoe.es
UDC	*Unió Democràtica de Catalunya*	Democratic Union of Catalonia	www.uniodemocratica.org

Batasuna is the pro-ETA Basque radical nationalist organisation that recently emerged from its predecessor, *Euskal Herritarrok*. Given that *Batasuna's* website was created only recently, in this analysis we have used the websites of both organisations to produce the final indicators.

Notes

1 The literature that has considered southern Europe as a region with character-istics of its own (be it in historical, anthropological, economic, institutional or political terms) is too large to be mentioned here extensively. However, some examples are Arrighi, 1985; O'Donnell and Schmitter, 1986; Malefakis, 1995; Gunther, Diamandouros and Puhle, 1995; Sapelli, 1995; Linz and Stepan, 1996; Ferrera, 1996.

2 A tendency that stretches from Edward Banfield's (1958) notion of 'amoral familism' in the 1950s, through Almond and Verba's (1963) 'civic culture' study, to the more recent notion, among analysts of environmental policy and policy-making, of a 'Mediterranean syndrome'.

3 See, for example, the figures provided by NUA Internet Surveys at http://www.nua.ie/surveys/how_many_online/europe.html.

4 Donovan (2002) defines a 'quasi-party' as 'a non-institutionalised formation, for example, a parliamentary elite without a stable territorial organisation ("a party on the ground"), or a social movement with politico-electoral ambitions which has not achieved, or sustained, significant parliamentary representa-tion'. Italy saw the birth (and in some cases, short-lived existence), from the early 1990s, of a large number of such 'quasi-parties', this consequent upon the party-system transformation that took place in the wake of the *Tangentopoli* (Bribe City) corruption scandal from 1992 and a new electoral law introduced in 1993. See Newell (2000).

5 See Note 3. See also references in Norris (2001: Chapter 1, Note 10, page 3, and Chapter 11, page 6) and the Eurobarometer data in Table 4.3.

6 During spring 2001, Greek parties were contacted for webmaster interviews. Two of the main parliamentary parties, ND and KKE, either did not answer or did not accept the request. Therefore, the webmaster comments reflected in this chapter exclude them. In addition, the KEP, whose webmaster was inter-viewed, is a new party that was founded only three months prior to the inter-view.

7 One would expect parties' coding scores to be higher during an electoral cam-paign, but that is not always the case. The PS, for example, overhauled its site so that it focused exclusively on the campaign. As a result, many of the features included in the index we are using were ignored, leading to lower scores for those variables. Similarly, the PSD had all surfers forwarded to a newly created campaign site with an obscure link to the main party site. And given the party's concentration on the campaign, its traditional site stagnated, also leading to lower scores.

8 Vote share would normally be more informative of the relevance of a party in the national arena. However, in the case of one of the countries considered here – Italy – the electoral system is such that parties do not always present candidates in their own name but do so as part of broader electoral coalitions. In such cases, vote shares for individual parties do not exist, and their seat shares will be as much a function of the number of candidacies they have managed to negotiate with coalition partners as the number of votes that the coalition then goes on to win.

9 The correlation for Greece should be interpreted with caution. The second largest party, Nea Dimocratia, has a website that is less developed than would be expected of the main opposition party. The reason for this may lie in the controversy surrounding its website. In early May 2001 the Greek Prime Minis-ter, Mr Simitis, challenged the legitimacy of the historical, non-democratic ND governments. The basis of the Prime Minister's argument could be found in the laudatory language of the ND website regarding the economic results

achieved during those non-democratic periods. The refusal by those in charge of the ND's web pages to be interviewed was probably due to the considerable sensitivity of the issue during the spring of 2001, when the rest of the interviews were conducted.

10 EA's webmaster, when interviewed in the winter of 2001, stressed that the party sought to be at the forefront of the political and social changes being wrought by the Internet's growth, and that it was seeking to exploit the distinctive characteristics of the technology to experiment with new forms of organisation.

11 Webmasters of small, and 'excluded', parties are clearly aware of the equalisation potential of the new medium. For example, in Portugal the webmaster of the extreme-leftist MRPP/PCTP stated that one of the main purposes of its site was to 'get the message out because the traditional media censors its message'. This view was echoed, in Italy, by the spokesperson for the National Alliance, who clearly felt that, owing to the party's historic roots in the fascist experience, it had an uphill struggle in overcoming what it regarded as biased media messages about the party. The great advantage of the Internet, from this point of view, was that it allowed parties to reach voters directly, bypassing the traditional media.

12 Google is used by typing the following into the search box: *link:www*[remainder of web address]. For example, if one were searching for the number of back-pointers to the *Rifondazione Comunista* site, one would type *link:www. rifondazione.it*. Google then shows the number of pages linking to http://www.rifondazione.it.

13 Interviewed summer 2000.

14 In Spain a further institutional feature is relevant. That is, the well-developed system of sub-national autonomy and regional government means that many of the parties whose political influence in the national arena is quite modest are nevertheless influential governing parties within their own regions. They thus have an additional incentive to attempt to enhance their impact by deploying the web and other communications tools.

15 Though the statements may have been rhetorical, it is significant that EA's webmaster claimed that one of the party's principal goals in engaging with the new technology was to use it 'to foster the political participation of members and supporters'; while IU's webmaster said that 'The people leading IU in 1994 had the vision that the Internet could become a very good tool for participation and social mobilisation'.

16 For a critical discussion of these issues and claims, see Lipow and Seyd (1996).

17 Interviewed summer 2001.

18 However, they also mentioned that the same kind of control – by using word-filters – is offered as a service by the public telephone company.

19 The webmaster of Portugal's PSD, for example, explained that the party had concluded that it was not worth spending the money that would be required 'to have a moderator to keep discussion organised'. Meanwhile, Catalonia's IC-V noted that while the new ICTs implied a number of opportunities to raise levels of participation, they thereby also implied increased management costs.

20 However, only the Fileleftheroi, the liberal party, considered people's participation the main objective of their website. This is obvious from perusal of the several discussion fora and surveys that appear on their site.

21 This point has been noted in Nixon and Johansson (1999: 145).

22 The webmaster of the Italian party, Communist Refoundation, expressed this idea very well when he explained that his party's objectives were to integrate the new technology into the life of the party without letting it substitute

impersonal, for face-to-face interaction; for instructions from above are accepted if, and only if, there is consent from below. Therefore, face-to-face mediation cannot be dispensed with. Interestingly, however, the webmaster also explained that his party had sought to recruit new members via the web and had found that most of the new members thus recruited apparently lived in areas where the party was organisationally weak. His party was thus exploring how it could use the web to engage with these persons in a way that would compensate for the lack of physical contact consequent upon the party's weakness in the areas in which they were living. This idea that parties might potentially use the web to recreate the kind of party-member interaction that was once possible through the old mass parties – and thus to reinvigorate their organisations – was one that was expressed by a number of the Italian webmasters interviewed, not just those representing parties of the left.

23 Interviewed summer 2001.
24 Interviewed summer 2000.
25 France is also amongst this group, but its peculiarities with regard to use of new ICTs are very different from those of Greece, Italy, Portugal and Spain. See Chapter 6.
26 Unfortunately, the Eurobarometers do not contain information about visits to political parties' websites for those who access them from somewhere other than their homes (such as the workplace, cybercafés, etc.).

References

Almond, G. and Verba, S. (1963) *The Civic Culture*, Princeton: Princeton University Press.
Arrighi, G. (1985) *Semiperipheral Development: The Politics of Southern Europe in the Twentieth Century*, Beverly Hills, CA: Sage Publications.
Banfield, E. (1958) *The Moral Bases of a Backward Society*, New York: The Free Press.
Bentivegna, S. (1999) *La politica in Rete*, Roma: Meltemi.
Bosco, A. (2000) *Comunisti: Trasformazioni di partito in Italia, Spagna e Portogallo*, Bologna: il Mulino.
Diamandouros, N.P. (1997) 'Southern Europe: A Third Wave Success Story', in Diamond, L., Plattner, M.F., Chu, Y. and Tien, H. (eds), *Consolidating the Third Wave Democracies*, Baltimore and London: The Johns Hopkins University Press, 3–25.
Donovan, M. (2002) 'The processes of alliance formation', in Newell, J.L. (ed.), *Berlusconi's Victory: The Italian General Election of 2001*, Manchester: Manchester University Press, 105–123.
Ferrera, M. (1996) 'The "Southern Model" of Welfare in Social Europe', *Journal of European Social Policy*, 6(1): 17–37.
Gibson, R., Newell, J. and Ward, S. (2000), 'New Parties, New Media: Italian Party Politics and the Internet', *South European Society and Politics*, 5(1): 123–142.
Gibson, R. and Ward, S. (1998) 'UK Political Parties and the Internet: Politics as Usual in the New Media?', *Harvard International Journal of Press Politics*, 3(3): 14–38.
Gunther, R., Diamandouros, N. and Puhle, H.J. (1995) *The Politics of Democratic Consolidation: Southern Europe in Comparative Perspective*, Baltimore and London: The Johns Hopkins University Press.
Linz, J.J. and Stepan, A. (1996) *Problems of Democratic Transition and Consolidation:*

Southern Europe, South America, and Post-Communist Europe, Baltimore and London: The Johns Hopkins University Press.

Lipow, A. and Seyd, P. (1996) 'The Politics of Anti-partyism', *Parliamentary Affairs*, 49(2): 273–284.

Malefakis, E. (1995) 'The Political and Socioeconomic Contours of Southern European History', in Gunther, R., Diamandouros, N. and Puhle, H.J. (eds), *The Politics of Democratic Consolidation: Southern Europe in Comparative Perspective*, Baltimore and London: Johns Hopkins University Press, 33–76.

Melich, A. (2001) Eurobarometer 53: Racism, Information Society, General Services, and Food Labelling, April–May 2000 [computer file]. ICPSR version. Brussels, Belgium: INRA (Europe)[producer], 2000. Cologne, Germany: Zentralarchiv für Empirische Sozialforschung/Ann Arbor, MI: Inter-university Consortium for Political and Social Research [distributors].

Morlino, L. (1995) 'Political Parties and Democratic Consolidation in Western Europe', in Gunther, R., Diamandouros, N. and Puhle, H.J. (eds), *The Politics of Democratic Consolidation: Southern Europe in Comparative Perspective*, Baltimore and London: The Johns Hopkins University Press, 315–388.

Morlino, L. (1998) *Democracy Between Consolidation and Crisis*, Oxford: Oxford University Press.

Newell, J. (2000) *Parties and Democracy in Italy*, Aldershot: Ashgate.

Newell, J. (2001) 'Italian Political Parties on the Web', *Harvard International Journal of Press/Politics*, 6(4): 60–87.

Nixon, P. and Johansson, H. (1999) 'Transparency Through Technology: The Internet and Political Parties', in Hague, B. and Loader, B. (eds), *Digital Democracy: Discourse and Decision Making in the Information Age*, London: Routledge, 135–153.

Norris, P. (2001) *Digital Divide? Civic Engagement, Information Poverty & the Internet in Democratic Societies*, Cambridge: Cambridge University Press.

O'Donnell, G. and Schmitter, P. (eds) (1986) *Transitions From Authoritarian Rule: Southern Europe*, Baltimore and London: The Johns Hopkins University Press.

Pridham, G. and Lewis, P.G. (1994) 'Introduction: Stabilising Fragile Democracies and Party System Development', in Pridham, G. and Lewis, P.G. (eds), S*tabilising Fragile Democracies: Comparing New Party Systems in Southern and Eastern Europe*, London and New York: Routledge, 1–22.

Sapelli, G. (1995) *Southern Europe Since 1945: Tradition and Modernity in Portugal, Spain, Italy, Greece and Turkey*, London: Longman.

Sartori, G. (1976) *Parties and Party Systems: A Framework for Analysis*, Cambridge: Cambridge University Press.

Torcal, M., Gunther, R. and Montero, J.R. (2002) 'Antiparty sentiments in Southern Europe', in Gunther, R., Montero, J.R. and Linz, J. (eds), *Political Parties: Old Concepts and New Challenges*, Oxford: Oxford University Press, 257–290.

Ward, S.J. and Gibson, R.K. (2003) 'Online and on message? Candidate Websites in the 2001 general election', *British Journal of Political Science and International Relations*, 5(2): 1–18.

5 A marriage made in cyberspace?

Political marketing and UK party websites

Julian Bowers-Brown

Introduction

Although still an emerging field of study, 'political marketing' has pro-vided an informative addition to the available literature on party-political behaviour. It follows a long and distinguished line of academic work, all of which points towards a collective rationalisation of strategy in response to changes in voter behaviour.[1] Whilst the competitive nature of politics has grown, so too have the media formats on which much of it is played out. Unsurprisingly, television continues to dominate but, since its emergence into politics in the early 1990s, the Internet has gained an increasing role. Yet, despite a growing body of work by political marketing scholars in the UK, any meaningful exploration of the medium has been noticeably absent.

This chapter examines the potential of interactive information and com-munications technologies (ICTs) for political organisations and develops a 'cyber-specific' political marketing analysis to explore the online efforts of the main British parties. It provides a business model for marketing on the World Wide Web and examines whether a relational philosophy has informed the evolution of Internet campaigning in Britain. The analysis concludes that, whilst political parties have come to recognise the potential of the Internet in re-engaging a politically alienated electorate, they still have some way to go in realising the full marketing potential of the web.

Political marketing: a relationship between parties and the people

Parties are seemingly faced with an ever more discerning electorate. The relationship between them is one of 'exchange' (Harrop, 1990: 277) and is characterised by a noticeable shift in power away from politicians as the principal definers of policy priorities. A process of 'modernisation' of society (Swanson and Mancini, 1996: 7) and declining political interest (Putnam, 2000: 36) suggests that parties can no longer rely on the certainties of ideology or class alignment to deliver them to victory.[2]

In order to survive in this new environment party organisations must act like successful businesses able to understand the needs and preferences of a more critical and discerning electorate. At the heart of this argument is the notion that parties now need to be 'customer-focused' (Scammell, 1995: 8; Webb, 2000: 155). It is this element above all that will lead to electoral success (Lees-Marshment, 2001: 1) and allow us to describe the process as one of 'political marketing'. In this scenario, where business practice is pervasive and a plethora of media formats have replaced previous forms of political socialisation, it is possible that the electorate may be reduced to the role of spectators (Swanson and Mancini, 1996: 16). Yet, even in this analysis, the electorate remain 'consumers' of proposed polices and government services (Harrop, 1990: 278; Scammell, 1999: 723). The result of this is that there is an opening out of the political market and a requirement for parties to alter the conduct of their relationship with the electorate.

From 1994, when Tony Blair was elected as party leader, Labour introduced a strategy to re-engage with sections of the electorate that it had failed to address in previous years. The emphasis was on changing the party itself, rather than seeking to change the voters' values and preferences: 'Making Labour a new party was the core, the absolute heart, of Labour's strategy; both for electoral success and success in government' (Gould, 1998: 6). What becomes clear is that parties need to be market-oriented rather than assuming they know 'what the customer wants' or where the centre ground lies. In this scenario, a commonality of approach is possible and we are able to draw on models of business practice to provide greater understanding of those areas common to the political environment.

Understanding the political marketing concept

There is now broad academic recognition that political marketing represents both an illustrative description of modern party activity and a model of analysis. There is, however, often a difference of terminology and of opinion as to the consequences of this process.[3] Early (social-scientific) studies were primarily focused on the promotional and campaigning nature of marketing (Bowler and Farrell, 1992; Franklin, 1994). Others have borrowed directly from marketing theory to emphasise the wider impact on strategic philosophy and organisational culture (Scammell, 1999; Lees-Marshment, 2001).

One of the problems of this emerging discipline continues to be that the meaning of marketing may vary between, and even within, different schools of thought. Here, the perception is one of political parties as potential providers of (governmental) *services*, seeking to engage with the electorate over the long term, rather than conceiving of elections as 'one-offs', or 'single-transaction dates' (Lock and Harris, 1996: 21). This broader philosophical analysis allows us at least three advantages over previous cognitive efforts:

- acknowledgement of the importance of voters' perceptions and experience, as well as a transactional focus on organisational objectives,[4] in developing productive relationships;
- awareness of the importance of 'reputation', 'customer (voter/ supporter) focus' and policy 'delivery' as factors influencing voting decisions, as much as an ideological divide or the policy proposals;
- recognising that 'service', rather than 'product orientation', may provide a significant element in determining voting decisions, which allow us to appreciate the potential role of the Internet in replicating, or even establishing, lucrative party–public interaction.

Although not necessarily uniform in its application, a political-marketing perspective will impact on the party organisation as a whole. As a practice, it is primarily an (implicit) management strategy that is influenced by 'market position' and informs party behaviour (Lock and Harris, 1996: 28). As such, any attempt to offer a more specific definition is open to considerable debate. However, in recognising a service–consumer dynamic between parties and the electorate, I would suggest the primary elements of political-marketing analysis can be stated thus: the study of the generation and development of relationships with voters, for electoral advantage and the benefit of all stakeholders, so that organisational objectives are achieved by mutual exchange and fulfilment of promises.[5]

From this perspective, it is clear that the primary concern is with the nature of the relationship between voters and political parties. However, conceiving of voters as electoral consumers is not without problems. Instead, it becomes important to develop a more precise reference to organisational models. The work of Keith (1960) in developing an evolutionary model for business practice has been influential in the work of several political-marketing scholars (Wring, 1997: 101; Lees-Marshment (2001: 4–5).[6] For our purposes, the framework is adapted (below) in order to explore differences of approach and sophistication within the broader application of party political-marketing. In short, it allows us to determine more accurately the degree to which party strategy is informed by a marketing philosophy.

- *Product orientation.* This approach assumes a 'fordist' view of customer relations (Wring, 1997: 101). The product is regarded as superior and will, therefore, sell itself. When applied to politics this would describe a party as having an ideological orientation and is exemplified in recent history by the Labour election campaign of 1983. This model may be seen to have been appropriate in a society where voting patterns largely followed class alignment.

- *Sales or Transactional orientation.* Again the product is regarded as largely correct but effort is concentrated on selling it to the consumer (Lees-Marshment, 2001: 29), with the 'sales pitch' existing over a relatively short time frame (Egan, 2001: 17). Similarly, a political party may attempt to *persuade* voters of the benefits of its policies and organisation. This approach may examine market research to understand people's concerns but will attempt to focus on those policies that are popular and shift the agenda from those that are not. At its most basic, this model concentrates on political communication, rather than informing the organisation as a whole, and is open to comparisons with propagandistic approaches (O'Shaughnessy, 1999: 738).

- *Market or Service orientation.* Organisations that employ this approach to philosophy and practice are primarily consumer-focused in order to create and maintain customers. Lees-Marshment suggests where parties are similarly acculturated they will seek 'to identify voter demands, then design the product to suit them. It does not attempt to change what people think, but to deliver what they need and want' (2001: 30). In strategic terms, we may expect such a party to be engaged in a process of 'relationship marketing' (Scammell, 1999: 726).

  In this model, an analysis of the political environment will create the opportunity for leaders to promote flexibility of approach and adaptation of organisational response. By adopting a customer-focused ethos, parties can adapt business practice that will 'treat sales, not as one off purchases, but as "exchange relationships" where the customer invests trust (as well as money) and the producer fulfils his promises' (Scammell, 1999: 728). To the extent that a party actively focuses on the demands of its target market, builds positive relationships and reputation, and employs a strategic approach to operational implementation, it can be described as a marketing-oriented organisation.

Internet marketing and business practice.

Business, like politics, is in part about ideas and as such companies may be product- or sales-focused in approach. It can be argued, however, that, in mature markets especially, it is the successful businesses that adhere to the 'marketing concept' (O'Cass, 1996: 45) by focusing on meeting the needs of their customers (Scammell, 1999: 728). For such organisations the issue is not merely establishing a web presence but utilising the Internet as a relationship-building medium, encouraging potential customers to become 'interactors', gradually developing both the customer's interest and trust, creating and, crucially, maintaining consumer loyalty (Berthon *et al.*, 1998: 693).

In the marketing-oriented organisation, the website will function as part of the overall business strategy. The organisation will need, therefore, to co-ordinate its 'online' and 'offline' marketing strategy. In successfully positioning the website the organisation will need first to establish:

- why it has created a web presence and how this will interact with its corporate image;
- what the primary purpose of the website is;
- who controls the website content and strategy;
- how the organisation can measure the effectiveness of the website.

(Morgan, 1996: 767)

In terms of its communication potential, we may assume that the website will act as something of a hybrid between the organisation's promotional efforts (advertising, sponsorship) and 'one-to-one' contact through sales representatives. Indeed, the advantage of a website is that it can incorporate many of the functions of offline marketing activity in one location. This provides advantages of cost and efficiency and points to the potential for expansion of this medium. For the purpose of analysing marketing effectiveness, however, it suggests that an evaluative model will need to incorporate broader marketing features within a web-specific framework.

Berthon *et al.* (1998: 697–704) provide a six-point conceptual framework for marketing a website to Internet users, as shown below:

- *Awareness efficiency.* This refers to the ability of the host organisation to generate awareness of its website. Strategies may include advertising the website address on organisational literature or sponsored events.
- *Locatability/attractability efficiency.* This is a measure of 'how effectively the organisation is able to convert target surfers into website hits, either by facilitating active seeking behaviour (surfers who actively look for the website), or by attracting passive seekers' (ibid: 697). 'Locatability' is, in part, determined by registering the site with Internet Service Providers (ISPs) and search engines. 'Attractability' refers to features that help construct the early impressions of 'visitors' and will be primarily determined by homepage content.
- *Contact efficiency.* This is the requirement of websites to turn 'hits' into 'visits',[7] which occurs if the site can generate interest and encourage visitors to remain on the site for some time. Here, we may expect easy readability of text and early opportunities to interact.
- *Conversion efficiency.* With the visitor engaged, the site should aim to convert him or her into a customer. Where this is not an explicit goal, 'conversion efficiency' can include membership and registration facil-

ities as well as the encouragement of an 'offline' customer relationship.

• *Retention efficiency.* This final phase of the process conforms to a 'relational-marketing' strategy and, therefore, aims to maintain these customers as long-term consumers. Those people that are customers and already established in an exchange relationship represent a particularly valuable group to the future marketing efforts of the organisation. Relevant features should be regularly updated to encourage development of visitors and repeat purchasers.

• *Website efficiency.* The host organisation will have a particular strategic focus when assessing the site. A basic commercial aim may be to achieve promotional value from a website. A more sophisticated approach will use a web presence to develop returning customers and engage in evaluation of online services (James, 2001: 35).

The measures outlined above allow us to break down the marketing elements within the business website at a more specific level and permit further understanding of the marketing nature of the organisation. The 'Efficiency' Framework provides a model that demonstrates the primary features of a web-marketing strategy: the facilitation of organisational goals by concentrating on the user and potential user of the site.

Internet marketing and political websites.

Politics, for the main parties at least, continues to be dominated by the offline world of television studios and photo opportunities. An emphasis exists, even within a political-marketing approach, that favours mass-communication methods such as advertising and election broadcasts.[8] It may be that these 'political tools' provide the certainties that familiarity brings. In strategic terms, they enable parties to extend their marketing reach in a way that the Internet is, as yet, unable to do. In fact, there are a number of problems for the practice of political marketing on the web.

• It is a 'pull' technology rather than a 'push' technology such as television and, as such, is reliant on members of the public actively seeking out websites rather than being passively open to receiving political information or party PR that typically may occur in the offline media.

• The number of people with access to the Internet is less than half the population (around 40 per cent) and significantly lower than in the United States. Plainly, if people are not able to access the World Wide Web, they are not open to the online material that is available.

• Declining turnouts at successive elections may be indicative of a civic disengagement generally and this seems to have transferred to the web. An 'iSociety' report, produced shortly after the election and using focus-group research, suggested people were likely to have low expectations of party website content. The presumption was that sites would be dull and text-heavy, be 'amateurish' in approach and contain propaganda (Crabtree, 2001: 18).

For parties that have invested significantly in their websites and online campaigns, it may now seem a questionable investment of organisational resources.[9] Yet, television underwent a similarly underwhelming introduction to politics in the USA in 1956 and in Britain in 1959. Internet use is increasing, however, and creates methods of active engagement and information provision not replicated elsewhere. Indeed, there are a number of possibilities for political marketing on the Internet.

- In developing a website and the features it can provide, parties are able to extend 'marketing reach' and engage with potential supporters and voters in areas where their physical presence is low or with those who would otherwise not be visited by party workers.
- A website can act as multi-media information resource, providing content that cannot be gained elsewhere.
- Immediacy – websites are easily updated and can therefore be developed as a first-choice medium for up-to-date information and improved content. Its immediacy can also encourage customer feedback, where this is an explicit aim of a party and will also allow for the construction of a 'supporter' database.
- Internet technology allows for targeting of specific groups, from development of specialised page content to individual sites and narrowcasting of relevant material.
- Because the Internet is primarily a 'pull' rather than a 'push' technology, this means those that choose to view web content are likely to be more open to the information. They have 'consumer control' and can manage their participation online and do so in their own time.
- Websites can be 'interactive' and allow users to engage with the providers, giving them information on their needs and their experience, thus enabling the development of a 'customer'- or 'voter'- focused provision of service.

It is only now, however, that any meaningful discussion of 'political cyber-marketing' can be considered for serious discussion. The early efforts of parties in the UK can be best described as experimental and, if anything, primarily concerned with presenting a 'modern' image (Ward and Gibson, 2000: 31). Between 1994 and 1995, all the main parties achieved an online presence, spurred on, it would seem, by the need to keep up with their competitors rather than a realisation of the potential this new technology could offer. The Liberal Democrats, for instance, regarded their initial website as a means of internal party communication rather than as an opportunity to build electoral support (Ward and Gibson, 1998: 95).

By the time of the 1997 General Election, party sites remained somewhat unsophisticated efforts and questions were being asked as to whether the Internet was just another ephemeral public interest (Coleman, 2000: 7). From a marketing perspective, the parties largely failed to realise the possibilities that web technology provided them (Auty and Nicholas, 1998). All three main parties did make some effort to encourage repeat visits by updating their websites on a daily basis. Though, any benefit this accrued may have been lost in the large quantities of policy detail that dominated the sites. There were limited opportunities for participation via email facilities but only in the form of invitations for general comments (Yates and Perrone, 1998: 5). Given the role of marketing within much of the national campaigns, it is perhaps surprising that the parties should fail to engage visitors or to use the data provided by them in any co-ordinated way. In this light, it is difficult to regard the 1997 web campaign as having been marketing-oriented.

The 2001 UK General Election: web marketing?

Four years on, the 2001 election held open the prospect of a 'new media' era in campaigning but will probably be remembered instead for the number of people that did not turn out. Those that did accounted for 59.4 per cent of eligible voters, the lowest turnout since the introduction of near-universal suffrage in 1918. For Labour, it, nevertheless, represented the first time that the party had been re-elected for a full second term. Moreover, the 2001 General Election was also the second in which all the main parties, and many of the smaller ones, had an established presence on the World Wide Web (WWW). Yet, like much else in a largely predictable result, many of the electorate barely noticed. Even the best estimates put likely use of the Internet for politics during the election at 15 per cent (Crabtree, 2001: 6).

Interactive marketing

It is clear that Internet technology provides an opportunity to reach voters who might otherwise feel ignored by parties. Potential interactivity means that websites represent a valuable resource in relational strategy. Indeed, the Conservative Party web manager stated that the party's web strategy was to recreate a 'one-on-one' relationship with the voter: 'The best you can do is use the technology to emulate that.'[10]

Whilst the online campaigns were largely led by the offline campaigns, each of the parties took a different approach to discovering the preferences of web users. The Conservatives claimed that the content of their site was focused on the 'end user'. Research was not specifically conducted on these users, however. Instead, party web staff spent time with various Republican organisations in the United States, learning from their approaches and experiences. The party rejected the use of focus-group research, claiming to use the interactive nature of the Internet as an ongoing source of online market research. The website was, in common with the other parties, constructed to meet the requirements of three separate 'customer' bases: the public, the media, activists and party representatives.

Labour was the only party to attempt to conduct market research into its website content, using three focus groups. These looked, primarily, at those elements specific to the website and visitors' experiences of its usability.[11] In addition, party staff also worked in the United States, this time with the Democrats.

The Liberal Democrats did not specifically attempt to discover the needs of online users. Instead the website was used to provide a broad range of information to supporters as well as the politically uncommitted. In common with the Conservatives, the party did not engage user-group research, instead making use of public research and its website to provide information on its current users.

Although all the parties demonstrated an awareness of the value of their websites in gathering market research, for the Conservatives and Liberal Democrats this does not appear to have been done in a systematic fashion. In addition to a 'customer focus', a relational-marketing approach identifies 'reputation' management to be of crucial importance in building trust with the consumer. Governing parties can attempt to do this through delivery of policy promises and demonstration of competence in administration. Online, parties can seek to enhance their organisations' image by discovering and meeting users' expectations. Examples include ease of use of the site, provision of the type of information and features that users require, and quality and speed of response to online feedback.

Co-ordination and campaign strategy

The election in 2001 saw the co-ordination of the parties' web strategies with the wider campaigns, both in terms of organisational factors and in media management. Under William Hague, the then leader, much of the work of the Conservative Party had been concerned with the internal restructuring of the organisation and in attempting to re-establish a trust relationship with the electorate. Both these strategies were evident in the party's web campaign, though in fact only 25 per cent of the project was dedicated to the public website. The remainder formed an 'Intranet' facility for internal organisational use and a media centre accessible by journalists. Levels of access were customised for different users, from shadow cabinet members and 'war room' staff to the wider membership. Both

Labour and the Liberal Democrats operated similar restricted-access areas for party members, representatives and staff, which aimed to facilitate efficient communication and co-ordination of campaigns.

Each of the campaigns was centrally driven. In maintaining control from the centre the web strategies were co-ordinated with parties' campaign grids. For Labour, web staff were involved in morning strategy meetings and web content and news stories co-ordinated with the mainstream campaign themes.[12] For the Conservatives, the web campaign was largely driven by the main themes and strategies of the party: 'Tackling the issues that matter to you' and 'Listening to Britain'. In the case of the Liberal Democrats, the web campaign was central to aiding the party's efforts to raise its media profile and, in particular, that of its leader, Charles Kennedy.[13]

Marketing efficiency of party websites

Awareness efficiency

Probably the greatest problem for any website is to create public consciousness of its existence. It is for this reason that established companies are often also the most successful on the Internet and 'web-only' companies such as Lastminute.com and Amazon spend millions of pounds in advertising their services.

So how did the parties seek to attract new users to their websites? All of the parties ensured that their domain names were well publicised in the offline world. None went as far as George Bush's campaign, in the US election of 2000, by dedicating an election broadcast to advertising their web presence but, in addition to the inclusion of web addresses on party literature, there was a concerted media-awareness strategy employed by all three parties.

The Conservative Party targeted media outlets by placing stories and devoting two dedicated press launches to its site.[14] For Andrew Saxton, Labour Website Editor, the advent of 24-hour news channels was a key to developing awareness of the party's website address: 'The best thing was we got it on lecterns, which we noticed the nine o'clock news had tried to cut out. But [on] the live news channels the logo was there.' Whilst using similar media tactics the Liberal Democrats also ensured publicity by including the party's web address on Charles Kennedy's battle bus and aeroplane. Once online, however, Labour produced the most features designed to attract new users (see Table 5.1).

All three parties asked users to forward content 'to a friend'.[15] Both Labour and the Liberal Democrats used e-postcards as a method of encouraging users and supporters to contact friends and colleagues with messages containing information on the parties' policy positions and inviting them to visit the websites. Only the Labour Party used its website to

Table 5.1 Awareness efficiency of website content (viral marketing features)

Party name	SMS text messaging	Page forwarding facility (by user)	E-postcard
Conservative		✓	
Labour	✓	✓	✓
Liberal Democrats		✓	✓

allow users to forward pre-prepared messages to others' mobile phones. These 'texts' allowed users to select from a range of fourteen options that highlighted policy proposals and encouraged the recipient to turn out and vote.[16] In addition, they contained the party's web address, where people could find out further information. The Conservatives decided against external use of SMS text messaging, claiming that they were concerned that it would be regarded as intrusive.[17]

Locatability/attractability efficiency

The purpose here is to establish the methods and website features used to convert 'surfers' on the web, both active and passive users, into 'hits' on the party sites and to gain their immediate interest in the homepage content. Firstly, an analysis of prominent search engines and Internet Service Providers (ISPs) was undertaken to discover the ease with which prospective users could locate the three main party websites.[18] Table 5.2 shows that all the parties achieved high prominence on all those sites surveyed, with the exception of 'Lycos.co.uk' and, for the Liberal Democrats, of 'AltaVista.co.uk'. However, whilst all the parties' main sites were less

Table 5.2 Locatability of UK party websites

Search engine/ISP	Conservative Party	Labour Party	Liberal Democrats
Yahoo.co.uk	1st	1st	1st
AOL.co.uk	1st[a]	1st	1st
Altavista.co.uk	1st	1st	✓[b]
Lycos.co.uk	2nd[c]	4th[d]	5th[e]
MSN.co.uk	1st	1st	1st
Freeserve.co.uk	1st[f]	1st	1st

Notes
1st, 2nd, 3rd, etc. = position amongst available data on search engine page.
a   Listed under alternative domain name or Universal Resource Locator (URL). E.g. '.org' or '.com'.
b   Local sites only.
c   1st domain is for Scottish Conservatives.
d   1st three domains are for local Labour sites.
e   1st four domains are for local Liberal Democrat sites.
f   Listed under alternative domain name or Universal Resource Locator (URL).

prominent on the Lycos site, they were contained on the first page of information provided.

All three main parties registered alternative domain names and URLs (Universal Resource Locator) such as 'Conservatives.org.uk', 'Labour.co.uk' and 'Libdems.org', so that those making a rough guess at the website address might be easily redirected to the official site and to avoid the problem of opposition or 'spoof' sites distracting potential supporters, as occurred in both the United States elections in 2000 and in Northern Ireland in 2001.[19]

The 'attractability' of the party websites was examined by identifying six potential features that would present a positive initial impression of the site, thus attracting the casual browser to enter the site (see Table 5.3). Visitors to each of the websites were presented with a positive impression, with all parties providing easy-to-use and clearly presented homepages from which users could navigate the sites. Again the Conservative site proved slightly more user-friendly with a home page that required minimal scrolling and news stories created for the public, rather than the press releases that appeared on the other two parties' sites.

The Conservative homepage was designed to conform to the party's brand values, which were defined by its advertising agency 'Yellow M'. The Labour Party home page also contained standardised branding and advertisements (as moving icons) used elsewhere but its development was informed by the use of several focus-group sessions prior to the election.

On entering the homepage of each of the sites, the user was invited to make use of various audio and video facilities. The Labour Party provided live links to press conferences and speeches, which were then archived for 24 hours, primarily for use by journalists. Another feature was an audio 'campaign diary' from (Deputy Leader) John Prescott's battle bus. Notably absent on the Labour site[20] but present on the Conservatives' homepage was an invitation to participate in live web-cast interviews with leading party spokespersons. The Liberal Democrats offered one web-cast interview with the party leader called 'Ask Charles'.

Table 5.3 Attractability of UK party website content (site design)

Party name	Home page	Website menu	Easy navigation	Readability/ fit to screen	Moving icons	Video/ audio use
Conservative	✓	✓	✓	✓	✓	✓
Labour	✓	✓	✓		✓	✓
Liberal Democrats	✓	✓	✓		✓	✓

Contact efficiency

The analysis here was again sub-divided into six categories by which to examine the online attempts of the parties to encourage users to remain on the sites. As Table 5.4 shows, both Labour and the Conservatives achieved the greatest number of features in developing contact efficiency.

It was noted above that crucial to the marketing-oriented party is a 'customer-focused' approach and that key to the marketing advantages of web technology is that it allows for a degree of interactivity not found in other media. During the election, whilst all of the main parties used interactivity to develop user relationships, their approach was not uniform.

The Conservative Party Web Manager identified the interactivity of the party's site as particularly important: 'It's any way you can interact with the Party, whether it's face to face, by phone, by fax, whatever. You should be able to do it electronically.' The Conservatives' site contained two main interactive features, in addition to email feedback. These were 'My Manifesto', and the live web interviews. The 'My Manifesto' feature was launched to the press by the party chairman, Michael Ancram, and as a result received a direct link from the BBC website. Its interactivity was derived from its ability to present a personalised version of the main party manifesto, based on individual details inputted by the online user. Thus a pensioner would be presented with details of the 'Growing Older' section of the manifesto.

Labour's main interactive feature was its 'Interactive Map', which asked users to type in their postcodes. Those that did were presented with 'Local Contact Information', including details of the local candidate, 'What Labour's Done for You', listing a variety of government achievements impacting locally, and 'Tories in Your Area', which warned of the alleged negative impact a Conservative administration would have on the local area.

Labour also offered a 'Mortgage Calculator'.[21] This asked users to input their mortgage details and work out 'How much you save under Labour compared to the Tories'. The Liberal Democrats did not have the depth of interactive features of the other parties, offering a single webcast with the party leader, which invited participants to 'Ask Charles'. The Party

Table 5.4 Contact efficiency of UK party website content (make 'visit' worthwhile)

Party name	Interactive features	Dialogue facilities	Policy/ manifesto	Fun items	Candidate info	Web casts	links
Conservative	✓	✓	✓	✓	✓	✓	✓
Labour	✓	✓	✓	✓	✓	✓	✓
Liberal Democrats	✓	✓	✓		✓	✓	✓

Web Campaign Manager argued that this was for strategic reasons, as well as a question of resources: 'Charles Kennedy's image was very simple, honest, etcetera and we tried to reflect that in the website rather than having fancy gimmicks.'

A key feature of Internet technology is that it is dialogical and a political web-marketing strategy will look to exploit this feature to discover user needs and build relationships. All three parties used their websites to provide invitations for feedback and enable users to submit questions and had dedicated correspondence units co-ordinating responses to public enquiries via letter, facsimile, telephone, as well as email.

In order to gauge the effectiveness of this feature on the party websites a survey was conducted in which sample policy or campaign questions were submitted, one each week for four weeks of the election period.[22] The Conservatives responded to two of the four questions on Health and Education. Both replies were made within 24 hours. They contained detailed policy information and were sent from a named individual.[23] No response was received to questions on crime and policing or on tactical voting.

Labour responded to three of the four email enquiries, all within 24 hours. However, these were all automated responses that did not refer to the questions submitted but explained that whilst the election was a busy period 'we value all the comments and feedback we receive and can assure you that all concerns raised are read and passed on to the relevant people'.

The Liberal Democrats responded to three of the four email enquiries and took between one and three days to do so. Two of these, on crime and policing and on health issues, were sent as policy-document attachments to the email. The party provided a personal response from an Information Officer on the question of tactical voting.[24] Whilst the Conservatives responded to only 50 per cent of enquiries compared to the others' 75 per cent, their detailed and personalised responses created the most favourable impression. The Labour Party, in this survey, failed to interact with the user and thus created the impression of not being 'consumer-focused'.

All of the parties' sites contained detailed policy information and online versions of their manifestos. In the case of the Conservatives, this was available in several languages, whereas the Labour Party produced separate documents aimed at business and young people. Both the Conservatives and the Liberal Democrats claimed that their manifestos were amongst the most popular features on their websites.

One of the more noticeable trends from the election campaign was the number of irreverent and 'fun' political sites. Both Labour, especially, and the Conservatives also attempted to encourage users to remain on their websites with various features, such as screensavers and 'wallpaper',

available to download. The Labour Party used 'fun' features most extensively, offering games and humorous emails.

The parties all provided information on candidates. The Liberal Democrats made this a prominent feature of their campaign and provided a
search facility, which allowed users to find candidate biographies and
contact details by inputting either the candidate's name or constituency.
Labour provided contact details of candidates via its 'Interactive Map' and
the Conservatives included a 'Find my Candidate' facility on the home
page, searchable by postcode. Both Labour and the Liberal Democrats
stated that local and candidate information were amongst the most
popular sections of their public websites.

All three parties provided links to other organisations that they considered to be of interest to users. However, overall, the lack of opportunity
on Labour's main website to 'dialogue' with party representatives and a
failure to respond personally represented a missed opportunity in terms
of the Internet's relational potential.

Conversion efficiency

Building on those who had first been attracted to the site and had decided
to explore, a relational web-marketing model will attempt to develop the
support of visitors to the party website (see Table 5.5). All the parties presented opportunities throughout their sites. This was explicit in the
Labour strategy. The Party Web Editor suggested that the approach to
users was that: 'if they were browsers, turn them into supporters, if they
were members, turn them into activists'. A 'Make a Difference' bar at the
top of each page headed the Conservatives' website. This presented users
with a number of opportunities to offer support, including options to join,
volunteer and donate to the party.[25]

Labour was the only party to attempt a professionally produced website
targeting support from young people and first-time voters, entitled
'Ruup4it.org.uk'. The site contained games and competitions as well as
information on the party's youth manifesto and details of celebrities who
were endorsing the party. Given that a large number of the online population are under 30, this was an admirable attempt to capture their inter-

Table 5.5 Conversion efficiency of UK party website content (support-creation
facilities)

Party name	Joining facility	Volunteering facility	Donation facility	Postal vote application	Youth site
Conservative	✓	✓	✓	✓	
Labour	✓	✓	✓	✓	✓
Liberal Democrats	✓	✓	✓	✓	

est. However, it was let down by a limited marketing campaign that largely centred on university campuses.

Retention efficiency

Each of the parties claimed that its site's news section was updated at least several times a day, and 'hourly' in the case of Labour.[26] In addition, for those that had registered, both Conservative and Labour provided updates using WAP and PDA technology. The take-up of these facilities was, however, mainly confined to journalists. The Conservatives also used PDAs to transmit the party's campaign guide to candidates.

All the parties ensured that new features were added to their sites throughout the campaign (see Table 5.6). However, for the Liberal Democrats this occurred only twice, when the election was declared and in order to coincide with the party's manifesto launch. Both Labour's and the Conservatives' web campaigns were designed largely to follow the broader campaign grids. This negated the possibility of narrow-casting messages to target groups but ensured the co-ordination of wider political marketing strategy with the introduction of new elements to the election.

The parties made use of email to inform recipients of updates on the main websites. For the Liberal Democrats, emails mainly contained press releases and invitations to 'find out more' by visiting the website. The Labour Party primarily used email updates to complement its campaign strategy and, again, invited recipients to visit their website. The Conservatives' Web Manager argued that the party's strategy was, in part, a pro-active one, which enabled it to contact voters, highlighting new website features.

Web efficiency

All three parties' websites conform to a commercial web-marketing model and demonstrate some use of relational strategy, with sites containing features designed to take the online browser through a process of awareness of a website to using and reusing it and, where possible, offering support. There were variations amongst the parties in approach and the number of

Table 5.6 Retention efficiency of UK party website content (reasons to revisit site)

Party name	Daily (or more) news updates	Creation of new features during campaign	Email updates	WAP/PDA updates
Conservative	✓	✓	✓	✓
Labour	✓	✓	✓	✓
Liberal Democrats	✓	✓	✓	✓

features, with each needing to consider its relative strengths and weaknesses within the five-stage web-marketing process.[27]

The final (sixth) stage of the model is to classify and contextualise the strategic approach of the host organisation. What do the parties' web strategies and the website data collected above say about their organisation's approach to web marketing and campaigning?

In 1997 all three parties' websites had been party-centric in approach and largely failed to exploit the potential advantages for campaigning offered by the Internet (Ward and Gibson, 1998: 110). Greater investment has meant professionally produced content. The websites are constructed with three primary target 'markets' in mind: public, media, supporters and members. As we have seen, the contents of 'public-access' websites act as 'stand-alone' web-marketing exercises. Strategic implementation is, though, largely 'normalised' by the parties' offline organisational functionality.

Conservatives.com

The Conservatives conducted research into developing their web content by focusing on the Republican Party's experiences in the United States. As an opposition party, the focus of web strategy on the image and, thus, reputation of the site demonstrates a strategy to reconstruct the party as 'efficient and modern' in the eyes of the voter. User feedback formed part of an ongoing process and was part of an explicit strategy to develop a 'one-on-one' relationship with the user. These strategic goals were demonstrated in the personal response to submitted feedback. Whilst the party demonstrates a clear 'user focus', where web strategy incorporates systematic use of market intelligence, it can be broadly classified as adopting a 'market orientation'.

Labour.org.uk

Whilst all the parties have produced content that is designed to build relationships with users, this was the explicit strategy for Labour. The party's market orientation is reinforced by its use of market research prior to the election-website launch. However, this will need to be an ongoing process if the site is to develop alongside the likely increasing Internet access levels. Whilst the website was designed to demonstrate an 'open approach', poor response to submitted feedback damaged the party's attempts to implement a relational strategy.

Libdems.org.uk

Whilst approaching this study through a political-marketing perspective, it should be remembered that a party's online campaigning is, in part, a matter of resources, and as such the Liberal Democrat website did not provide the number or quality of marketing features of the other sites. However, it can be seen from the table content above that the party provided broadly similar if sometimes less-sophisticated content. Moreover, the party drew on knowledge of its 'market position' and experience of offline campaigning to inform its web content, resulting in an emphasis on local and candidate features. In identifying the website as an information resource from which users could select predetermined content, it cannot be classified as marketing-oriented but did complement the party's broader strategy of highlighting the Kennedy 'brand' and the themes of 'honesty' and 'straight talking' (Denver, 2001: 82).

Conclusions

The emergence of marketing continues to be an evolutionary process for business and politics alike. Service-based companies, with which comparisons were made earlier, have emerged from the product orientation and short-term sales focus often associated with a 'transactional approach' (Egan, 2001: 24), instead developing a long-term service orientation that seeks to develop customer loyalty. Similarly, in the 'post-modern' era of permanent campaigning (Norris, 2000: 312), parties need to develop as media-conscious and political-marketing organisations.

As a growing proportion of the electorate have become politically de-aligned, and therefore open to persuasion, so parties have consciously and unconsciously adopted competing marketing strategies to win over this electorally significant group. This has resulted in a relationship of exchange with the public acting as electoral consumers and parties as professional organisations and (potential) providers of government services.

Political marketing as party strategy

The exchange relationship between 'consumer' and 'producer' has led to a marked response by parties to focus on appealing to their target 'markets' within the wider electorate. All three main parties occupy different positions within the political market-place and have differing political traditions. Each one will therefore adopt its own strategies in seeking to win voters' support. In order to do so, however, policy, party and personnel are regarded as malleable factors, rather than the values of the potential voter.

The nature of exchange between people and the parties has resulted in two central features of post-modern politics: the emergence of a relational philosophy in political-marketing approaches that inform political campaigning; and the significance of 'reputation' – parties need to be seen as competent organisations.[28] As a consequence, organisational activity has been devoted to developing 'open-arm' initiatives, such as reducing party membership fees, extension of voting rights to members, consultative exercises and single-issue campaigns.[29] Additionally, the parties have focused greater attention on news management and message development.

Web marketing and political campaigning

Whilst the media and media management continue to preoccupy political parties, the rise of the Internet provides the most recent and interesting location from which to observe such changes. This chapter has argued that political marketing represents an appropriate analytical model from which three strategic party goals emerge:

- to encourage target groups to visit their websites;
- to use the websites to complement the main campaign grid;
- to use the websites to build multi-level support.

Political web marketing has two central functions: it is concerned to build the website as a separate and identifiable area of organisational activity; and it seeks to apply organisational strategy to online activity in developing party support. Political 'normalisation' means that websites are effectively used by parties as strategic marketing tools. As such they are co-ordinated with 'brand' values, media management and advertising campaigns.

Although criticised in terms of website design elsewhere,[30] parties are beginning to show an awareness of the advantages of the Internet over other media. They have begun to demonstrate a limited, but growing, use of interactive and dialogical features, which add value to the marketing potential of websites. By the time of the next general election, Internet and digital technology use will be likely to have grown still further (Coleman, 2001: 8). Thus, parties will need to exploit the relational-marketing potential of this technology to a much greater degree if they are to encourage and develop this new audience in online engagement.

Notes

1 These include Downs's Economic Theory of Democracy (1957), Kirchheimer's 'Catch-all' party (1966) and, more recently, the work of Panebianco in noting the emergence of the 'Electoral-Professional' party (1988), and the 'Cadre-party' observed by Katz and Mair (1994).
2 In the UK, evidence is further provided by Webb, who notes that, since the 1960s, the proportion of these claiming to be 'strongly partisan' has declined from 44 per cent to 16 per cent, on a national scale (2000: 151).
3 For instance, Franklin (1994) refers to 'packaged politics' and provides a critical analysis of party-political communication. Remaining in this academic

perspective, Scammell (1995) terms political marketing as 'designer politics' and Maarek (1995) refers to 'promotional politics'.

4 Where parties seek to employ such a focus the strategic emphasis will recognise the existence of voter and supporter, as well as policy, 'life-cycles'.

5 Adapted from Gronroos' explanation of relationship-marketing philosophy (1994: 9).

6 Lees-Marshment has reapplied the original work to develop a model of 'Comprehensive Political Marketing'.

7 A 'hit' occurs when an Internet user lands on a site but does not necessarily stay. A 'visitor' is defined here as someone that uses the information or resources on the site.

8 The combined total spend of the three main parties was over £10 million during the 2001 General Election.

9 It is estimated that the parties spent an aggregate figure of £3 million (Simon Quicke, 'How Voters Slip Through the Net', *The Independent*, 14 May 2001).

10 Interview with Justin Jackson, Conservative Party Web Project Manager, 8 August 2001.

11 Two groups of 'young people' and one group of people aged around 40–50 were consulted to find how easy it was to discover required information or features and their feedback was then used to make adjustments to website design and navigation.

12 Interview with Andrew Saxton, Labour Website Editor, 8 August 2001.

13 Interview with Mark Pack, Liberal Democrat Internet Campaign Manager, 2 August 2001.

14 The first was to attract publicity for the re-launched election website and the second was dedicated to highlighting the party's central interactive feature 'My Manifesto'.

15 The Labour Party Web Editor Andrew Saxton claims that this was an underused facility but this may have been because people preferred to use 'cut-and-paste' facilities to forward content by email.

16 Examples included 'TB 4 PM on jun7' and 'Cldnt give a XXXX 4 last orders? Vote Labour'.

17 The Conservative Party's Web Project Manager Justin Jackson states that this had originally been budgeted for but in the end was used for internal organisational purposes only.

18 These were selected from a suggested sample provided by Bickerton *et al.* (2000): 298. Additionally, AOL and Freeserve were added to the list as popular ISPs.

19 Mark Pack, for the Liberal Democrats, states that these alternatives were not used very often. Only 'Libdems.org' received significant usage.

20 According to Andrew Saxton this was due to pressure of time on party leaders and he points out that both Tony Blair and Gordon Brown were present at all press conferences.

21 This was similar in principle to the 'Tax Calculator' that appeared on the Bush website in the US presidential election.

22 Four questions, relating to issues of crime, health, education and tactical voting, were submitted, one each week, on 8, 15, 24 May and 2 June.

23 These claimed that William Hague had asked the representative to reply.

24 A misspelling of the recipient's name marred the positive impression created.

25 Neither Labour nor the Conservative Party was able to provide information on the numbers that had used these facilities. Only the Liberal Democrats were able to confirm that 1.5 per cent of the party's total membership had joined online between January and June 2001.

26 When web staff were on duty between 06.30 and 00.00.

27 For future strategic development and design, web managers may wish to engage in a 'SWOT' analysis on the basis of this model.
28 For instance, party management may be an especially important factor for opposition parties who are unable to point to policy delivery.
29 The Conservatives have operated campaigns to 'Save the Pound' and 'Save our Countryside' whilst the Liberal Democrats have initiated petition campaigns that have focused on the London Tube and the NHS.
30 VoxPolitics' 'End of Term Internet Reports' (Phil Cain, 31 May 2001) (http://www.voxpolitics.com/news/voxfpub/story272.shtml).

References

Auty, C. and Nicholas, D. (1998) 'British Political Parties and their Web Pages', *Aslib Proceedings*, 50(10): 283–296.

Berthon, P., Lane, N., Pitt, L. and Watson, R.T. (1998) 'The World Wide Web as an Industrial Marketing Communication Tool: Models for the Identification and Assessment of Opportunities', *Journal of Marketing Management*, 14: 691–704.

Bickerton, P., Bickerton, M. and Pardesi, U. (2000) *Cybermarketing: How to Use the Internet to Market Your Goods and Services*, Oxford: Butterworth-Heinemann.

Bowler, S. and Farrell, D. (eds) (1992) *Electoral Strategies and Political Marketing*, Basingstoke: Macmillan.

Coleman, S. (ed.) (2000) *Elections in the Age of the Internet: Lessons from the United States*, London: Hansard Society.

Coleman, S. (2001) *2001: Cyber Space Odyssey – The Internet in the UK Election*, London: Hansard Society.

Crabtree, J. (2001) 'Whatever Happened to the E-lection: A Survey of Voter Attitudes Towards New Technology During the 2001 Election', *An iSociety Report*, The Industrial Society, http://www.indsoc.co.uk/isociety/Election%20designed1.pdf.

Denver, D. (2001) 'The Liberal Democrat Campaign', in Norris, P. (ed.), *Britain Votes 2001*, Oxford: Oxford University Press.

Downs, A. (1957) *An Economic Theory of Democracy*, New York, Harper & Row.

Egan, J. (2001) *Relationship Marketing: Exploring Relational Strategies in Marketing*, Harlow: Prentice Hall.

Franklin, B. (1994) *Packaging Politics*, London: Arnold.

Gould, P. (1998) 'Why Labour Won', in Crewe, I., Gosschalk, B. and Bartle, J. *Political Communications: Why Labour Won the General Election of 1997*, London: Frank Cass.

Gronroos, C. (1994) 'From Marketing Mix to Relationship Marketing: Towards a Paradigm Shift in Marketing', *Management Decisions*, 32(2): 4–20.

Harrop, M. (1990) 'Political Marketing', *Parliamentary Affairs*, 43: 227–291.

James, M. (2001) 'Putting the User First', *e.Business*, July 2001: 32–37.

Katz, R. and Mair, P. (eds) (1994) *How Parties Organize: Change and Adaptation in Party Organisations in Western Democracies*, London: Sage.

Keith, R.J. (1960) 'The Marketing Revolution', *Journal of Marketing*, 24 (January): 35–38.

Kirchheimer, O. (1966) 'The Transformation of West European Party Systems', in Lapalombara and Weiner (eds), *Political Parties and Party Development*, Princeton, NJ: Princeton University Press, 177–200.

Lees-Marshment, J. (2001) *Political Marketing and British Political Parties*, Manchester: Manchester University Press.

Lock, A. and Harris, P. (1996) 'Political Marketing – Vive la difference!', *European Journal of Marketing*, 30(10/11): 21–31.

Maarek, P. (1995) *Political Marketing and Communication*, London: John Libbey.

Morgan, R.F. (1996) 'An Internet Marketing Framework for the World Wide Web (WWW)', *Journal of Marketing Management*, 12: 757–775.

Norris, P. (2000) *A Virtuous Circle: Political Communications in Post-industrial Societies*, Cambridge: Cambridge University Press.

O'Cass, A. (1996) 'Political Marketing and the Marketing Concept', *European Journal of Marketing*, 30(10/11): 45–61.

O'Shaughnessy, N. (1999) 'Political Marketing and Political Propaganda', in Newman, B.I. (ed.), *The Handbook of Political Marketing*, Thousand Oaks: Sage.

Panebianco, A. (1988) *Political Parties: Organisation and Power*, Cambridge: Cambridge University Press.

Putnam, R.D. (2000) *Bowling Alone: The Collapse and Revival of American Community*, New York: Touchstone.

Scammell, M. (1995) *Designer Politics: How Elections are Won*, Basingstoke: Macmillan.

Scammell, M. (1999) 'Political Marketing: Lessons for Political Science', *Political Studies*, XVVII: 718–739

Swanson, P. and Mancini, D.L. (eds) (1996) *Politics, Media and Modern Democracy*, Westport, Connecticut: Praeger.

Ward, S.J. and Gibson, R.K. (1998) 'The First Internet Election? UK Political Parties and Campaigning in Cyberspace', in Bartle, J., Crewe, I. and Gosschalk, B. (eds), *Political Communications: Why Labour Won the General Election of 1997*, London: Frank Cass, 93–112.

Ward, S.J. and Gibson, R.K. (2000) 'The Politics of the Future? UK Parties and the Internet', in Coleman, S. (ed.), *Elections in the Age of the Internet: Lessons from the United States*, London: Hansard Society, 29–35.

Webb, P. (2000) 'Political Parties: Adapting to the Electoral Market', in Dunleavy, P., Gamble, A., Holliday, I. and Peele, G. (eds), *Developments in British Politics 6*, Basingstoke: Macmillan.

Wring, D. (1997) 'Reconciling Marketing with Political Science: Theories of Political Marketing', *Journal of Marketing Management*, 13: 651–663.

Yates, S.J. and Perrone, J.L. (1998) 'Politics on the Web', *paper presented to IRISS '98 International Conference 25–27 March 1998*, Bristol, UK, 1–13, http://www.sosig.ac.uk/iriss/papers/paper46.html.

6 Moving towards an evolution in political mediation?

French political parties and the new ICTs

Bruno Villalba

Introduction

The French political system, as with many others in western Europe, is currently in a state of flux. It appears that we are in a period of democratic transition as the traditional model of representative democracy is increasingly criticised and demands for more direct forms of participation are becoming more commonplace (Budge, 1996; Rousseau, 1995). Political parties have long been considered as the central component of the representative democratic model. However, their institutional role is evolving (Katz and Mair, 1995), to the point that it is becoming possible to question the importance of their pre-eminence in the representative system (Rosanvallon, 1998). Arguably, the party system no longer seems to assure the link between society and government.

In response to this transition, parties are looking for new resources or new practices to re-legitimise their role and to reassert their position. The rapid development of new information and communications technologies (ICTs) has coincided with this new period of turbulence for political parties. Undoubtedly, new forms of communication are likely to be important in this process. As has been noted in earlier chapters, investment in new ICTs was often carried out to serve two major objectives: to renew the mechanisms for partisan identification, and to give new life to internal grassroots organisational practices (see Chapters 1 and 2; Hoff, *et al.*, 2000).

This chapter studies such debates in the context of the French political system. New ICT usage by parties was undertaken with the goal of developing a new form of political mediation, both in the relations between parties and party members, and also between parties and the electorate at large. An evaluative and longitudinal study of party websites will be used to allow us to gain an appreciation of the different discourses and strategies being adopted. The theoretical framework will thus focus on the way political parties adapt their rules of political communication (Hague and Loader, 1999), but also on the way they adapt techniques for political mobilisation (Fishkin, 1991), notably during election-campaign periods.

Parties and political participation: the social and technological context

To understand the way in which French political parties have reacted to the Internet requires some background understanding of the general technological and political context into which the technology emerged. This context is characterised by two principal aspects: the emergence of a strong demand for new forms of participation within the democratic framework, and the apparently declining interest in, and respect for, political parties amongst the French public.

New demands for participation

Since the mid-1980s, the French political system has seen strong demands from citizens to find new means of political participation. This has led to a number of legislative initiatives ostensibly designed to increase citizen input into the democratic process: for example, extension of referendum practices; parity laws allowing women equal access to electoral offices; and reforms of local administration (Baguenard and Becet, 1995; Paoletti, 1997; Blondiaux *et al.*, 1999; Balme *et al.*, 1999). The broad objective has been to bring decision making closer to the citizen through the development of new practices that allow better representation of political expression.

It would be reasonable to think that the new ICTs could play a central role in this process, since during the 1970s, the French put a vast programme into place in order to gain a footing in the information society (Nora and Minc, 1978). The Minitel became the symbol of this new policy.[1] As Joyandet *et al.* (1997) comment:

> Faced with the emergence of this new world, our country, with its *Minitel*, was one of the pioneers. This incredible experience put France in the leading group of nations, among those with massive experience in the management of an information system using telephone technology, and its requirements.

Minitel was not only a technical success, but also had political and economic ramifications since one could access administrative data and place online orders. But, paradoxically, this success has arguably made it difficult for French government to objectively assess the technological advances of Internet. French authorities were hesitant with regard to this new communication medium. They appeared more concerned with attempting to regulate the development of the Internet. Much energy was expended on trying to establish ethical guidelines and on considering how to apply them to the Internet. They paid particularly close attention to the judicial framework. A minister was delegated in 1997 to deal with '*la*

Poste, les Télécoms, et l'Espace with two principal concerns: respect for human rights (Braibant, 1998), and respect for consumers' rights (Lorentz, 1998). Equally, there was considerable debate as to which administrative authority should be given the responsibility for regulatory policy – The Superior Committee on Telematics,[2] The Superior Council on Audio-visual Technology, or the National Commission on Computer Technology and Freedoms (Paul, 2000).[3] In the end, the government began debating a vast parliamentary bill that was meant to organise the information society in France. In particular, it dealt with: free public diffusion of essential public information; transposition of the June 2000 European directive on electronic commerce; the responsibility of ISPs; electronic advertising; the exercise of the right of reply on Internet; encryption and ciphering; and the legal status of 'online communication services'.

By the end of the 1990s, official reports were unanimous: 'The general view is that Internet penetration in France is behind schedule' (Lafitte, 1997; Martin-Lalande, 1998). Although universities were satisfactorily covered, the linking of companies, administrations and individuals was still little developed (poorly equipped in terms of personal computers and modems, a poor supply of telecommunication public services and relatively high transmission costs). As early as August 1997, the Prime Minister had established the entry of France into the information society as an essential priority, and he re-affirmed this commitment in May 1998 during the Innovation Conference (*Les Assises de l'Innovation*, http://62.23.2.50/fr/p.cfm?ref=25518). The objective is 'to democratise the Internet and make it accessible to the whole population'. Technological evolution has become associated with a new dimension of collectively exercising freedoms of information and expression, in associations, in professional situations and in the political realm. A more positive image of the technical possibilities of Internet in terms of democracy is being developed (Levy, 1997; Premier Ministre, 1999; Rodota, 1999). The general political context seems to be favourable to a major innovation in terms of citizen participation, in which the new ICTs would be required to play an important role (Loiseau, 1999). However, it is important to note that the rate of Internet penetration is still low in European terms, and that the user population consists largely of social elites (Vedel, 2000).

Reforming the way parties function?

Political parties cannot afford to remain insensitive to these developments for they continue to be held in low public esteem. In 1997, 83 per cent of the French public stated they did not trust political parties (Brechon, 2001: 9). Public opinion is often critical of their distance from the realities of everyday life, their tendency to be bogged down in internal debates, and sees them as having outdated, extreme practices (Mossuz-Lavau,

1994). Moreover, their grassroots organisation is weak, since they have few active party members, limited financial means and some trouble in renewing their ideological programmes (Brechon, 2001). The commitment of party members has undergone a major transformation whereby they have become more distant from the party (Perrineau, 1994). According to Jacques Ion (1997), members are now more concerned with preserving their personal independence and, as a result, less inclined to blindly follow the party line.

Aware of their weaknesses, parties have been trying since around the early 1990s to reform their organisational practices and to renew their political programmes. They have also tried to enhance the role of party members (Rihoux, 2001). At an individual level, members are now more often involved in crucial party decisions such as the selection of leaders and debates concerning general ideological orientation. This can be seen as being a reflection of the general concern with democratic values and practices in society at large.

Clearly, new technologies bring a number of classic debates back into the limelight, such as the necessity for mediating political organisations as a prerequisite for a smooth functioning of democracy (Bellamy and Taylor, 1998; Bimber, 1998). The question of communication seems to be of increasing importance in representative democracy and the parties have to adapt themselves to this new configuration. In making use of the potential of new ICTs, parties can contribute to the renewal, or even to the widening, of their communication capabilities. This could also allow them to widen or transform the different types of collective mobilisation (see Chapter 1). The political class, which was initially reluctant to change, now seems to see the necessity of gaining a foothold on the Internet.

Parties and the new ICTs: an evaluative and longitudinal approach

This chapter seeks to understand how far the Internet can assist parties in adapting to a new vision of political participation. In particular, its goal is to determine how the potential of the Internet has been used in reference to the idea of broader and deeper participation. As a result, it is not the intention to assess the technical sophistication of party websites (Gibson and Ward, 2000; Greffet, 2001). The undeniable technical development of national-party sites is simply reiterated here. The chapter will focus on the way in which participatory opportunities such as online interaction, dialogue and responsiveness have been put in place. Beyond the stated goals in their political discourse, have political parties really implemented a participatory policy via the Internet? In order to fully comprehend the process involved in setting up this policy, it is important to compare two levels: the official national-party websites, and sub-national sites set up by

local political personnel. This evaluative dimension will allow us to determine whether websites reflect different discourses operating at the local
or national level.

In addition, a longitudinal approach has been adopted focusing on the
electoral campaigns since 1998. Election campaigns present an excellent
example of a discourse that brings together mobilisation and participation, directed towards party members, but also towards the electorate as a
whole. The time period covered offers a fairly complete picture of the different levels of elections (national and local). It has also been possible to
examine the manner in which Internet use has spread into the realm of
electoral mobilisation. However, the longitudinal approach complicates
the comparison of the different levels. During a national election, the
electoral campaign on the Internet is mainly run via the central party
website. It gives us the relatively unified image of organisations apparently
speaking with one voice. However, at the local level, it is striking to
observe the extreme heterogeneity of situations.

In total, thirteen national sites have proved to be continually
active between 1998 and 2000 (*Les Verts, Le Parti Communiste, Le Mouvement
des Citoyens, Le Parti Socialiste, Le Parti Radical de Gauche, Le Mouvement
des Ecologistes Indépendants, Génération Écologie, Le Parti Radical, l'Union
pour la Démocratie Française, Force Démocrate, Le Rassemblement pour la
République, Démocratie Libérale* and *Le Front National*). The study focused
mainly on the official national website for each of these parties. This
allowed us to reveal the continuity in the relations between these parties
and the new ICTs, and thus to understand more fully the evolutionary
significance.

Beyond this list, we should not forget the diversity of the political landscape present on the web. Political portals (institutional or private)[4] provide
differing levels of access to a wide variety of supposedly national parties.
Some place both major political parties and curious little-known structures
such as the *Pied-noir* Party (http://www.partipiednoir.net/) or The
Party for the Recognition of Spoiled Ballots (http://www.partiblanc.fr/;
http://ligue.savoie.com) on the same level. However, indexing of local-party
activity online is still extremely patchy.

The origins and development of party websites

The first party online in France was the National Front in 1994, quickly
followed over the next eighteen months by all the main French political
parties. The origins of these sites are difficult to establish. The principal
creators range from the party leadership, a special delegation within the
party, a group of parliamentarians or a group of party members. Outside
of a special page dedicated to this subject by the Greens in 1996, and
another on the same theme by the PS in 1997, none of the parties
explains online why it has set up a website or deals with the link between

democracy and the new ICTs. It appears that the goal is simply to remain visible in cyberspace.

Following the initial moves into cyberspace, it was the 1997 general election that solidified the process. Parties that were already online rapidly developed online campaigns and expanded the information available. Parties that had previously hesitated now decided to join the trend (*Parti radical de gauche* or PRG, *Parti radical, Génération Écologie* or GE, *Force démocrate* or FD, *Démocratie libérale* or DL). Other small parties also moved online at the same time (*Convention Alternative Progressiste, Convergences Ecologie Solidarité, Mouvement pour la France, Rassemblement social et libéral, Mouvement des écologistes indépendants, La Ligue communiste révolutionnaire*), along with esoteric political movements such as *Parti de la Loi naturelle*.

The regional elections of 1998 continued this process through a reinforcement of the importance and the role of national-party sites, and a development of personal websites for local candidates. At the national level, the arrival of the Citizens' Movement (*Mouvement des citoyens* or MDC), meant all of the major parties were now online. In total, twenty-five parties provided candidates for this election and eighteen of them had websites.

In terms of information provided, the websites generally presented the political programmes, political news and press releases. More rarely, a forum for discussion was presented (often little used during the period of this study), or an address by party leaders was given with the possibility to contact the leader directly via email. A nationalisation of the sites can also be observed, notably through the integration of information from local-party structures (links and regional contacts).

However, it was during the European election campaign of 1999 that party websites were deemed to have come of age. The political landscape on the web became fairly similar to the real political landscape. The French press unanimously heralded the birth of this new era that they had been expecting for so long.[5] The variety of political portals that emerged are testament to this keen interest.[6] The 1999 campaign and its aftermath is, therefore, an interesting period for more than one reason. First, we see the arrival online of the last of the important parties – *Lutte ouvrière*, which was actively involved in this election, and *Mouvement National* under Bruno Megret, which was created following the internal schism in the National Front. Of course, some movements were still absent from the web, notably the National Centre for Independents and Farmers, which, though small, still retains some influence on French politics, the Workers' Party, the autonomous Corsican parties, and the Party for French Democracy, which finally created a site at the end of 1999. It is worth noting that the existence and the form of political websites reveals the power redistribution among parties. Small parties appear less worried about their web presence. Among the smallest parties with candidate lists in 1999, five had no site at all. Others experienced internal political difficulties that created problems for their sites (*Génération Ecologie* and the FN, for example, whose sites were inaccessible for about a month). However, other small movements showed they could create a durable relationship with this medium (*Vivant Energie France, Parti fédéraliste, Parti de la loi naturelle*).

Second, this campaign presented the opportunity for the parties already present on the web to give more prominence to this tool. This is shown in the use of special pages dedicated specifically to the European election (PS, PCF, *Verts*, UDF, RPR notably). The site became a space for offering specific information in response to the political questions at stake during the election.

The period in question also sees a diversification of strategies for the use of this media. For the twenty lists presenting candidates, the campaign for the European parliamentary elections presented the opportunity to form alliances (PS–MDC–PRG; LO–LCR; RPR–DL–UDF; *Rassemblement pour la France–Mouvement pour la France*). Yet, on the Internet there was little or no evidence of such a strategy. Only two sites (see Table 6.1) reveal such a strategy. As a result, except for general indications (united front discourse made accessible online), or at best a special page, alliances lacked visibility on the net. This reveals an interesting case of asymmetry with regard to the real campaign. The strategy of alliances does not automatically have its corollary on the web. Furthermore, it can be difficult for divergent strategies to co-exist on the same site from one election to another. While in 1997 the left-wing parties united to form the 'majority of plurality' (*'la majorité plurielle'*, composed of PS–MDC–PC–*Verts*–PRG), in 1999 the Greens and the Communists created their own separate candidate lists.

The specialised sites dedicated to promoting the national leaders provide another example of the diversification of uses. The leaders of the main parties created pages that focused exclusively on themselves (J.-M. Le Pen and D. Cohn-Bendit). This type of diversification shows how politicians are learning how to make use of the net, but it also reveals that they are subordinated to political interests determined outside of the hypertextual logic of the Internet, notably in the alliance lists.

The development of party campaigning outlined above would appear to support the idea of an irreversible trend towards cyberspace. Yet, in 2001, as Greffet (2001) has pointed out, out of twenty-four parties receiving public financing,[7] there were still six that did not think it necessary to develop a website. Official recognition by the state and universal suffrage do not automatically go together with a presence in cyberspace. At the local level the situation is even more striking. Getting involved in the net remains a marginal strategy for local politicians. However, without a doubt, national elections provide a stimulus to the development of political propaganda on the network. Six months before the next presidential election, roughly forty new sites were created (candidate sites, support or opposition to candidates sites, portals).

From this brief look at recent history, three conclusions can be drawn. First, although parties were relatively slow to get on to the Internet, today almost all have their own window on the net. This would seem to indicate that most parties consider it necessary to have a website at least for electoral purposes. Second, all elections are affected by this process: supranational elections (European Parliament), national elections (presidential and legislative) and local elections (regional, county and municipal). New ICTs have been appropriated by political personnel at all levels but with enormous disparities in terms of the priority accorded, the means invested and the quality and quantity of information posted. Third, there has been a diversification and growth of political sites including both specialised sites for each election and personal sites. However, this still represents a tiny minority among the 300,000 websites created by businesses and organisations, to which can be added the close to 2 million 'personal sites' created by individuals (Kaplan, 2001). Political websites are, therefore, very much a minority interest.

Overall, political elites, at the national level at least, can now be considered to have begun to integrate the Internet into their communication strategies and there has been an undeniable technological development of party websites. But perhaps the more important question to ask is how far this has affected their relationships with voters and members. Has it begun to alter the style of internal party democracy and also systemic models of representative democracy?

A limited and supervised participation

If we are to believe the rhetoric of French politicians, then the Internet has already become an essential tool for political communication and is predicted to become one of the key elements of future elections. For example, René Monory, former President of the Senate, stated in 1997:

> I am certain that five years from now the President of the Republic will be elected thanks to the Internet. In 2002 . . . each candidate will have a specialised team for the Internet. The one who knows how best to handle the network will be elected.

Similarly, François Hollande, Socialist Party Secretary, argued at the annual PS convention in September 2000, 'the 2002 election campaign will consecrate the Internet as both an essential theatre and vector of political competition'. These two quotes, coming from well-placed figures in French political life, are not only witness to the importance granted to the new medium, but also to its influence. However, in order to assess the reality of such claims it is important to know whether the uses made of the net are really adding to the widening of grassroots participation and the

Table 6.1 French political parties' websites: 1999 European parliamentary elections

Party name	Specific election website	Website with pages on the European parliamentary election
LO-LCR. *Pour une autre Europe* (*Ligue Communiste Révolutionnaire et Lutte Ouvrière*)	(none)	http://www.lcr-rouge.org/ (LCR website) http://rafale.worldnet.net/~lo-uci/fra/jlo/hom-jlo.htm (LO website)
Bouge l'Europe (Robert Hue and the *Parti Communiste Français*, with input from personalities outside the party)	http://www.bouge-leurope.org/	www.pcf.fr
L'écologie, les Verts, (Daniel Cohn-Bendit)	http://www.les-verts.org/ (complete reorganisation of the site)	D. Cohen-Bendit's personal website: www.enviedepolitique.org
Construisons notre Europe (PS, MDC and PRG, under the direction of François Hollande)	(none) www.france-elections.org (non-official website for the list)	Page on the PS website: http://www.europeennes99.parti-socialiste.fr/ Page on the MDC website: www.mdc-france.org Page on the PRG website: www.radical-gauche.org
L'Union pour l'Europe, l'opposition unie avec le RPR et DL (RPR under Nicolas Sarkozy)	http://www.union-pour-europe.org/	Page on the RPR website: www.rpr.asso.fr Page on the DL website: www.democratie-liberale.asso.fr
Avec l'Europe, prenons une France d'avance (*Union pour la Démocratie Française*, François Bayrou)	(none)	http://www.nouvelle-udf.org
Rassemblement pour la France et l'indépendance de l'Europe (Charles Pasqua, and his movement *Demain la France*, with Philippe de Villiers, and his *Mouvement Pour la France*)	http://www.pasqua-villiers.org/	Website MPF Website Demain la France

Party	Website	Notes
Front National (Jean-Marie Le Pen).	(none)	Website J.-M. Le Pen: www.lepen.net; Pages on FN website: http://www.objectif-fn-20.com/
Européens d'accord, Français d'abord, Mégret l'avenir, Mouvement National (Bruno Mégret)	http://www.mouvement-national.org/	Website Mégret: http://www.m-n-r.com
Ecologie, le choix de la vie, Mouvement Ecologiste Indépendant (Antoine Waechter)	http://www.novomundi.com/mei/ (reorganisation of the website)	
Combat pour l'Emploi (Pierre Larrouturou)	http://www.combat-emploi.org/index.htm	
Vive le fédéralisme!, Parti Fédéraliste. (Jean-Philippe Allenbach)	http://www.dalmatia.net/parti-federaliste/ nouvel url: http://www.parti-federaliste.com/	http://www.dalmatia.net/parti-federaliste/elections_europeennes.htm
Parti de la Loi Naturelle (Benoît Frappé)		http://members.aol.com/f6dyw/index.htm
Parti Humaniste (Marie-Laurence Chanut-Sapin)	http://www.parti-humaniste-france.org/	Pages on website: http://www.parti-humaniste-france.org/europeennes/index.phtml
Vivant: Energie France (*La voix des sans parole*, Gérard Maudrux)	http://www.vivantef.org/	Note that in their statement of principles, the Internet address given is wrong (http://www.vivantef.fr)
Moins d'impôts maintenant! (Nicolas Miguet, *Liste indépendante des partis*)	No website	No website
Chasse, pêche, nature et Tradition (Jean Saint Josse)	No website	No website
97-2: mi ou, mi muen (Joseph Jos)	No website	No website
Liste de la Ligue nationaliste (Guy Guerrin)	No website	No website
Politique de vie pour l'Europe, collectif associations citoyennes (Christian Cotten)	No website	No website

diversification of participation practices. This implies two fundamental dimensions:

- that the citizen be able to gain access to information which will help him or her to think independently with the aim of shedding new light on his or her political choices (Rosanvallon, 1998) – participation therefore presupposes setting up a 'transparent' relationship between a citizen and this person's political representative;
- that the citizen be able to play an effective role in the construction of political debate, and that s/he be able to influence the final decision (Budge, 1996).

These two indicators will now be used to test the way in which parties put in place new methods of participation via the web.

Transparency: accessibility and availability of information

This policy of transparency is conveyed by various mechanisms. First, the presentation of the party (or candidate) assumes an ever-increasing importance. Whatever the level examined, national or local, it would appear that a site's primary objective is to spread information. The webmasters and also the candidates interviewed insist on the importance of supplying information that allows citizens to make a choice. All of the national sites have some elements in common: a general presentation of the party (commonly historical background, election results, and so on), electoral programmes (strategic positions, platform alliances), the campaign schedule (meetings, press points), a presentation of ideological position varying in detail (statements, principles), the party's organisation (structures, leaders) and, in the case of election campaigns, the candidates and the lists are given. It is clear, as Kamark's (1999) analysis shows, that the sites represent an important source of information for experts in political communication (political journalists or academics), although it should be noted that the content of the information given remains rather general in its nature. Few parties really offer the opportunity to obtain precise information about certain areas of internal activity, such as financial accounts (only the Green Party publishes these) or membership data.

Similarly, the information given does not always reflect the differing organisational and ideological traditions of the parties. The net unquestionably produces a uniformity and standardisation of political discourse on the official sites. In this way, disputes within parties are minimised, giving the decidedly false picture of a unified party. The diversity can be seen away from the official site by studying the sites devoted to the diverging currents of thought within a party. Information is diffused more in the manner of a network of sites that communicate and relate to each other in varying degrees. A party's principal official site may find itself in the 'centre' of a vast galaxy of politically active sites. It can include sites created by branches and regional federations, the institutional sites of elected members and senior party officials, election candidates' sites and other internal groups, for example youth sections. This process has been strengthened since 1999 through the development of temporary sites given over to events such as annual party conferences.

Access to information is no longer only instantaneous (through an improved updating of information on the national sites and even more frequent updates during election periods), but also tends to become permanent. The sites develop a policy of archiving available information. This policy rests largely on a desire to make official the information on offer. The advantage of this information is that it has been approved internally. Consequently, one can argue that transparency results from this increased ability to question the collective memory of the party.

Moreover, the widespread growth of national sites is regularly kept up through the addition of new pages. It is becoming more frequent to find certain tools that increase the efficiency of information searches (small search facilities in the site itself, for example). There is a concomitant improvement in terms of internal and external connections. The objective seems to be to enlarge the party's identity. What the party is cannot be limited to the available information. The party extends itself through its hypertextual representations. The party cannot be reduced to the space occupied by only its own web pages. Its general coherence is found in the contacts and links it presents to the Internet user.

It should also be noted that the strategy of transparency runs up against a classic limitation. It covers up the distinction between party members and those who simply support the party. An Intranet, however, allows parties to create a space reserved for members. Some information, and some party documents, are only then accessible to those who have a password.

Political parties are therefore trying, without external mediation, to offer Internet users a more complete and more intense representation of what they have been, what they are and what they propose to be in the future. More information is now in the public domain than was previously. As a result, the primary objective of these sites, namely to allow Internet users to have access to some of the general resources of the party, seems to have been partially achieved. However, such diffusion of political information still works on the classic top-down model with information moving from the parties towards the citizens rather than vice versa.

Bringing the citizen into the political process: the interactive myth

It is not simply a question of communication guaranteeing a more participatory society; rather, the idea of interactivity is associated with the construction of a new type of political mediation. In this model, the Internet-citizen would truly become the agent of his or her information. Such citizens could obtain considerable information by comparing the different party programmes. By gaining access to a large source of information ('transparency'), they would be able to engage in a discussion directly with political officials. Websites could then become a forum for direct exchanges. Citizens could play a direct role in political debate. This idealist, even naïve, vision is associated with the discourse on renewal of democratic practices.

The technology necessary for establishing a truly interactive process between parties and citizens via the Internet user do exist. It is possible to interact in real time through Internet Relay Chat (IRC) or I'll Seek You (ICQ). A second category is closer to traditional written exchanges, in the sense that it does not allow the user to react in real time. A bulletin-board forum can allow a discussion to develop on a particular theme in this way. FAQs (Frequently Asked Questions), mailing lists or, more simply, email can be used to establish general contacts between Internet users and politicians. All of these possibilities can be used to increase the Internet user's potential for expressing him or herself and for getting involved in debate (Beaudoin and Velkovska, 1999). The Internet presents a new avenue for citizens to make themselves heard, to react to information and, crucially, to contribute something new to the debate. However, French political parties are still very hesitant about making use of these techniques. This can be seen in relation to five areas with interactive possibilities, as detailed below.

- *Email and email lists.* Today, whether at the local or national level, almost all the French party websites present users with the possibility of sending an email to the party, or at least to the webmaster. However, the possibility of getting in direct contact with party officials, particularly with political leaders and candidates, is less common. IRC was used for the first time by a few candidates at the municipal level, but not on any local-party sites (Magniant and Villalba, 2001; Benvegnu, 2001: 40). Mailing lists are being used more and more often by the national sites. Only two parties do not currently use mailing lists. The goal is to allow a wider distribution, and better accessibility, of official party positions (press releases, speeches, dates for public meetings). Yet during the municipal campaign of 2001, local websites that created mailing lists made little use of them. The same can be said of the FAQs. This section of a site can be seen as a memory space for the principal exchanges between Internet users and the party. It maintains the idea that there is efficient interaction, as there would be the need to avoid repeating the same message. But, once again, the FAQs section is controlled exclusively by the site officials. Archiving is subject to internal considerations of the party.

- *Discussion fora.* These can allow interaction to develop between the party and the Internet user, but can also allow interaction between different users. This type of space for discussion has proved difficult to set up and to manage. Parties are concerned, above all, about maintaining control over the content of debate, avoiding offensive language and also allowing too much public criticism to appear on their site. Most party discussion fora are therefore 'moderated', that is, the webmaster decides on content, either *a priori* or *a posteriori*. However, this type of space is rare. Moreover, when this type of space does exist, the themes are controlled by the party, the guidelines for content are pre-established and quite often the discussion space is taken up primarily by party members. At the local level, discussion fora remain the exception (only one was found for the *Nord-Pas de Calais* region in 2001) and where they exist, they are little used. For example, there were fewer than a dozen messages on the local sites studied here.
- *Online polls.* The use of polling techniques online, or of other types of questionnaire, is also very rare, except for the case of the party *Démocratie Libérale* (DL) which developed 'cyberpolls'. However, these types of online polls remain problematic in terms of scientific reliability and are of dubious quality. Where they have been employed, the questions used are generally designed to reinforce the pre-existing political position of a given party or candidate. Furthermore, the results of these 'studies' or 'polls' are then rarely made available to the Internet user. As a result, these techniques are often no more than electronic fripperies.
- *Narrowcasting.* Similarly, this technique is little used. The information provided by French parties online is not aimed at any particular group of the population. Even if some icons appear to be targeting certain groups, for example 'Youth', 'Identity', or 'Women', the content is often shallow and generalist in tone.
- *Online membership.* Finally, in contrast to studies in other European countries, encouraging visitors to become members is not a common practice in France. Becoming a member directly online is not possible and membership often requires an array of tasks, including filling out forms, answering questionnaires, and sometimes having to be in direct contact with party officials.

In sum, the interactive possibilities, with the exception of email, have hardly been developed. Party and candidate websites add only moderately to the opening up of participation that is supposedly highly prized. As a result, two conclusions can be reached. First, publication of the opinions and judgements of Internet users is still uncommon. The circulation of information remains a unidirectional process, where the content is controlled by the parties from their sites. Communication by users is channelled and the classic mechanisms of political mediation still operate (selection, reconstruction, hierarchical classification of public-opinion messages and incorporation into a pre-existing ideological framework). Second, collective input into party platforms and debates remains insignificant. Opposition and dissent to the main party line remains low despite the supposed openness of the Internet. When it does exist, it does not manage to modify the content of party policy. Party platforms are still an internal concern for the party, its members and its leadership.

In explaining the lack of online participatory input into party debates, two factors appear particularly important; notably, the costs of website campaigning and the low audience for political sites.

Although the possibilities for dialogue are multiplied through online methods, this implies that party organisations would have to provide the means to meet the new requirements in terms of financial and human resources. Yet, increasingly, political party accounts have to meet more and more rigid conditions, with overall spending limitations and financial audits. Parties, and especially candidates on the campaign trail, cannot afford to put significant funds into this new medium. Yet, it is the technological sophistication of a site that explains to a great extent its ability to draw visitors (Margolis *et al.*, 1997), and the creation, management and running of a sophisticated web presence requires considerable resources. Even if competent party members can be used (*Parti Radical, Verts*, LCR, PLN), or helped by a firm specialising in multimedia (DL, FD), the trend in the large parties is to increasingly use the services of specialised personnel in web design and management (UDF, RPR, PS, PCF). During the European parliamentary elections of 1999, five parties recruited firms that specialised in the creation and management of websites. Five others used the services of specialists found within the group of party members and staff. This created a situation of formal inequality between the parties that had the financial means to draw on professional organisations for help, and the others. This was notably to the detriment of small parties. Whilst it is true that this type of communication requires a relatively limited basic investment in computer equipment, modems and URL domain purchases, functioning costs, however, can vary according to the priority given to this medium. The cost of a national website can vary between 45,000 and 100,000 francs per year. At the local level, website activity is essentially amateur. In the *Nord–Pas de Calais* region of France, among the 'small list' and the leaders' personal sites, only three were found to have used the services of paid professionals.

It is not just the costs of the Internet that restrict party activity but perhaps more importantly the limited returns in terms of an audience for the sites. Internet users do not consult political web pages very often. According to the firm Médiamétrie, 23.5 per cent of the French population over 11 years of age hooked up to the Internet at least once during the first quarter of 2001. Among this population of Internet users, men are over-represented (62 per cent of Internet users), as well as young people between 16 and 34 years of age (50.7 per cent) and the higher socio-cultural categories (37.8 per cent).[8] Approximately 25 per cent of the French electorate had access to the Internet by mid-2002. Although parties do not want to neglect reaching one elector in five or one in six, for the time being, access is low and targets a select social elite of mainly younger, urban, male professionals. This is typically the type of group who are already political active. Hence, it does not encourage parties to develop new communication methods to reach a group that already has access to traditional political-communication techniques.

Conclusion and prospects

Since 1997, we have been going through a formative period in the use of the interactive media. The technical infrastructure has begun to be put in place and the political will has been affirmed. However, the citizens will require a period of adjustment to the new media. Already, though, certain kinds of uses, especially commercial uses, have become common place. The political world has been slower to adapt and any significant correlation between Internet usage and improved political participation has yet to be established.

Internet sites certainly allow parties to improve their communication channels with supporters, to develop practical techniques for exchanging documents/information and even to establish elementary forms of online political debate. Certainly, the different Internet tools offer the possibility of a new form of mediation, which may increase the quantity and the permanence of partisan information. So far, however, online partisan representation has remained quite conventional, simply reproducing the same political patterns that were traditionally presented in the press, or in internal party literature. As yet, it does not seem to have produced any major changes in classic participatory practices. As such, the use of this new tool has had no impact on one of the key functions of parties – the selection of the political elite and the professionals who govern. The web is not used for internal candidate selection procedures (even if some candidates set up personal websites). Even if political parties still declare that the Internet is going to produce a major change in the way they organise their grassroots activities, the fact remains that, at this time, this is an illusion (Lyon, 1988).

Notes

1   Minitel was a monochrome teletext service allowing users to access a range of information and services via special phone-based terminals.
2   *Le conseil supérieur de la télématique* (CST) and *le comité de la télématique anonyme* (CTA), created by decree on 25 February 1993, are responsible for assuring that service providers respect their engagements.

3   *Commission nationale de l'informatique et des libertés* (http://www.cnil.fr).
4   http://www.adminet.com/poli/presents no fewer than 100 websites under the title 'French politics', but the list includes groups ranging from parties present in parliament to associations fighting against racism. The site http://www.france.diplomatie.fr/france/fr/instit/instit08.html: provides a panorama of what it qualifies as the 'principal' parties (PS, PCF, RPR, UDF, *Les Verts, Le Rassemblement pour la France* (RPF), FN), but without giving any links.
5   http://www.liberation.fr/europeennes/index.html; http://www.lemonde.fr/elections/europe/index.html.
6   Newsletter in journaldunet.com (http://www.journaldunet.com) and especially the files in the European election campaign (http://www.journaldunet.com/99mai/dossiereurope.shtml; www.lafranceelectorale.com; http://www.france-elections.net/; www.lapolitique.com; the Election 2000 Collection at http://archive.alexa.com).
7   Public aid is calculated on the basis of legislative results in 1997. (*Décret n°2000-166 du 28 février 2000, publié au* Journal Officiel *du 1ᵉʳ mars 2000*).
8   See the statistical results for the first trimester at www.mediametrie.fr; see also: http://www.ilo.org/public/french/bureau/inf/pr/2001/03.htm; www.canalipsos.com.

References

Baguenard, J. and Becet, J.-M. (1995) *La démocratie locale*, Paris: PUF.

Balme, R., Faure, A. and Mabileau, A. (dir.) (1999) *Les politiques publiques locales*, Paris: Presses de Sciences Po.

Beaudoin V. and Velkovska, J. (1999) 'Constitution d'un espace de communication sur Internet (forums, pages personnelles, courrier électronique...)', in Réseaux, 97: 121–177.

Bellamy, C. and Taylor, J.A. (1998) *Governing in the Information Age*, Buckingham: Open University Press.

Benvegnu, E. (2001) *L'extension du domaine de la lutte politique. Les sites de candidats en campagne, Mars 2001, Nord-Pas-de-Calais*, IEP de Lille: Mémoire.

Bimber, B. (1998) 'The Internet and Political Transformation: Populism, Community, and Accelerated Pluralism', *Polity*, XXXI(1): 133–160.

Blondiaux, L., Marcou, G. and Rangeon, F. (dir.) (1999) *La démocratie locale*, Paris: PUF.

Braibant, G. (1998) *Données personnelles et société de l'information*, Rapport au Premier Ministre sur la transposition en droit français de la directive no 95/46.

Brechon, P. (2001) *Les partis politiques français*, Paris: La documentation française.

Budge, I. (1996) *The Challenge of Direct Democracy*, London: Sage.

Fishkin, J.S. (1991) *Democracy and Deliberation*, New Haven: Yale University Press.

Gibson, R.K. and Ward, S.J. (2000) 'A Methodology for Measuring the Function and Effectiveness of Party Websites', *Social Science Computing Review*, 18(4): 301–319.

Greffet, F. (2001) 'Les partis politiques français sur le Web', in Andolfatto, D., Greffet, F. and Olivier, L. (eds), *Les partis politiques: quelles perspectives?* Paris: L'Harmattan (coll. Logiques politiques), 161–178.

Hague, B. and Loader, B. (eds) (1999) *Digital Democracy: Discourse and Democracy in the Information Age*, London: Routledge.

Hoff, J., Horrocks, I. and Tops, P. (eds) (2000) *Democratic Governance and New*

Technology: Technologically mediated innovations in political practice in Western Europe, London and New York: Routledge.

Ion, J. (1997) *La fin des militants?*, Paris: Editions de l'Atelier.

Joyandet, A., Herisson, P. and Türk, A. (1997) 'L'entrée dans la société de l'information', Rapport d'information 436, Mission commune d'information sur l'entrée dans la société de l'information, 'La télématique en France: un essai à transformer', http://www.Internet.gouv.fr/francais/textesref/rapce98/accueil.htm.

Kamark, E.C. (1999) 'Campaigning on the Internet in the Off-Year Elections of 1998', John F. Kennedy School of Government: Harvard University.

Kaplan, D. (2001) *La France dans la société de l'information*, étude disponible sur le site du Premier Ministre. Available at: http://www.Internet.gouv.fr/francais/textesref/fsi99/accueil.htm.

Katz, R. and Mair, P. (1995) 'Changing Models of Party Organization and Party Democracy: the Emergence of the Cartel Party', *Party Politics*, 1: 5–28.

Lafitte, P., Sénateur 'La France et la société de l'information', Rapport de l'Office parlementaire d'évaluation des choix scientifiques et technologiques, 7 février 1997. Volume 1.

Levy, P. (1997) *Cyberculture*, Paris: Odile Jacob.

Loiseau, G. (1999) *Municipalités et communication numérique. Les sites Internet des grandes villes de France en 1999*, Paris: Université Paris I (Rapport de recherche réalisé par local avec le concours de l'Association des Maires de Grandes Villes de France, http://www.multimediaville.tm.fr/pages/multi2000/Synthese.html.

Lorentz, F. (1998) 'Commerce électronique: une nouvelle donne pour les consommateurs, les entreprises, les citoyens et les pouvoirs public', Rapport du groupe de travail.

Lyon, D. (1988) *The Information Society: Issues and Illusions*, Cambridge: Polity Press.

Magniant, S. and Villalba, B. (2001) 'Les préaux virtuels, ou les candidats locaux en campagne sur le net. Approche comparative France-Etats-Unis', Serfaty Viviane (dir.), Colloque 'Campaigning on the Net', Strasbourg: Institut d'Etudes Politique.

Margolis, M., Resnick, D. and Tu, C.-C. (1997), 'Campaigning on the Internet. Parties and Candidates on the World Wide Web in the 1996 Primary Season', *Harvard International Journal of Press Politics*, 2(1): 59–78.

Martin-Lalande, P. (1998) *L'Internet, un vrai défi pour la France. Rapport au Premier Ministre*, La Documentation française: Collection des rapports officiels.

Mathias, P. (1997) *La cité Internet*, Editions Presses de Sciences Po: Collection La Bibliothèque du citoyen.

Mossuz-Lavau, J. (1994) *Les Français et la politique. Enquête sur une crise*, Paris: Odile Jacob.

Nora, S. and Minc, A. (1978) *L'informatisation de la société*, Paris: La Documentation Française.

Paoletti, M. (1997) *La démocratie locale et le référendum*, Paris: L'Harmattan.

Paul, C. (2000) *Du droit et des libertés sur l'Internet. La corégulation, contribution française pour une régulation mondiale*, Rapport remis au Premier Ministre, http://www.Internet.gouv.fr/francais/textesref/pagsi2/lsi/rapportcpaul/sommaire.htm.

Perrineau, P. (dir.) (1994) *L'engagement politique, déclin ou mutation?* Paris: Presses de la fondation nationale des sciences politiques.

Premier Ministre (1999) *La France dans la société de l'information*, Paris: Documentation Française.

Rihoux, B. (2001) *Les partis politiques: organisations en changement. Le test des écologistes*, Paris: L'Harmattan, coll. Logiques Politiques.

Rodota, S. (1999) *La démocratie électronique, de nouveaux concepts et expériences politiques*, Paris: éditions Apogée.

Rosanvallon, P. (1998) *Le peuple introuvable*, Paris: Gallimard.

Rousseau, D. (1995) *La démocratie continue*, Paris: LGDJ-Bruylant.

Vedel, T. (2000) 'Public policies for digital democracy in the European Union and the United States', in Hacker, K. and Van Dijk, J. (eds), *Digital Democracy: Issues of Theory and Practice*, London: Sage, 184–208.

7 Letting the daylight in?

Australian parties' use of the World Wide Web at the state and territory level

Rachel Gibson and Stephen Ward

Introduction

The World Wide Web (WWW) is used increasingly for communication by citizens and governments in most advanced democracies. Systematic study of its uses by, and effects on, traditional political actors such as parties and their voters, however, have generally been confined to the national level (Margolis *et al.*, 1997, 1999; Gibson and Ward, 1998, 2000b, 2000c, 2002; Tops *et al.*, 2000; Newell, 2001). This chapter seeks to address this deficit by investigating the use of online technologies for parties at the state and territory level in Australia. Specifically, the goals of the chapter are three-fold: first, to profile the overall levels of web activity by parties at the state level and the ease with which those sites can be accessed; second, to show how far the sites focus on opening the parties up to greater democratic scrutiny through information provision and feedback; and, finally, to compare parties' performance online across states and consider how far other social and political factors are influencing their uses of the Internet. In doing so, not only will we provide a fuller picture of the enthusiasm of political actors in Australia for the new media technologies, but we will also begin to build a theoretical understanding of why some are more enthusiastic than others. Does party outlook drive the move to get wired? Does federalism play a role at all in the diffusion of new ICTs? Do certain states and territories have a greater web activity than others and, if so, is this related to demographic characteristics, such as the size of the urban population, or institutional factors, such as the electoral cycle or which party is in power? Perhaps none of these is significant and it is party outlook that determines most often who is online. In order to address these questions we focus on the federal, state and territory websites of the two major parties plus those of the most active online minor party, the Australian Greens.

While answers to such questions provide insight into the technological adaptability of the parties, addressing such topics is also of broader significance for understanding the health of Australian politics more generally. Although not discussed in the same 'crisis' terms as in the USA and European countries (McAllister, 1997), the party system in Australia has become a cause for concern given the evidence of weakening party identification and increasing numbers of floating voters (McAllister, 2002), growing support for independent candidates (Sharman, 1994), and the rise of fringe players such as One Nation (Gibson, McAllister and Swenson, 2002). Internally, both major parties stand accused of leaving much to be desired with regard to levels of accountability and scrutiny. Johns (2000), focusing on the particular issue of candidate selection, has argued that the parties could clearly let more 'daylight' into the selection process to comply with 'basic democratic standards' (Johns, 2000: 423). Certainly, continuing allegations of branch stacking (Robinson, 1996) have done nothing to alleviate perceptions of internal corruption and cronyism. While we are not suggesting that establishing a website means parties can reverse these trends, we do think that by doing so parties have the chance to present themselves as more transparent and open to popular input, and that these are valuable assets given the current concerns about parties' increasing failure to connect with the electorate. Email and websites clearly allow organisations to engage in a more sustained and direct dialogue with voters and members. Furthermore, such opportunities may prove particularly appealing to parties at the state and local level who are naturally 'closer' to the voters than their national counterparts but lack the budget to engage in big publicity drives or 'listening' exercises.

Parties and the use of new ICTs

The emergence of new ICTs in the 1990s has led to consideration of a number of trends in parties with a more public persona. Much of the reflection has focused on the implications of the new ICTs for campaign style and its ongoing professionalisation and globalisation. Is the Internet a tool for standardising campaign conduct across liberal democracies? (Gibson and Ward, 1998; Gibson *et al.*, 2000). Does it link to the new so-called postmodernised or professionalised phase of campaigning whereby voters are regarded more as customers and policies as products to be shaped with continuous opinion polling to better reflect voter preferences (Norris, 2000; Farrell and Webb, 2000; Gibson and Römmele, 2001; Chapters 1 and 5 of this volume)?

In terms of the more public uses of the net, that is, the WWW, the evidence of most national studies generally regards parties as limited in their interactive uses of the medium. Most parties present static sites combined with targeted information provision. Websites largely remain mechanisms for feeding information to activists and journalists and for symbolising parties' 'cutting edge' credentials, rather than providing any meaningful interaction with voters (Stone, 1996; Gibson and Ward, 1998; Davis, 1999; Gibson, *et al.*, 2000; Tops *et al.*, 2000; Chapter 1 of this volume). Such findings were endorsed in a recent study of the federal party websites in Australia, which concluded that:

> In terms of party functions it would seem that the Internet is seen as a tool for top-down information provision. Attempts by sites to gather information from voters or offer interactive experiences were very limited. While attesting to the potential for such devices, party communications personnel confess to not seeing much scope for them currently. Particularly for the major parties, the sites are seen primarily as an adjunct to existing communication devices, a useful extra promotional tool, but not a central focus for mobilisation efforts.
>
> (Gibson and Ward, 2002)

Such trends clearly challenge the widespread technological optimism that greeted the advent of the Internet and its expected revitalising effects for democracy (Rheingold, 1995; Grossman, 1995). In the article cited above, however, we questioned whether these result were the product of focusing on the national-level sites and missing the series of 'smaller pictures' at the state level that might show a more active pattern of political activity. While Australia's federal system may be perceived to have become more centralised over time, particularly since the 1970s (Summers, 1996), the states and state parties are still considered to be powerful players in shaping political outcomes.

Certainly, the differences in population characteristics, socio-economic status and political-institutional design of the states would lead us to expect some variance in their proclivity towards online 'politicking'. The stronger legacy of referenda in New South Wales, for example, may mean that citizens are more oriented towards direct-feedback mechanisms, and so parties may be bolder in experimenting with online polls and email. Alternatively, perhaps it is more a question of numbers and the most intensive web campaigning takes place in those areas with the highest proportion of Internet-connected voters. While national surveys indicate a rapid growth of Internet access, with almost 50 per cent of Australians reporting that they had used the Internet by the end of 2000,[1] regional variations do exist between states. Statistics from 1998 available from the Australian Bureau of Statistics show a marked disparity, with the ACT emerging as the most 'wired' state (27 per cent of households reported having access to the Internet) and Tasmania the least (8 per cent of households). The reasons for such distinctions lie most obviously in socio-economic factors or the so-called digital divide, since a key reason given among those reporting no access to the net was that the 'costs were too high'.[2]

As well as seeking to profile the activity taking place below the national level of web campaigning, investigation of state and territory web campaigning also allows us to analyse questions about the implications of the new ICTs for the internal life of political parties. Thus far, only limited attention has been given to the 'inward' effects of the new ICTs, a result possibly of the more difficult task of gaining information from the parties on these more 'private' uses of the technology. What little evidence has been gathered so far indicates that parties do not necessarily see the Internet as a tool for democratisation. Rather, it is viewed as a means of modernisation and increased efficiency of party administration (Smith 1998, 2000; Gibson and Ward, 1999).

The Internet and party democratisation

It is clear that the Internet's impact on parties' internal life is potentially highly significant. In order to understand these effects more clearly we divide the applications into two distinct areas: (1) the purely internal arena – meaning the application of new ICTs to communication between leaders, staff and activists through specialised Intranets, and a range of other more private matters such as data management, distribution of campaign materials, and voting on policy issues or leadership positions; and (2) the external arena – relating to parties' use of the Internet in the public sphere, that is, in terms of the World Wide Web and email.

The internal applications of the new technology carry the most obvious implications for levels of intra-party democracy. Interactive uses of the Internet could facilitate wider and more inclusive discussions within the parties on matters of policy and procedure. Publication of minutes and alerts about forthcoming important meetings could help improve scrutiny and accountability of the party hierarchy. Offering voting online could open up the numbers involved in key party decisions. Of course, the democratic potential of the technology depends on how the parties structure opportunities for feedback. Simply offering online referenda with options for approval or rejection does not necessarily provide for meaningful control over the direction of the party. As Katz (2001) has pointed out, democratising reforms within parties often lead to real decision-making shifts to other non-institutionalised fora. Indeed, moving communication into electronic form may actually raise possibilities for new and more effective ways for centralised monitoring and regulating of party communication – measures that, if taken to an extreme, could result in power becoming more concentrated in the organisation rather than dispersed.

In terms of the external applications of the new technology it is clear that there are features that, if utilised, could affect internal party power relations and enhance levels of democracy. We consider there to be four major applications in this regard.

- *Information dissemination.* In making information freely and readily available on the web, parties open themselves up to greater scrutiny from members and voters. This could even extend so far as setting up specific email lists for disseminating news of internal party business as discussed above.
- *Interactivity.* This can come in two basic forms: parties could set up special channels to structure upward feedback from the public on key issues of internal business or policy questions, or offer some facility for interactive discourse between themselves and their supporters. This could be done in a simply deliberative or 'talking shop' sense or be made more consultative or even decisive. In offering bulletin boards, email and chat rooms, for example, the parties could allow such groups to play an enhanced role in party policy and structure by providing direct access to party minutes and leaders. Parties at the sub-national level, one can argue, would have a smaller and more manageable constituency to target for input than the national-level organisations.
- *Networking.* Using hypertext links from their websites, organisations such as parties can provide a 'one-stop shop' for the public and their own activists to access other branches of the party. Such internal net-working arguably would lead to a higher frequency of cross-party consultation and thus a stronger sense of group identity and internal coherence.
- *Factional fora.* The web can also be seen to offer groups or factions within the party an alternative and highly public platform to air their views, which might be converted into an outlet for dissenting factions within the party. Of course, one needs to remain aware that the use of websites and email can also allow for more centralisation of control over the party's message. A 'one size fits all' templated approach to web design is a tempting option for a party seeking to place stricter limits on freedom of expression. Finally, one can argue that the web through the hypertext link can promote a stronger degree of inter-party linkage and, thus, a stronger sense of group purpose and internal coherence.

Clearly both the internal and external areas of new ICTs have implications for internal power relations in the party. For the purposes of this chapter, we focus largely on this second, more public, arena, although where data are available we also refer to the former.

Australian parties and internal democracy

Questions about the implications of the new ICTs for parties' internal functioning and democracy are expected to yield interesting results in the Australian context. The parties are considered to follow rather different models of internal organisation, resulting in differing tendencies towards factionalism and centralisation. Taking the two major parties, it is fair to say that the Liberal Party has generally been seen as the most decentralised and pro-federalist and the ALP as favouring a more centralised and nationalised style of management of state-level branches (Lloyd, 1996; Warhurst, 1996). Thus, as a starting point one might expect the Liberal Party to favour more decentralist uses of the technology and the ALP to display a greater propensity to use it in more centralised and nationalised ways. Of course the geographic or lateral dispersion of power across organisations does not necessarily translate into any greater accountability of elites to members. Indeed, the reforms initiated during the 1970s within the ALP that established more participatory structures at the state and local level were actually induced by the party's national executive body (Warhurst, 1996). Thus, participatory uses of the new technology by Labour might be expected to be structured in a more vertical way, with the websites of regional parties designed to bring the members and national elites into closer communication, and spreading power downwards. In terms of the categories of innovation discussed above, therefore, ALP state and territory websites would be expected to place more emphasis on interactivity and networking than the Liberal counterparts, the latter, in turn, displaying greater autonomy and possibly dissent with its site and focusing more on transparency, or the top-down communication of party information.

Of course, expectations of variance in the internal and external uses of the technology between the major parties should not be overstated. Both parties in general have experienced an increase in the prominence and power of the national level of organisation since the 1980s, such changes occurring in tandem with the overall increase in power of the Commonwealth government (Summers, 1996). However, they also follow trends observed among parties globally towards a more professionalised and homogenised model of party campaigning. Since the 1980s, observers in numerous countries have reported the growth of tighter controls over ideological debate within parties and an increased use of external media consultants and pollsters (Swanson and Mancini, 1996). While at first glance such changes might lead one to downgrade expectations for participatory innovations with new ICTs, one can argue that, conversely, such developments actually mean that the incentives for both parties to make participatory uses of the new technology are running high.

Among the smaller parties, in terms of levels of centralisation there is more of a spectrum, with the Democrats being the most nationalised party and the Greens occupying the other highly federalist pole. The Greens combine their highly decentralised territorial structure with a commitment to a more radical grassroots participatory philosophy. With such features, one would expect the Greens to display a greater proclivity to use the net in ways that would promote more internal party democracy on all four dimensions of transparency, interactivity, networking and factional-ism/dissent. Certainly, following the path of Green parties in the Euro-pean context, one would expect them to exploit the participatory opportunities in their uses of online technologies (Voerman and Ward, 2000).

Data and methodology

The goal of this chapter is to establish the overall level of internal and external online activity within state and territory parties in Australia and whether such activity is oriented towards increasing intra-party democracy. The parties chosen for analysis are the two major parties and the Greens. While the sheer size and influence of the Liberals and the ALP make them obvious cases to include, the Greens present an additional and inter-esting study. Although they are a smaller party in terms of resources and members, their more educated and postmaterialist support base, along with their commitment to intra-party democracy, gives them a strong incentive to use the new ICTs, particularly in participatory ways. In study-ing these three organisations, therefore, we can begin to see how far it is party ethos or ideology that determines the extent of innovation with new ICTs compared with basic capacity and the desire for efficiency. In order to do this we gathered a variety of data from the WWW during August 2001 and also some more specific attitudinal data from party elites them-selves during Autumn 2001. Specifically:

- (a) the web was surveyed for the presence of state and territory parties using the federal sites for all three parties plus the three major indices of Australian party sites;[3] and (b) a search-engine count was under-taken of the number of links or 'backpointers' in to the sites;[4]
- federal and state party websites were content analysed using a coding scheme designed to score sites on the three elements of: transparency (information provision); interactivity (one-way and multi-directional participation opportunities); and internal and external organisational networking (hypertext links), relevant to enhancing internal demo-cracy. The coding scheme was adapted from that developed specifi-cally for candidates and party sites (Gibson and Ward, 2000c) and is listed in the Appendix to this chapter. We also looked for evidence of internal dissent or factionalism being made public on the site. Lastly, we measured the design of the site in terms of its level of glitziness (multimedia use), and features relating to ease of navigation, and freshness.

Findings

Website presence and visibility

While the federal sites of all three parties prominently displayed links to their state and territory branches, not all were accessible. Of the twenty-four possible sites available, three were offline and one was totally outdated. The Queensland and Western Australia Liberals sites were 'under construction', as was that of the Tasmanian Green Party. The Queensland Labour Party site, while accessible, was actually just an old electoral site. Most of these sites promised further developments soon.[5] Of the remaining twenty sites that were 'live', as Table 7.1 reveals, the Liberal Party sites proved the most difficult to locate. The Liberals in the Northern Territory and Tasmania were not listed on Yahoo, the Federal Parliament site or that of The National Library.

The search for links in to the sites provided a similar story (see Table 7.2). The ALP and Green state parties enjoy a significantly higher profile on the web than their Liberal rivals. While the latter averaged 37 links in per branch, the Greens had over a third as many (61) and the ALP almost ten times as many, with over 350 links in to each state and territory website.

Table 7.1 Australian state party online visibility: presence on major indexes

Party	Index	ACT	NSW	VIC	WA	QLD	NT	TAS	SA	Fed
Liberal	Yahoo		✓	✓						✓
	Parl Lib	✓	✓	✓	✓	✓			✓	✓
	Nat Lib	✓	✓	✓		✓			✓	
ALP	Yahoo	✓	✓	✓	✓	✓	✓	✓	✓	✓
	Parl Lib	✓	✓	✓	✓	✓	✓	✓	✓	✓
	Nat Lib	✓	✓	✓	✓	✓	✓	✓	✓	✓
Green	Yahoo	✓	✓	✓	✓	✓	✓	✓	✓	✓
	Parl Lib	✓	✓	✓	✓	✓	✓	✓	✓	✓
	Nat Lib	✓	✓	✓	✓	✓	✓	✓	✓	✓

Table 7.2 Australian state party online visibility: number of links in to websites*

Party	ACT	NSW	VIC	WA	QLD	NT	TAS	SA	Mean	Fed
Liberal	48	31	56	–	–	34	6	46	37	538
ALP	374	303	399	336	–	389	336	364	357	939
Green	44	139	74	55	83	43	18	32	61	355

Note
*Calculated using Google search engine.

Such patterns are no doubt a reflection of the more international nature of the social democratic and environmental movement. However, they also confirm that the web is certainly offering smaller parties such as the Greens the chance to punch above their weight in terms of comparisons with exposure granted in the traditional media. In addition, in terms of state variation it seems that parties in Victoria had the highest international profile, while those in Tasmania had the lowest.

Website functionality

Moving to compare the parties' sites in terms of their openness with information, opportunities for interaction and level of connectivity and conflict expressed, we find a rather mixed picture. Table 7.3 presents the summary of findings for each of the functions of the websites. Detailed scoring on each index is listed in the tables in the Appendix.

Transparency and interactivity

In terms of transparency we applied a 0–17 point index that registered how much basic information parties made publicly available on their site, ranging from organisational history and structure to events and newsletters. None of the state sites, except the Queensland Greens, however, scored particularly highly for information provision. Most of the sites offered only around half of the information items. The Liberal Party overall performed better than the other two, with the state parties actually outperforming its national site in terms of the range of information provided. The type of information being offered by all the parties was fairly similar, however, with organisational history, policy and basic contact details being the most common forms of content. No attempt was made to post details of party meetings or minutes for public consumption on the site, although some did advertise upcoming party events and had a password-protected section for members, which possibly contained information on these matters. The media were the clear target audience, with most sites having press releases, speeches, archives and/or media centres. The ALP gained the most consistent scores, a product of the fact that all state and territory sites adhered to a similar design, based on the national-level model. Interestingly, several ALP sites directed visitors to official government sites or state leader sites for information on policy and news.

The parties performed even less well in regard to opportunities for interaction, on average featuring only around a third of the items measured, with a mean score of 4 out of a possible total of 14. In the main, while sites commonly allowed for interaction with the site in terms of information gathering with search engines and encouraged visitors to

Table 7.3 Summary of scores by Australian state party: transparency, interactivity and networking

Party	Transparency/ info provision	Interactivity	Networking internal/external	
Liberal Party				
Federal	8	4	2	2
Canberra	9	4	2	2
NSW	9	6	3	2
VIC	8	3	4	2
WA	site offline	site offline	site offline	
QLD	site offline	site offline	site offline	
NT	9	2	2	1
TAS	3	1	1	2
SA	11	7	1	0
Mean score	*8.2*	*3.8*	*2.2*	*1.2*
Labour Party				
Federal	14	8	2	2
Canberra	7	3	2	2
NSW	5	3	3	1
VIC	8	4	2	2
WA	6	4	2	1
QLD	3	1	0	0
NT	7	3	2	2
TAS	7	3	2	2
SA	7	3	2	2
Mean score	*6.25*	*3.0*	*1.9*	*1.5*
Green Party				
Federal	9	7	1	2
Canberra	6	5	2	2
NSW	9	7	3	2
VIC	7	5	2	2
WA	7	4	2	1
QLD	12	10	2	2
NT	3	4	1	2
TAS	site offline	site offline	site offline	
SA	4	3	2	2
Mean score	*6.9*	*5.4*	*2.0*	*1.9*
Overall Mean	*7.0*	*4.0*	*2.0*	*1.6*
Range	0–17	0–14	0–4	0–3

send money or volunteer help, few sites offered any two-way communication or novel participatory features. Less than a quarter of the sites had member-only areas or bulletin boards and none had chat rooms, and few were running active online issue campaigns. There were more variations between the parties on this dimension, however, with the Greens lifting the average considerably by their mean score of 5.4. The Queensland and

NSW Greens in particular offered extensive participatory opportunities. In contrast, none of the ALP sites scored more than 4 for interactivity. In addition, the Victorian Liberals did encourage offline participation by offering application forms to those interested in being considered as candidates in the forthcoming elections and directing voters to electoral-commission sites for further information about registering and voting.

Overall, comparing federal and state sites on transparency and inter-activity dimensions, a further interesting picture of variance emerges. In the case of the Liberal Party, the regional sites generally outscored the national site, particularly in terms of transparency. In contrast, the ALP federal site far exceeded its state counterparts in terms of its infor-mativeness and participatory components. Indeed, it may have been that given the amount of information available on the federal ALP site, the state parties felt less need to provide their own alternative sources. The Greens displayed a more even balance between the regional and national sites, with the latter performing slightly better but not markedly so.

Networking

For networking we examined the extent of intra-party linkages made by the state and territory parties to one another via their websites and also to other units within the parties, namely, the federal and local parties and the national leader pages. We compared this with a measure of the extent of external links to outside organisations divided into three categories – educational, partisan and commercial. The results reveal less variation among the parties on this measure than those reported above, although this is related largely to the narrower range of scores available (0–4 and 0–3 respectively). On average, most parties scored around the mid-point for internal networking, with most sites linking upwards to the federal party and laterally to other state parties and state representatives, but with hardly any providing links or information about local-level branches. Only three of the sites provided any links to branch parties (NSW Greens, ALP and Northern Territory Liberals). Links to the federal leader were a uniquely Liberal phenomenon with three state parties displaying links to John Howard's home pages. The Victorian Liberals also had a particular section of their website devoted to the federal Campaign 2001 that pro-moted Howard and attacked Beazley for his profligacy. While the Greens' decentralist culture and eschewing of national leadership helps explain their reluctance in this regard, the failure of the state ALP sites to link to their national leader make for a rather conspicuous absence. Internally, therefore, there was some exploitation of the technology as infrastructure with sites serving to guide users to other parts of the party. This was not as extensive as it might have been, however, and overall there does not appear to be any concerted effort towards organisation building online.

Most parties included some external links to other national and international organisations. Most commonly these were partisan links to sister parties around the world and like-minded pressure groups and campaigns, and the Greens in particular favoured these types of links. Links to government departments at the state, territory and federal level were also common, particularly among those parties, such as the Canberra Liberals, holding government office.

Dissent/factionalism

There was little evidence of dissent or factionalism highlighted by these websites. Public websites were not really a forum for internal party debate. In fact, sites followed remarkably similar patterns. In the case of the ALP the state sites were mainly of templated design with largely standard content across all the states.[6] Where there was variance between party sites it tended to be in terms of pages focused on the state party leader. If the sites have any impact on internal party debates it is generally to promote state leaderships or elites. Equally, below the state level the penetration of the web into internal party affairs is negligible. For example, two ALP state parties reported that they only knew of one of their constituency parties being online in each of their states.[7]

Presentation and delivery

In addition to focusing on particular functions of the party sites, we also gathered some basic information on their appearance and stylistic merits. This included information on the design of the home page and use of multimedia, the frequency of updates of the site and the ease of accessing and navigating through it. While some of these were fairly straightforward to measure, accessibility was assessed in two ways. The first method assessed the site's accessibility in principle using an additive index that counted a variety of features such as language translation and text-only options. The second method assessed it in practice by the size of the home page in kilobytes. Generally speaking, a page larger than about 30 Kb will take a long time to load. Ease of navigation was also measured using an additive index based on features such as the presence of search engines, site maps and having a fixed menu bar. For a full listing of the methodology used see the Appendix.

On the whole the sites were quite basic. Scores for the ALP parties on site-design features were again highly similar since they all followed a pared-down version of the national model. In terms of home page, all the parties offered some colourful graphics on their home page and some had moving icons although only four sites made use of audio or video, mainly for campaign broadcasts. The Northern Territory Greens, for instance, had some sound clips of leading Liberal politicians 'in their own words' as

Table 7.4 Summary of scores by Australian state party: site presentation and delivery

	Glitz/ Multimedia	Access/Kb home page		Navigation	Freshness
Liberal Party					
Federal	2	0	21	5	4
Canberra	2	0	15	3	2
NSW	3	0	20	5	6
VIC	3	0	45	2	2
WA	site offline	site offline		site offline	site offline
QLD	site offline	site offline		site offline	site offline
NT	3	0	7	2	6
TAS	2	0	10	2	4
SA	4	0	14	4	6
*Mean score**	*2.8*	*0*	*18.5*	*3*	*4.3*
Labour Party					
Federal	2	3	NA**	7	6
Canberra	2	2	15	6	5
NSW	4	1	4	3	?
VIC	2	0	14	6	?
WA	2	3	NA	6	?
QLD	3	0	NA	1	0
NT	4	3	15	6	?
TAS	2	3	14	6	4
SA	2	3	NA	6	5
Mean score	*2.6*	*1.9*	*12.4*	*5*	*3.5*
Green Party					
Federal	2	1	NA	5	5
Canberra	2	0	13	1	5
NSW	2	0	NA	2	5
VIC	2	0	14	2	2
WA	2	0	5	2	1
QLD	2	0	NA	4	5
NT	2	0	7	1	0
TAS	site offline	site offline		site offline	site offline
SA	2	1	13	1	2
Mean score	*2*	*0.1*	*10.4*	*1.9*	*2.9*
Overall Mean	*2.5*	*0.7*	*14*	*3.3*	*3.6*
Range	0–6	0–6	0–n	0–n	0–6

Notes

*All mean scores are calculated without federal party scores.

**NA = not available.

part of their negative attack on NT Liberal government. For ease of navigation and access to information the templated ALP sites generally outperformed both Liberal and Green sites, with navigation tips, site maps, text-only versions, search engines and printer conversion for documents. Some Liberal and Green sites had search engines and fixed menu bars; however, none of the Liberal sites and only one Green site offered more enhanced accessibility options such as language translation, blind software or text only. In general, the parties, displayed a rather casual attitude towards keeping the site fresh with just less than half the sites being updated either daily or every few days. For many of ALP sites it was impossible to distinguish when they were last updated since news sections were often simply links to information updates on the State Premiers' site (where the ALP held office). Of those that could be judged, however, a third were considerably dated, not having been altered for at least a month. A clear gap emerges here with the federal sites, which tended to be updated at least every few days.

Summary

So what do our findings tell us about the three aims of the research outlined in the beginning? In terms of the level of web activity among the Australian parties, overall it appears to be rather patchy. A minority of parties actually lack any web presence at all, or prove very difficult to locate. Of those sites up and running, it does not appear that a strenuous effort is being made to let the daylight in, however, and promote intraparty democracy. Overall, there is little evidence that parties are focusing on their sites as an opportunity to promote a more transparent, interconnected and interactive 'face'. The main purpose is a general level of information provision for interested voters. Of course, such generalisations often hide some subtle yet important differences. Indeed, in line with our expectations the Greens emerged as the best all-round performers, particularly in the area of interactivity. The Liberal parties did appear to place a greater emphasis on transparency and information provision than the ALP and also more independence in terms of site content and design. ALP sites were notable primarily for their monotony, all being clones of the mother ship based in Canberra. Contrary to expectations, however, Labour sites were not more likely to offer interactivity, nor did they display a strong degree of networking. Indeed, Liberal sites were actually more likely to link upwards to the national leader. In general, however, most parties engaged in some form of internal networking, but none really offered the site as a virtual 'meeting point' or a 'hub' of coordination for the party as a whole.

Conclusions: towards a theory of parties' use of new ICTs – systemic versus organisational determinants

Taking these findings as a whole, we can begin to address the third aim of this chapter – speculation on some of the causal dynamics at work here. Dividing party factors into two basic dimensions – capacity or resources and incentive or outlook – it would appear that it is the latter that is more important in determining a party's level of engagement with new ICTs. Having a larger budget, more staff and a bigger membership base, as the major parties do, does not necessarily make them more likely to have a web presence or to use the web to reach out to supporters and, more significantly, invite them in. However, having a commitment to the participatory needs of one's support base, as the Greens do, appears to engender more of such activity online. Equally, having a more centralised understanding of party organisation is also manifest here with the ALP and its templated approach to state and territory branch sites. Liberal Party sites, following the party's more decentralist mantra, are clearly more variable in quality, with some states not even bothering to run a site at all. Of course, not all the differences observed can be put down to the influence of party ethos. There do appear to be some other aspects of parties' online presence and performance that suggest the influence of broader geographic, demographic and political-institutional factors.

If we compare the parties' performance on each of our functional indicators by state (see Table 7.5), for instance, there does appear to be some systematic variance emerging.

Parties in Tasmania generally score lowest on the coding scheme with those in NSW performing much better. Tasmania, as reported earlier, reported the lowest rate of Internet access across Australia, whereas New South Wales has one of the highest. Thus, one can argue based on these data that parties' innovation with ICTs is propelled to some extent by

Table 7. 5 Mean party scores for website functions within Australian states and territories

State	Information provision	Participation	Internal networking	External networking	Overall mean
ACT	7.3	4.0	2.0	2.0	3.8
NSW	7.6	5.3	3.0	1.7	4.4
VIC	7.6	4.0	2.7	2.0	4.1
WA	6.5	4.0	2.0	1.0	3.4
QLD	7.5	5.5	1.0	1.0	3.8
NT	6.3	3.0	1.6	1.7	3.1
TAS	5.0	2.0	2.0	2.0	2.8
SA	7.3	4.3	1.3	1.3	3.6
Mean	7.0	4.0	2.0	1.6	3.7

perceptions of the viability of the market. With fewer voters online, parties' investment in a more sophisticated web presence is more likely to seem an extra cost that does not offer significant benefits.

In addition to socio-economic differences it appears that some of the variance is related to the particularities of the political context within the states. Of those places where sites were either inaccessible or left derelict, this occurred in states where the party had recently undergone an electoral shock, losing government office and significant electoral support. The Queensland and West Australian Liberals had both sustained heavy losses in the elections earlier in 2001. For those states where an election was looming, the Northern Territory and the ACT, parties were all online and the performances of the incumbent Liberal parties or Country Liberals were above average on most indicators. However, such parties had the added advantage of being able to link to a range of government-produced sites rather than offering only 'home-grown' party-based sites.

Thus, while data collected here clearly do not allow us to sustain any clear-cut conclusions about the determinants of party behaviour online, they do provide a start. Overall, if state-level parties are really occupying a frontline role in Australian politics and getting closer to the electorate, then our evidence would suggest that they are choosing to do so by means other than electronic. However, while the parties appear to be similarly unambitious in their use of the web, those differences that did emerge do appear to follow some logical contours of explanation extending from the party level to the systemic environment. Such findings are useful in offering a basis for future research to build a more formal understanding and ultimately an empirically testable model of factors promoting parties' use of the new ICTs.

Appendix: coding scheme for party websites

Transparency/information provision

Additive index – 1 point assigned for each item present (0–17) of:

- organisational history;
- structure;
- values/ideology;
- policies;
- documents (i.e. manifesto, constitution);
- newsletters;
- media releases (i.e. speeches, statements, interview transcripts, conferences);
- people/Who's Who;
- leader focus (picture, text on home page);
- candidate profiles;

- electoral information (statistics, information on past performance);
- event calendar (prospective or retrospective);
- conference information;
- Frequently Asked Questions;
- privacy policy;
- article archive or library;
- group pages.

Interactivity

Each of the following can be assigned a value of 1 if present, yielding a score range of 0–14.

Information gathering (1)

The site offers search engines, cookies, games/gimmicks, audio and video, etc. whereby the user can gather more information about the organisation.

Information gathering (2)

More active engagement is required, with users signing up for direct email updates and newsletters.

Talking about politics with friends

The site offers some kind of bulletin board or chat room for interested visitors to exchange views with one another.

Trying to influence others' opinions

The site offers or encourages individuals to send some kind of email postcard or message to friends to attempt to get them to support the organisation.

Advertising

The site offers downloads of wallpaper or screensavers, which, like bumper stickers or badges, can be used to promote the organisation publicly.

Leafleting

The site offers leaflets to download and print that can be distributed offline.

Contacting

The site offers email contacts for itself and/or other individuals/organisations that encourage people to express opinions and provide feedback.

Petitioning

The site offers some kind of online petition to sign.

Dialogue

The site offers online chat Q&A sessions with leaders.

Donating

You can donate financially to the organisation directly on the site.

Joining (associate)

The organisation offers associate membership or a 'friends of' status directly on the site.

Joining (full)

You can join the organisation directly on the site.

Campaigning

The site offers a facility for taking a more formal role in an e-campaigning strategy, e.g. becoming an e-precinct leader.

Membership section

Members-only pages are available that require an ID and password to enter.

Networking

Internal

Additive index: 0–4:

- federal party;
- federal party leader home page;
- state parties;
- local parties.

External

Additive index: 0–3 (3 ordinal indices):

- partisan links are those to other parties and organisations that are supportive of the party's goals; for example, if the Labour Party links to the Trades Union Congress site, or the American Democratic party;
- reference links are those to neutral or news/educational sites such as news broadcasters, newspapers, parliamentary/government sites, national libraries etc.;
- commercial links are those promoting business services such as book-sellers, web designers.

Presentation and delivery

Glitz factor

Cumulative index (0–6) comprises two additive indices.
Homepage design index awards 1 point for each item present (0–3):

- graphics;
- frames;
- moving icons.

Multimedia index awards 1 point for each item present (0–3):

- sound;
- video;
- live streaming.

Access

This consists of two dimensions, access in principle and access in practice.
   In principle index awards 1 point for each item present (0–6):

- no-frames option;
- text-only option (entire site);
- text-only documents to download and print (clearly listed as such);
- WAP/PDA 'wireless' enabled;
- foreign language translation;
- software for the blind/visually impaired.

In practice:

- size of home page in Kb (>25 slows site loading time significantly).

Navigability

Additive index awards 1 point for each item present (0–n):

- navigation tips;
- no. of search engines;
- home-page icon on lower-level pages;
- fixed menu bar on lower-level pages;
- site map/index.

Freshness

Ordinal index (0–6):
Updated: daily (6); 1–2 days (5); 3–7 days (4); every two weeks (3); monthly (2); 1–6 months (1); +6 months (0).

Notes

1   For details see ABS report 'Household use of Information Technology', http://www.abs.gov.au/ausstats/abs@.nsf/94713ad445ff1425ca25682000192af 2/6aa7090c5912730eca256b360012b83f!OpenDocument. Also see http://www. nua.com for more Internet demographics and access statistics. See also Curtin, J. (2001) 'A Digital Divide in Rural and Regional Australia', Current Issues, Brief 1 2001–2002, available at: http://search.aph.gov.au/search/ParlInfo. ASP?action=view&item=0&resultsID=IToBy.
2   Australian Bureau of Statistics, Special Article, 'The Information Society and the Information Economy in Australia' (Year Book Australia, 1999), available at http://www.abs.gov.au/ausstats/abs@.nsf/94713ad445ff1425ca25682000192af2 /485fd68c254fd5eeca2569de0028de90!OpenDocument.
3   The major sites used for party listings were those of: the National Library of Australia (www.nla.gov.au/oz/gov/party.html); the Parliamentary Library (www.aph.gov.au/library/intguide/pol/polparti.htm); Yahoo (http://dir. yahoo.com/Regional/Countries/Australia/Government/Politics/Parties/).
4   This was done using the search engine Google (www.google.com). The method was simply to enter link:www.name of party into the dialogue box and hit enter.
5   For instance, the two Liberal Party sites presented the visitor with a message to 'Watch This Space For Exciting New Development' and one gave a link back to the Federal party's home page.
6   It is worth noting that for most state ALP sites if you want to contact the webmaster then the email address directs you to the national party webmaster.
7   Personal communication with ALP state-level officials, August 2001.

References

Davis, R. (1999) *The Web of Politics: the Internet's Impact on the American Political System*, Oxford: Oxford University Press.

Farrell, D. and Webb, P. (2000) 'Political Parties as Campaign Organisations', in Dalton, R. and Wattenberg, M. (eds), *Parties Without Partisans*, Oxford: Oxford University Press, 102–128.

Gibson, R.K., Newell, J.L. and Ward, S.J. (2000) 'New Parties, New Media: Italian Party Politics and the Internet', *South European Society and Politics*, 5(1): 123–142.

Gibson, R.K., McAllister, I. and Swenson, T. (2002) 'The Politics of Race and Immigration in Australia: One Nation Voting in the 1998 Election', *Ethnic and Racial Studies*, 25(5): 823–844.

Gibson, R.K. and Römmele, A. (2001) 'Political Parties and Professionalized Campaigning', *Harvard International Journal of Press Politics*, 6(4): 31–44.

Gibson, R.K. and Ward, S.J. (1998) 'UK Political Parties and the Internet: Politics as Usual in the New Media?', *Harvard International Journal of Press Politics*, 3(3): 14–38.

Gibson, R.K. and Ward, S.J. (1999) 'Party Democracy Online: UK Parties and New ICTs', *Information Communication and Society*, 2(3): 340–367.

Gibson, R.K. and Ward, S.J. (2000a) 'New Media, Same Impact? British Party Activity in Cyberspace', in Gibson, R.K. and Ward, S.J. (eds), *Reinvigorating Government? British Politics and the Internet*, Aldershot: Ashgate, 106–129.

Gibson, R.K. and Ward, S.J. (2000b) 'An Outsider's Medium? The European Elections and UK Party Competition on the Internet', in Philip Cowley *et al.* (eds), *British Parties and Elections Review Vol. 10*, London: Frank Cass, 93–112.

Gibson, R.K. and Ward, S.J. (2000c), 'A Proposed Methodology for Studying the Function and Effectiveness of Party and Candidate Websites', *Social Science Computer Review*, 18(3): 301–319.

Gibson, R.K. and Ward, S.J. (2002) 'Virtual Campaigning: Australian Parties and the Internet', *Australian Journal of Political Science*, 37(1): 99–129.

Grossman, L. (1995) *The Electronic Republic*, New York: Penguin Books.

Johns, G. (2000) 'Party Democracy: An Audit of Australian Parties', *Australian Journal of Political Science*, 35(3): 401–425.

Katz, R. (2001) 'The Problem of Candidate Selection and Models of Party Democracy', *Party Politics*, 7(3): 277–296.

Lloyd, C. (1996) 'The Liberal Party', in Parkin, A., Summers, J. and Woodward, D. (eds), *Government Politics, Power and Policy in Australia*, Melbourne: Addison Wesley Longman Australian Pty Ltd: 5th edition, 124–138.

McAllister, I. (1997) 'Australia', in Norris, P. (ed.), *Passages to Power: Legislative Recruitment in Advanced Democracies*, Cambridge: Cambridge University Press.

McAllister, I. (2002) 'Rational or Capricious? Late Deciding Voters in Australia, Britain and the United States', in Farrell, D. and Schmitt-Beck, R. (eds), *Do Political Campaigns Matter?*, London: Routledge, 22–40.

McAllister, I. and Bean, A. (1996) 'Long Term Electoral Trends and the 1996 Election', Australian National University, Mimeo.

Margolis, M., Resnick, D. and Tu, C. (1997) 'Campaigning on the Internet: Parties and Candidates on the World Wide Web in the 1996 Primary Season', *Harvard International Journal of Press Politics*, 2(1): 59–78.

Margolis, M., Resnick, D. and Wolfe, J. (1999) 'Party Competition on the Internet:

Minor Versus Major Parties in the UK and USA', *Harvard International Journal of Press Politics*, 4(4): 24–47.

Newell, J. (2001) 'New Parties, New Media: Italian Political Parties and the Web', *Harvard International Journal of Press Politics*, 6(4).

Norris, P. (2000) *A Virtuous Circle*, Cambridge: Cambridge University Press.

Rheingold, H. (1995) *The Virtual Community: Finding Connection in a Computerised World*, London: Minerva.

Robinson, S. (1996) 'Remarks', in Simms, M. (ed.), *The Paradox of Parties: Australian Political Parties*, Sydney: Allen & Unwin.

Sharman, C. (1994) 'Political Parties', in Brett, J., Gillespie, J. and Goot, M. (eds), *Developments in Australian Politics*, Melbourne: Macmillan Education Australia Pty Ltd.

Smith, C. (1998) 'Political parties in the Information Age: From Mass Party to Leadership Organisation?', in Snellen, I. and van de Donk, W. (eds), *Public Administration in the Information Age: A Handbook*, Amsterdam: IoS Press.

Smith, C. (2000) 'British Political Parties: Continuity and Change in the Information Age', in Hoff, J., Horrocks, I. and Tops, P. (eds), *Democratic Governance and New Technology*, London: Routledge, 57–70.

Stone, B. (1996) 'Politic 1996', *Internet World*, November: 38–48.

Summers, J. (1996) 'State and Federal Politics', in Parkin, A., Summers, J. and Woodward, D. (eds), *Government Politics, Power and Policy in Australia*, Melbourne: Addison Wesley Longman Australian Pty Ltd.: 5th edition.

Swanson, D. and Mancini, P. (eds) (1996) *Politics, Media and Democracy*, Westport: Praeger.

Topf, R. (1995) 'Electoral Participation', in Klingemann, H.-D. and Fuchs, D. (eds), *Citizens and the State*, Oxford: Oxford University Press, 27–51.

Tops, P., Voerman, G. and Boogers, M. (2000) 'Political websites during the 1998 Parliamentary Elections in the Netherlands', in Hoff, J., Horrocks, I. and Tops, P. (eds), *Democratic Governance and New Technology*, London: Routledge, 87–100.

Voerman, G. and Ward, S. (2000) 'New Media and New Politics: Green Parties, Intra-Party Democracy and the Internet (An Anglo-Dutch Comparison)', in Voerman, G. and Lucardie, P. (eds), *Jaerboek Documentatiecentrum Nederlandse Politieke Partijen 1999*, Groningen: University of Groningen, 192–215.

Warhurst (1996) 'The Labor Party', in Parkin, A., Summers, J. and Woodward, D. (eds), *Government Politics, Power and Policy in Australia*, Melbourne: Addison Wesley Longman Australian Pty Ltd.: 5th edition, 139–159.

8 The democratising potential of the Internet and political parties in Romania

Rodica Mocan, Gabriel Badescu and Cosmin Marian

> It is impossible to be simultaneously blasted by a revolution in technology ... and a worldwide revolution of communication without facing ... a potentially explosive political revolution ... all our tools to make and enforce collective decisions ... are obsolete and about to be transformed.
>
> (Toffler, 1980: 392)

Introduction

More than a decade ago, John Naisbitt was already heralding the death of representative democracy, as we know it, owing to the development of communications technologies (Naisbitt, 1989: 235). From the 1970s onward, American politics had entered a new era with an unprecedented number of referendums and initiatives regarding local politics initiated in a number of states and participation rates of 80 to 90 per cent. This form of consultation was seen to satisfy a need for 'direct democracy', the 'heart and soul of participative democracy' (Naisbitt, 1989: 234).

If we see participatory politics as the direct involvement of each individual in the formal decision-making process of the state via a vote or consultation, then new technologies clearly do offer the possibility for radical change in our democratic system. Because of the decentralised character of the Internet, information flows become more free and open. Closed societies that depend on downward flows of communication are challenged as civil society finds a new means to engage in an open dialogue with one another, with elites and with the international community. Such a challenge, however, raises a host of additional questions about the ability of individuals to access and to use it effectively.

As Romania makes its transition to democracy, the importance of communication with citizens has become increasingly important. New communications technologies, such as the Internet, are particularly appealing given their facility for two-way flows of information. The Internet is also perceived as valuable since it forms a relatively inexpensive means of communication. Printed materials are costly to produce and also face distribution problems. As such, they are of limited availability and can rarely be obtained upon request. Information on the Internet does not present such problems given that web addresses are freely available and the amount of information offered is as extensive as one's server permits.

The role of new communications technologies in participatory democracy

Politics, like many other areas of life, is being influenced by Internet technologies. Parliaments and governments now regularly publish information online, provide services and engage in consultation with citizens. Political parties are using the Internet to voice their agendas and communicate with their members. Given that communication is an essential element in the political processes, such change will have consequences for political discourse and for democracy as a whole. At the more radical and optimistic end of the spectrum, the Internet is seen as an instrument that can transform the democratic system from a representative democracy to a more participatory model. In practice, we already see burgeoning movements for more direct democracy emerging across the world (the United States, Canada, Great Britain, Australia, and some other European countries). The campaign for Direct Democracy in Great Britain considers that 'it is now both desirable and possible for citizens to take part in the decision making process themselves, rather than always relying upon the selected few to do it for them' (Harvey, 1998). While these movements do not underestimate the role of the citizen in realising this new model of government, they also invariably see the new technology as a vital tool to help them towards this goal.

Parties and the new technologies

To provide a more specific understanding of the impact of the Internet on representative democracy and particularly political parties it is perhaps most useful to start from a more technologically determinist position and focus on the inherent characteristics. Following the work of Zittel (2000), we draw attention to three basic properties of the Internet that distinguish it from other forms of communication: *bandwidth, interactivity* and the *decentralisation* of the communication structure. By focusing on these three essential features we are provided with a useful basis for beginning to map or pinpoint the effects of the net on political structures such as parties. Essentially, we can argue that there are three main areas of change in political communication: first, through the much greater *bandwidth* provided by the Internet, parties have the opportunity to offer greater access to documents such as internal agendas, parliamentary initiatives and daily press releases and news.

Another specific characteristic of the Internet is *interactivity*. Information may be exchanged between political institutions and constituents with little effort and almost instantaneously. This amount of interactivity has never been possible before, being limited to letter exchanges or, at the most, public radio or television interventions. Innovations in this area include websites with automated email replies or email newsletter sub-scription and opinion surveys. Even further along the interactivity scale are websites hosting bulletin boards that facilitate online exchanges or comments. Such features facilitate a more participatory dimension to communication with the electorate, and show the party as willing to engage in an open dialogue.

The third characteristic of net-based communication is its *decentralised communication structure*. Through hypertext links and email, users can move around parties and gain access to all levels of the organisation, such as local party affiliates and representatives of the party in the parliament-ary or executive structures. Decentralisation of communication should lead in time to a level of communication with the citizens that would enable them to directly participate in the decision-making process (Zittel, 2000: 9). Such a development is even more important for a country where the former dictatorship emphasised the unique leadership and centralised control of information.

Use of new ICTs in Romania by political parties

Political context in Romania

Until the overthrow of the Communist Party in 1989, Romania had been a one-party state for over fifty years. Despite the existence of democratic structures, the system was essentially a dictatorship run through a cult of personality surrounding Nicolae Ceauçescu. Following the collapse of the Communist system, Romania like other countries in Eastern and Central Europe began to look to the West and its democratic values as a model for governance.

The first and biggest new political force to be established after the Romanian revolution was the Democratic Front of National Salvation (FSN), which was essentially the reconstituted Communist Party. Its struc-ture and leadership were unclear, but, following the communist pattern, many branches were formed. At the same time, many other parties were officially registered. These can be divided into two categories: the first group contains the historical political parties that existed before the communist regime was established and were banned during its rule. This includes the National Christian Democratic Farmer's Party (PNTCD), the Social Democratic Party (PSD) and the National Liberal Party (PNL). These parties represent the traditional European political values of Christian democracy, social democracy and liberalism. The second group of parties comprises those newly formed in the aftermath of the overthrow of Ceauçescu. These parties covered a broader range of ethnic and cultural issues alongside more radical economic programmes for market reform.

The first democratic election held in Romania after the fall of Communism in 1990 saw the FSN led by Ion Iliescu win with a huge majority. As early as 1991, however, conflict erupted within the FSN that led eventually to its division into the Democratic Party (PD), under the leadership of Petre Roman, prime minister at that time, and the Romanian Social Democracy Party (PDSR), led by Romanian president Ion Iliescu. In 1991–1992 a flood of new parties entered the political arena so that by the end of the year, more than 250 parties had been registered (Bulai, 1999: 98). As small parties were proliferating, some of the larger parties were collaborating to shore up their strength. The Romanian Democratic Convention (CDR) was formed as an alliance of the three main historical parties along with the Hungarian party (UDMR) and other minor political formations. The strongest of the three was the National Christian Democratic Farmers Party (PNTDC). The Great Romania Party (PRM), the Party for the National Unity of Romanians (PUNR) and the Social Work Party (PSM), all parties with a social, right-wing, nationalist doctrine, joined with Ion Iliescu and the FSN in the 1992 elections, sharing the government for the next four years.

This process of merger and disintegration continued to make the Romanian party system highly fluid during the first few years of the 1990s. By the 1996 elections the field was reduced to forty-three parties, a significant reduction from the total of 250 in 1992. These elections saw the first major change in leadership with Emil Constantinescu, leader of the Romanian Democratic Convention, becoming president and Victor Ciorbea, of the National Christian Democratic Farmers Party (PNTDC), taking up the position of prime minister. While the number of parties may have been reduced at this point, instability in the system remained. During the next four years, although some opposition parties, such as the Social Democracy Party, managed to consolidate their strength, others fared less well. The PNTDC underwent serious internal convulsions, with two of its leading figures leaving to form new parties. Victor Ciorbea established the Christian Democratic Alliance (ANCD) and Radu Vasile, the Romanian Popular Democratic Party (PPDR). The Party for National Unity (PUNR), also a major player in the system, experienced a sharp decline in its popularity. Other strong new political forces continued to break through, however, such as the Union of Rightwing Forces (UFD) (Pocurar, 2000).

Profile of the ten most important Romanian political parties[1]

The last decade of the twentieth century represented a period of painful transition for Romania from a Communist regime with a centralised economy to a multi-party system with a free-market economy. Whilst the process was similar to that undergone by other former communist states, for Romania the process was perhaps even more difficult because of the dominating rule of party leader, Ceauçescu. Adaptation to the Western European democratic model has proved more difficult than expected and adoption by the population of the new civil and economic norms has been slow. It is from this highly controlled context for political communication, therefore, that we must understand the role of the Internet in Romania. On the one hand, one would expect these more interactive forms of communication to be welcomed as a way of opening up the authoritarian regime of the past. On the other, levels of socio-economic development and lack of democratic values present strong challenges to the effective use of the new media.

From the perspective of the political parties and following our theoretical approach outlined above we are interested to see whether they are using the Internet to facilitate a more genuine dialogue with citizens or whether they are content to focus on providing access to information. Does the *decentralisation of communication* increase the participatory role of citizens in terms of their participation in the decision-making process? (Zittel, 2000). How far are parties using the web to bring voters into direct communication with their representatives and local party structures? In order to address these questions, this chapter engages in a content analysis of the websites of ten key parties in the Romanian system during the election of 2000.

Christian Democratic National Farmers' Party (http://www.pntcd.ro) (Partidul National Taranesc Crestin Democrat, PNTCD)

The PNTCD has a long history, dating back to 1869 in Transylvania (which then was part of the Austro-Hungarian empire). The party continued to function clandestinely and illegally during the communist period and the new PNTCD was able to re-establish itself within one week of the bloody revolution of 1989. The party advocates moderate liberal ideas regarding the market economy and social questions. The PNTCD favours the re-establishment of the Romanian monarchy. The majority of the party's rank-and-file consists of elderly people.

Democratic Party (http://www.pd.ro) (Partidul Democrat, PD)

This party was formed from a group that broke away from the National Salvation Front (FSN) in March 1992. The group was led by Petre Roman who had been serving as prime minister for the FSN since May 1990 and who had often clashed with the Front's leader, President Iliescu. In May 1993 the Roman-FSN merged with the Democratic Party, after which the party took its current name. The DP-FSN advocates radical economic reform. Much of the party's rank-and-file consists of technocrats from the communist regime. The PD has since absorbed four small social-democratically oriented parties.

National Liberal Party (http://www.pnl.ro) (Partidul National Liberal, PNL)

The PNL was founded in January 1990 as the successor to the pre-communist-era liberal party. In 1992 it failed to pass the electoral thresh-old on its own, but in 1996 it re-entered the parliament and played an important role in the government between 1996 and 2000. The PNL advo-cates radical economic reform.

Democratic Union of Hungarians in Romania (http://www.rmdsz.ro) (Uniunea Democrata a Maghiarilor din Romania/Romaniai Magyar Demokrata Szovetseg, UDMR)

This party mainly exists to protect the interests of Hungarian-Romanians and the survival of Hungarian culture in Romania. The key issue of the party centres on autonomy for Hungarians living in Romania, which is considered an unconstitutional position by most of the other parties. On the issue of restructuring the Romanian economy, the party advocates more rapid reform.

Social Democratic Party of Romania (http://www.psdr.ro) (Partidul Social Democrat Român, PSDR)

The party was originally founded in 1893, banned in 1948 and then re-established in 1989. The first party-congress since 1948 was held on 8–9 March 1991. During the last parliamentary elections the PSDR and the PD presented themselves at a joint list in order to strengthen their electoral position.

Romanian Party for Social Democracy (http://www.pdsr.ro) (Partidul Democraiei Sociale din România, PDSR)

This party was originally founded as the Democratic National Salvation Front (FSN), which was itself the successor to the Communist Party. It was renamed in July 1993 after the faction led by Roman formed the PD. Iliescu continued as leader. Four remain close to the PDSR: the Demo-cratic Agrarian Party, the Socialist Labour Party, the Greater Romania Party and the Party of Romanian National Unity. The PDSR has estab-lished itself as one of the leading parties in Romanian politics, largely because it is the successor to the Communist Party. It headed the govern-ment for seven years during the 1990s. The PDSR defines itself as social-democratic, but the party retains many features typical of both a pre-1989 communist party and a popular front movement.

Greater Romania Party (http://www.romare.ro) (Partidul Romania Mare, PRM)

This is a nationalistic party. The PRM's main goal is to secure the (re)unification with Moldova. Beyond these nationalist claims, the party follows a policy line similar to that of the PSDR in economic matters.

Union of Rightist Forces (http://www.ufd.ro) (Uniunea Foretelor de Dreapta, UFD)

The UFD, formerly known as the Romanian Alternative Party (PAR), advocates radical economic reform and policies promoting the national identity of the Romanians.

The National Christian Democratic Alliance (http://www.ancd.ro) (Alianta Nationala Crestin Democrata, ANCD)

This party was formed by Victor Ciorbea and a group of dissidents from the Christian Democratic National Farmers' Party (PNTDC). While in the PNTDC, Ciorbea had served as prime minister; however, he was replaced after a series of conflicts within the Romanian Democratic Convention, the alliance the party had helped to form for the 1992 elections. After losing the support of his party, he formed the Alliance. Following the elections held in 2000 the party was absorbed back into the Christian Democratic National Farmers' Party.

Romanian Humanist Party (www.pur.ro) (Partidul Umanist Român, PUR)

The Humanist Party was formed in 1991 as a centrist political party aiming to coagulate political forces that were unhappy with the pace and timidity of the reforms under the Democratic National Salvation. Despite several attempts to form coalition with some small political forces (ecological movements, agrarians and others) to create a centrist alliance, these did not prove successful.

Romanian political parties' websites analysis

The websites of the parties were evaluated in spring 2000, three months prior to the local elections and eight months prior to the parliamentary and presidential elections. The first five parties analysed were members of the Romanian Democratic Convention (CDR), the political governing force at the time. From the opposition, we analysed the Party of Social Democracy in Romania (PDSR) and Great Romania Party (PRM). Three other non-parliamentary parties that were emerging at that time were also studied: the Union of Right Wing Forces (UFD), the Romanian Humanist Party (PUR) and the National Christian Democratic Alliance (ANCD).

Table 8.1 provides a schematic overview of the content of the websites of these parties and how far they emphasised access as opposed to interactivity and decision making. At the time of the research, some of the links in the pages were inactive or led to pages under construction. We included the inactive pages, considering that they show at the very least an intention of providing the specific information, but fail to do so because of technical reasons or lack of human resources.

From Table 8.1 we can observe that most of the parties realised the potential for communicating a large amount of information through their web pages. Seven parties (out of ten) included a complete statute of the party and nine of them intended to describe their leadership structures. However, three of them had inactive links to these pages. Six of the seven parliamentary parties gave a list of their representatives in the parliament and government, while only three parties (UDMR, PSDR, PDSR) presented their current agenda, among them the leading opposition party, PDSR. Updated news and press releases regarding the public life of the party were offered by seven out of ten, although the link to the agenda of the National Liberal Party did not work. Six parties offered general information such as the history of the party. Some offered details of international parties with a similar doctrine (PNTCD, PSDR, UDMR) and others promoted their youth organisation (PSDR, PDSR, PRM, PNTCD). The Hungarian Democratic Union's website was one of the most extensive in terms of political links, acting almost as a portal site to many Hungarian and international institutions, non-governmental organisations and news sources. Three parties, UDMR, PSDR and PDSR, provided information both in Romanian and English, and the Hungarian Democratic Union had also a Hungarian version of its website.

In terms of providing access to information, therefore, there was clearly a commitment on the part of the parties to such a goal. However, with the exception of the Hungarian Democratic Union, all the parties had some problems with inactive links in their pages.

In order to test the disposition of political parties to engage in open dialogue with the electorate, we searched for the presence of a contact email address, e-newsletters or discussion boards or forums. For responsiveness, we emailed all the addresses provided requesting information about the party and subscribed to the discussion board and to the e-newsletter. Since 2000 was an electoral year, some of the parties offered online-voting questionnaires. We included those under *voting info*,

Table 8.1 Website analysis of the ten most important Romanian political parties (spring 2000)

Information about	Governing parties Romanian Democratic Convention				Opposition			Non-parliamentary parties		
	PNTCD	PD	PNL	UDMR	PSDR	PDSR	PRM	UFD	ANCD	PUR
Access										
Statute	●	○	●	●		●	●	●		●
Structure	○	○	○	●		●	●	●		●
Representatives	●	●	●	●	●	○	●		●	●
Agenda	●		○	●	●	●			●	●
Other information	●	●		●	●	●	●		●	
News/events				●	●	●	●	○	●	
Multilanguage				●	●	●	●		●	
Interactivity										
Discussion board	○							○		
E-Newsletter		●							●	
Email address	●	●	●	●	●	●	●	○	●	●
Response		●								●
Voting info				●					●	
Decision										
Local affiliates	●			●		●		○	●	
Access to Representatives	●	○				○				
Youth organisations					●	●	●			

Note
● Black dots mean feature present and working.
○ White dots mean feature present but not working.

observing at the same time that there were no other issues or initiatives discussed.

All the parties offered a contact email address; however, almost all did not seem to have the human resources to respond to the messages. The Humanist Romanian Party was the only one to respond, while all the other attempts to engage in dialogue with the parties, be it through email, e-newsletter subscription or discussion board, failed. Three parties acknowledged the importance of discussion groups but only the National Christian Alliance had an active open discussion board with approximately fifty postings from North America and other European countries as well as Romania. Only the Democrat Party issued an e-newsletter, but two months after subscribing, no newsletter had been received. The Democratic Party, the Hungarian Democratic Union and the Christian Democratic Alliance all offered some kind of online poll for users to fill in but did not provide any results. Such findings reveal that the parties surveyed placed a much higher premium on providing access to information via their websites than on facilitating dialogue with the electorate.

The *decentralisation of communication* offered by the web is another dimension that could increase the participatory role of the citizen in a democracy. To investigate this we observed the direct access of the electorate to local affiliates, youth organisations and representatives of the party. Opportunities for direct communication with these key sections of parties provides a way to increase the role of the electorate in the decision-making process (Zittel, 2000: 9).

The study revealed that four parties provided a list with the local affiliates of the party, but only two of the parties had links to local web pages of their affiliates. The National Christian Democratic Alliance (ANCD) had a link to one branch and the Social Democracy Party (PDSR) had links to five web pages of their affiliates. The other two parties (PNTCD and UDMR) provided only a list of the affiliates while the Union of Right Wing Forces had an inactive link. While six parties, including the PDSR and the PD, provided a complete list of their representatives, only two of them had personal web pages, with a curriculum vitae and a picture, making it possible for the public to recognise them. However, none of these pages had a direct email address of the party representative, making direct contact impossible.

Overall, therefore, while parties vary in terms of how far they have developed their image on the Internet, none seems to be exploiting the potential of the Internet to pull citizens into more discursive and decisive forms of communication.

Internet users in Romania

Before drawing any final conclusions about the democratic impact of the Internet on political parties it is important to look at the response or user side of the equation. To what extent are these sites actually used by the Romanian public and do they have any impact on the political scene?

If we use electoral outcomes as our guide then the evidence appears highly positive. The sites were analysed prior to the November 2000 elections, which the PDSR went on to win with a small majority. After forming a single-party government, the PDSR went on to strike up an informal parliamentary alliance with the UDMR. From our analysis presented above it is clear that these two parties offered by far the most complete and well-maintained sites. Deriving a causal relationship between web proficiency and electoral success from such evidence is, of course, stretching the implications of these findings too far.

To probe the issue of impact and effect more seriously we need to examine how many people are using the web, who they are and whether they are interested in politics online. To answer some of these questions, data from the November 2001 Romanian Barometer Survey is assessed.[2] These data allow us to focus on two basic aspects of Internet use: first, how widespread is it? And second, how active and oriented towards politics are Internet users?

How widespread is Internet use?

The question used to identify people using the Internet was: 'Do you have access to the Internet in your household, or at your job?' According to the data, while just over 10 per cent of the Romanian population have a computer at home, just under 5 per cent report using the Internet at home or at their office (Romanian Public Opinion Barometer, November 2001, sample size 2,029). It should be noted that these figures do not include those people who access the Internet from public spaces such as Internet cafés, which can be found in many Romanian towns. These findings show a slight increase over time from the May 2001 Romanian Barometer Survey, which revealed that just 4 per cent of respondents had Internet access (from home or the office of the company they were working for).

Political orientations and attitudes of Internet users

Here we look at how politically informed and interested Internet users are in Romania. Looking first at the question of news consumption in newspapers and television, we can see it is higher for users than non-users. The proportion of those who read newspapers every day is more than double than among those that do not use the Internet, around 38 per cent compared to 17.5 per cent. Only around 3 per cent of Internet users do not read newspapers at all, compared to 28.3 per cent of non-Internet users. Just over 90 per cent of Internet users watch television every day, compared to 74.6 per cent of the non-users.

Table 8.2 'Discuss politics frequently'

	Internet users	Non-Internet users	All sample
with family	49.5% (48)	35.4% (684)	36.1% (732)
with friends	37.1% (36)	26.8% (518)	27.3% (554)
with colleagues	30.9% (30)	14.1% (272)	14.9% (302)
with employer	12.4% (12)	5.2% (100)	5.5% (112)
with parliamentarians	7.2% (7)	2.2% (43)	2.5% (50)
Totals	100.0% (97)	100.0% (1,932)	100.0% (2,029)

Source: Romanian Barometer Survey, November 2001.

Beyond gathering information, Internet users are also more likely to engage in discussions about politics, as Table 8.2 shows. Overall, just over 60 per cent of Internet users discuss politics more than a few times a month, compared to 44 per cent of non-users. From these figures it is clear that those who use the Internet are, at least from a discursive sense, more politically active than those who do not. Significantly, Internet users are obviously more active in contacting their representatives, with over 7 per cent reporting that they discuss politics with parliamentarians.

Not surprisingly, the data also reveal that Internet users prove to be more informed about politics. Just under 70 per cent of Internet users can name their elected representatives compared with only a third of non-users.

Finally, the data in Table 8.3 show that Internet users are generally more in favour of weakening state controls over society. A greater proportion of Internet users see that parties should be protected against the state interference. Further analysis of the data reveals that such liberal attitudes are carried over into the economic realm with as many as 80 per cent of Internet users seeing the market economy as a good thing compared with just half of non-Internet users.

Table 8.3 'Should the Romanian state intervene in a very large extent, a large extent, only a little, not at all, in the activity of mass media?'

	Internet users	Others	All sample
Not at all	33.0% (32)	20.9% (404)	21.5% (436)
Very little	12.4% (12)	8.9% (172)	9.1% (184)
Little	20.6% (20)	15.0% (289)	15.2% (309)
Large extent	18.6% (18)	23.9% (462)	23.7% (480)
Very large extent	8.2% (8)	11.1% (215)	11.0% (223)
Don't know	7.2% (7)	16.6% (320)	16.1% (327)
No answer	0.0% (0)	3.6% (70)	3.4% (70)
Totals	100.0% (97)	100.0% (1,932)	100.0% (2,029)

Source: Romanian Barometer Survey, November 2001.

Note
$p < 0.000$.

Overall, therefore, Internet users in Romania comprise only a small minority of the population. Thus, any arguments about web pages having a significant electoral impact at this point are clearly unrealistic. However, following the patterns found in other countries, Internet users tend to be greater consumers of political information and more involved in politics (Norris, 2000, 2001). Also, Romanian Internet users tend to favour a more liberal political and economic stance. The implications are, therefore, that Internet use in the short term will largely provide an extra source of information and access to the most politically active and reformist-minded segment of the population.

Conclusions

Ten years after the Romanian revolution and the development of a multi-party system, Romanian parties certainly display an awareness of the communication possibilities provided by the Internet. All the parties active in the political arena have websites that can be easily accessed through mainstream search engines despite the low levels of access to the technology amongst the general population. The strategies adopted, however, are highly centralised and top-down, with most of the sites concentrating on providing access to information such as policy agendas, press releases and news. Little or no attention is given to a real dialogue with the electorate, with parties failing to respond to even the most simple of email contacts and exhibiting minimal interest in gathering citizens' opinions on specific issues. Opportunities for direct contact of local affiliates or representatives are basically nil, offering voters and party members no decision-making role.

While this lack of participatory uses of the web in Romania may be due to its level of technological advancement, other nations with more widespread Internet use present similar results. Zittel (2000), for instance, in his study of the German and American legislatures' websites, concluded that they paid far more attention to facilitating access than helping citizens get involved in decision-making mechanisms. Such findings indicate that political will is probably the most important force in putting these new technologies to work for the people. Electronic democracy, although it is a vague and all-purpose term, does suggest the possibility for new citizenship practices. While issues of access and inequality must be resolved for such practices to be realised in a meaningful and widespread manner, such problems are not insurmountable. The challenge, therefore, is for politicians and administrators to work more creatively with the possibilities presented by the new communications media, and harness them to the wider public good.

Notes

1   The survey has a small under representation of higher-education students.
2   The information on the Romanian political parties was taken from:
     http://www.europeanforum.bot-consult.se/cup/romania.

References

Abramson, J.B., Arterton, F.C. and Orren, G.R. (1988) *The Electronic Commonwealth: The Impact of New Media Technologies on Democratic Politics*, New York: Basic Books.

Bagdikian, B. (1990) *The Media Monopoly*, Boston: Beacon Press.

Branscomb, A.W. (1994) *Who Owns Information? From Privacy to Public Access*, New York: Basic Books.

Bulai, A. (1999) *Mecanismele electorale ale societii româniti*, Bucharest: Paideia.

Garnham, N. (1990) *Capitalism and Communication: Global Culture and the Economics of Information*, London and Newbury Park, CA: Sage.

Garnham, N. (1990a) 'The Media and the Public Sphere', in Garnham, N. *Capitalism and Communication: Global Culture and the Economics of Information*, London and Newbury Park, CA: Sage, 104–114.

Garnham, N. (1990b) 'Contribution to a Political Economy of Mass Communication', in Gillespie, A. and Robins, K. (eds), 'Geographical Inequalities: The Spatial Bias of the New Communications Technologies', *Journal of Communication*, 39(3): 7–18.

Harvey, J. (1998) *The Case of Direct Democracy in UK, in Direct Democracy Campaign*, Online. Available July 2001.

Lenert, E.M. (1993) 'The Virtual Public Forum: Society, Technology, and Democratic Possibilities', Kansas City, Missouri, Association for Education in Journalism and Mass Communication.

Levine, J.H. (1972) 'The Sphere of Influence', *American Sociological Review*, 37: 14–27.

Murdock, C. and Golding, P. (1989) 'Information Poverty and Political Inequality: Citizenship in the Age of Privatized Communications', *Journal of Communication*, 39(3): 180–195.

Naisbitt, J. (1989) *Megatendinte*, Bucharest: Politica.

Norris, P. (2000) *A Virtuous Circle*, Cambridge: Cambridge University Press.

Norris, P. (2001) *The Digital Divide*, Cambridge: Cambridge University Press.

Pocurar, A.M. (2000) 'Internetul – Instrument de comunicare intre partidele politice romanesti si cetateni', unpublished thesis, Babes-Bolyai University.

Sparks, C. (1993) 'Raymond Williams and the Theory of Democratic Communication', in Splichal, S. and Wasko, J. (eds), *Communication and Democracy*, Norwood, NJ: Ablex, 69–86.

Toffler, A. (1980) *The Third Wave*, New York: Bantam.

Wasko, J. and Mosco, V. (eds) (1992) *Democratic Communications in the Information Age*, Madison: University of Wisconsin Press.

Zittel, T. (2000) *Electronic Democracy – a Blueprint for 21st Century Democracy*, Online. Available from tzittel@rumms.uni-mannheim.de (July 2001).

9 Democratisation, parties and the net

Mexico – model or aberration?

Darren Wallis

Introduction

Recent contributions to debates on electronic democracy have challenged two perceived biases in the literature. According to Hoff *et al.* (2000a: 1–2) debate has focused 'too greatly on the technology itself' and has been 'highly Americano-centric'.[1] Their own work, along with that of a number of other authors, has sought to address this dual distortion, bringing human agency back into the equation and drawing on case studies beyond the United States, especially from Western Europe. Nevertheless, it is reasonable to argue that the literature continues to exhibit a narrow empirical focus, inasmuch as it is concerned principally with developments in the established democracies. There are two compelling reasons why this should be the case. First, the established democracies are generally the most technologically advanced countries, and they evince the greatest degree of penetration of information and communications technologies (ICTs). Second, they exhibit the classic symptoms of malaise of representative democracy that ICTs are purported to help cure or transform.[2] The technology needs to be there before it can have an impact; political systems have to be democratic before they can suffer a 'crisis of democracy'. Put the other way around, the reason why countries like Mexico have not been analysed to date is that they are insufficiently electronic and insufficiently democratic.[3]

Despite this, there are some good grounds for widening our empirical focus beyond the established democracies. For one thing, the penetration of new technologies may often be greater than is supposed. Brazil, for example, has rates of penetration that are not too dissimilar to those in some European countries. Even where penetration is currently low, we can expect rapid catch-up growth in the near future as technology advances and prices fall. Mexico in particular is well placed to take advantage of such developments because of its access to the United States through the North American Free Trade Agreement (NAFTA). Indeed, growth in the past three years in Mexico has been impressive and is set to accelerate.

More importantly, if the over-riding concern in the literature is to understand the extent to which ICTs present opportunities and constraints for democracy, it is not clear why democracy should be considered solely in one context, namely late modern politics in advanced capitalist countries. In much the same way as it could be argued that the early literature induced too readily from the United States case, so it can be argued that the later literature draws conclusions from a fairly similar set of political systems, albeit ones exhibiting differences of emphasis and 'culture'. Interesting questions might be posed, however, when we translate the study of ICTs to radically different contexts. The possibilities offered by the new technology to democratic actors in authoritarian regimes could constitute one such line of enquiry, and valuable lessons might also be learned from analyses of state responses to such developments.

For present purposes, the context shifts from the atrophy of the institutions of the established democracies to the opportunities and constraints posed by the democratisation of previously authoritarian regimes – what analysts have termed the 'dominant political trend of the last quarter of the twentieth century' (Huntington, 1991). Although many of the transitions in this 'third wave of democracy' occurred before ICTs had established much of a foothold, that in Mexico came later. The Mexican transition to democracy was only completed in 2000 following two decades of struggle,[4] and it is instructive to explore the dynamics of the impact of ICTs in such a context. To what extent do ICTs help to shift the balance of power between political actors and thereby give impetus to a move towards democracy? Conversely, we may ask to what extent is the development and use of ICTs by political actors itself contingent upon changes in the institutional rules of the game brought about through democratisation?

Beyond the transition to free and fair elections, the dominant concern in the democratisation literature has been democratic consolidation – or, more accurately, an absence of democratic consolidation. As Rose and Chull Shin (2001: 331) put it: 'conventional influences, such as the introduction of free elections, have not (or at least, not yet) created political regimes that match the standards of the established democracies'. In seeking to understand this problem of democratic consolidation, analysts have increasingly focused on the imperative of 'building democratic institutions', especially an institutionalised party system (Mainwaring and Scully, 1995). Weakly institutionalised party systems have been associated with the breakdown of governability and democracy.[5] Thus, while the centrality of parties in the established democracies has been called into question, powerful statements have recently been made on the indispensability of parties in 'third-wave' contexts (Mainwaring, 2000).

Although Mexico has now transited from its hegemonic party system, it is still not entirely clear what type of democratic party system is emerging in its place. Political competition in the decade leading up to the 2000 election was structured so strongly by the question of the regime's future that it is difficult to know exactly how 'normal' competition will shape up now that that issue has been resolved. In such circumstances, the Internet may be an important factor shaping the emerging patterns of competition. Will the Internet help to reinforce what appears to be a nascent three-party system, or will it provide opportunities for smaller, more marginalised parties to get their message across and provide wider choices to the population? What impact will the Internet have on the ways in which parties appeal to voters and conduct their campaigns? As we shall see, these are questions that are likely to be more important in future elections than they were in 2000, but we can discern some clues from present activity that provide pointers to future practice. Before exploring these clues, I provide a brief summary on the 'state of play' of the development of the Internet in Mexico.

Dot.mx

There is very little authoritative research on the Internet in Latin America, but it is clear that user levels are low, yet rising rapidly. Although Mexico is substantially more developed than many 'third-world' countries, with a GDP per capita of US$8,383 in 1999,[6] poverty and inequality, combined with infrastructure problems in the telecommunications industry, have conspired to keep levels of Internet use disappointingly low. With an estimated 1.5 million users (2.2 per cent of the population aged 14 and over) in 2000, the impact of the Internet on voting patterns in the election of that year was negligible.[7] Until 1999 at least, Mexico performed comparatively poorly in the region in terms of the number of users per domain, and its development of cybercafés and public booths has lagged that of other countries.[8]

On the other hand, sufficient fixed-line connections exist to suggest that greater penetration should follow fairly rapidly, and indeed there is evidence that this is occurring already. With outstanding infrastructural issues currently being addressed, usage is set to rise to 6.4 million people (8.6 per cent of the population) in 2004, while a number of sources suggest that both present calculations and future projections are substantially underestimated: for example, some put the 2000 figure at 2.5 million users.[9] Indications of recent expansionism include a growth of some 1,500 per cent in terms of the number of hosts, and over 1,100 per cent in domains, between July 1997 and January 2001. These rates are not only above those of the more developed countries (as we would expect with catch-up growth) but outstrip those of similar developing countries. Mexico's Internet usage (as measured by the number of hosts and domains) lagged behind that of Russia in 1997, for example, but is now substantially higher.[10] The new administration's e-Mexico initiative, supported by major industry players such as Microsoft, aims to bolster Internet use by widening access in schools and colleges, as well as in each of Mexico's 2000-plus municipalities.

In addition, Mexican demographics imply rapid growth. Thus, fully 70 per cent of the Mexican population are aged under 34 and one-third are under 14. As elsewhere, the younger age groups comprise the most enthusiastic users of the Internet: 67 per cent of current Internet users are aged under 34 and 37 per cent are aged under 24.[11] The political consequences of this demographic structure are obvious. There were 6 million potential first-time voters in the presidential election of 2000 and there will be a similar number in the 2003 mid-terms. Party engagement with the Internet evinces the need to try to form partisan attachments among a key section of the population.

Thus, while Internet penetration is lower than in most, if not all, of the other cases presented in this collection, it is likely to catch up with some of them in the medium term. Because usage has been so low to date, however, conclusions on its impact must remain tentative. Moreover, we must bear in mind that Internet development has occurred in the context of a momentous shift of political regime. Party and voter behaviour in the most recent election was fundamentally shaped by the question of the regime's future. Party policy positions were hard to discern because of the overwhelming impact of the pro-regime, anti-regime cleavage. We might anticipate more 'routine' political uses of the Internet, such as voters scrutinising party websites for policy positions, to be more important in future elections than would have been the case in 2000.[12] Certainly, the effort expended by parties in constructing their websites in 2000 suggests that they anticipate the medium to become increasingly important. Yet it remains an open question whether the threads that we may discern in the picture to date will be picked up in quite the same way in the future. Given these obvious caveats, we now turn to examine some of those threads, beginning with the question of regime democratisation.

Democratising Mexico

For most of the twentieth century, Mexico was governed by a hegemonic-party, semi-authoritarian regime, which was neither as repressive nor as closed as its military and communist counterparts.[13] There was at least some popular participation and government responsiveness to social demands, even if the procedural components of democracy were largely absent. The long-term causes of the regime's decline came, first, from socio-economic modernisation, which created political interests outside of the regime's corporatist structures, then, second, from economic crisis, which weakened the links between the ruling Institutional Revolutionary

Party (PRI) and its core constituents in unions and peasant leagues. The biggest shock to the 'perfect dictatorship' came in the 1988 election, when a breakaway left-wing movement from the PRI gathered sufficient momentum to pose a serious threat in the presidential election. On that occasion, however, information technology was on the regime's side: the federal electoral computer 'crashed' as negative results for the PRI started to mount. When it came back up, the PRI had won the election.[14]

The watershed election of 1988 set the stage for a series of political reforms that gradually led to freer and fairer elections. Electoral and party reforms of 1990, 1993, 1994 and 1996 allowed the opposition to compete more effectively. In 1997 the opposition managed to keep the PRI from control of the Chamber of Deputies for the first time in its history, and in 2000 an alliance of the right-wing National Action Party (PAN) and the Greens (PVEM) took the presidency under Vicente Fox. In between 1988 and 2000 rapidly expanding opposition representation at the state and local level reduced voters' fear of the unknown and boosted confidence in the competence of the opposition. Nevertheless, this was a gradual and at times bloody transition. PRI in-fighting led to some high-profile political assassinations and the left-wing Party of the Democratic Revolution (PRD) claims that several hundred members were killed or 'disappeared' in violent clashes in the early 1990s. The demise of the PRI was a protracted, 'slow motion' demise (Whitehead, 1995).

What role can be attributed to ICTs in bringing about democratisation in Mexico? In an obvious sense, the role was minimal. Mexico's techno-logical base following the economic crisis of the debt years lagged badly. Democratisation initially responded more to long-term shifts in the social structure than to short-term developments in technology. Parties appeared preoccupied with more pressing matters – the PAN with internal divisions and the PRD with its (and its members') survival. Moreover, all opposition parties faced resource constraints in investing seriously in information technology. The playing field was slanted heavily towards the ruling party and the use of technology by the mainstream parties was slow to start. A partial exception can be found in the computer centres established by PAN president Castillo Peraza between 1993 and 1996 to conduct opinion polls, gather and process electoral results and prevent electoral fraud (Mizrahi, 1998). For the PRI, the Internet represented a potential threat to the way in which it traditionally garnered its vote; its approach to the Internet was conditioned by the fierce battle for the soul of the party raging between 'the dinosaurs' and the modernisers.

The electoral process

One area where ICTs may have had an impact was in the newly established Federal Electoral Institute (IFE, created 1990). IFE was a semi-independent body, comprised of representatives from parties, the legislature and the executive, with a number of independent citizen members, staffed by a professional electoral bureaucracy, and chaired by the Interior minister. By 1996, this body – 'a model of its kind' according to the Carter Centre – was entirely controlled by its 'citizen-councillors', many of them prominent academics and psephologists.[15] Given the past evidence of abuse of the electoral system, especially in 1988, IFE's position as the guarantor of a free and transparent process was central. Few Mexicans were prepared to believe that the PRI would willingly cede victory.

IFE invested substantial financial and administrative resources in the development of its profile on the web. IFE's web page served as a focal point for party-political actors, civil-rights groups (such as the highly respected Civic Alliance), academics and journalists, as well as members of the public. It also served as a useful resource for the foreign media (many pages, as with those of parties and groups more generally, have an English-language version) and foreign observers, who were invited to observe Mexican elections for the first time in 1994. IFE provided a very comprehensive and contemporary range of information on the electoral process itself. This included full details on electoral legislation, a civic education and development programme,[16] details of training opportunities for the tens of thousands of polling booth officials (chosen by lot), as well as statistics on the electoral register and a programme to help voters obtain their voting credentials. IFE General Council decisions and reports are placed on the website instantly, in full document or stenographed form.

Although the management of the electoral process is usually taken for granted in established democracies, in transitional contexts it is itself an issue of political controversy, and IFE was the focus of much party-political conflict throughout the 1990s and during the 2000 election. Hence, its ability to provide full, accurate and contemporary information was critical for maintaining public confidence and assuring the transparency of the process. Although hits on the website would be low among the general public, it formed a valuable resource for academics and journalists who provided favourable cover through more conventional media in the run up to the election. The same point generally holds true for foreign observers.

IFE's site also contains full details of election results back to 1994, dis-aggregated to the municipal level, so it is possible for any member of the public to download and examine full election results. On election day itself, IFE used its website, operating through twenty-six domestic and international mirrors, to distribute the results of its Programme of Preliminary Electoral Results (PREP). The online dissemination of results as they came in, with projections of overall party and candidate support, ensured that domestic and international observers could follow the elections live and dramatically increased the costs to the ruling elite of replicating the type of fraud that had been used in the 1988 election. Moreover, it acted as a stimulus to the traditional media, especially the traditionally pro-regime Televisa, to have the courage of their convictions and report their own exit-poll findings showing the PRI to be losing.

To the extent that IFE had been a key demand of the opposition, its use of ICTs to help assure a transparent electoral process could be claimed to have had an impact on the development of the party system, even if it was just one of the multiple points of pressure on the regime that had made a repeat of 1988 extremely unlikely. In this sense, it could be argued that the Internet had been used to consolidate earlier democratic gains and secure further democratisation. It is certainly the case that IFE is one of the very few institutions in Mexico whose public-approval rating has been heading in the right direction in recent years and it makes full use of its website to disseminate, inform and educate.

Social movements

A second illustration of the use of ICTs in democratising Mexico comes from social movement activity. Even as parties were undertaking their protracted series of reform negotiations with the government in the 1990s, external pressure was being applied by newly self-confident sections of civil society standing outside the party's structures. Much of the new social movement activity in Mexico was centred around urban movements, women's groups, human rights' organisations and the debtors' movement, *El Barzón*. These groups quickly latched on to the opportunities offered by new technologies in the early 1990s to construct networks, alliances and common identities through which they could challenge the regime and advance their political position. Many of these groups were linked to sympathisers abroad, especially in the United States, and used Peacenet and Usenet bulletin boards, discussion groups and email to create networks of resistance to state power and in support of democratic reform (Cleaver, 1998). Quickly established archives of information and websites became readily available as permanent sources of reference for activists and the population more generally.

A particularly stark illustration of the potential of ICTs in this context, even allowing for its generally low level of penetration, can be had from the Zapatista rebellion that erupted in January 1994. This was a low-intensity insurgency among the indigenous population in the impoverished state of Chiapas. Lacking substantial military or financial capability, the Zapatistas have managed to hold domestic and international audiences in thrall for eight years.[17] They have organised conferences for democracy and against neo-liberalism and forced the pace of political reform in Mexico. The Zapatistas re-energised and recast much of the opposition to the PRI, shaking the foundations of the regime in 1994. Although not directly involved in the more general political-reform negotiations, the banner of the Zapatistas was taken up by many of those that were.

That the Zapatistas were able to achieve so much with such sparse resources is due in no small part to their use of the Internet as a communication tool to spread their message to domestic and inter-national sympathisers. The administrations of Salinas (1988–1994) and Zedillo (1994–2000) found themselves continuously frustrated by exogenous pressures applied within hours of the latest developments in the conflict, a consequence of the Zapatistas' ability to communicate with supporters through a rapidly burgeoning network of discussion groups, lists, newsgroups and web pages.[18] As Cleaver (1998) puts it, 'through their ability to extend their political reach via modern com-puter networks the Zapatistas have woven a new electronic fabric of struggle to carry their revolution throughout Mexico and around the world'. Earlier rebellions in Mexico had met with the familiar, repressive state response. Now, the government found itself obliged to maintain at least a façade of negotiation (although atrocities still occurred). Its attempts to control the flow of information and remove Chiapas from public consciousness have been largely ineffective. Government sites have not been able to successfully counteract the war of words emanating from the Zapatistas.

Not all observers view this instance of Internet power as positively as the Zapatistas' online support community, however. There are many (in Mexico at least) who would argue that the Zapatista case illustrates some of the potential dangers of the Internet. The Zapatistas are, of course, an armed rebel group and may provide an illustration of what Ferdinand (2000) sees as a developing trend of extremist or violent organisations using the Internet to spread their message.[19] Others would argue that the preponderance of the Zapatistas on the Internet has drowned the voice of the millions of other indigenous peoples in Mexico, especially on the issue of indigenous rights. Alternative indigenous images, including that of the umbrella National Indian Congress, often seem invisible compared to those of the Zapatistas. Finally, there are some suggestions that Zapatista accounts of government and paramilitary activities, distributed via the Internet, were at least partially fabricated, although these claims may themselves be open to contestation.

Nevertheless, the Zapatista rebellion has been eulogised as the first revolution of the twenty-first century. Certainly, it packed a political punch far above its potential weight and there is a solid case to be made that it would not have enjoyed the success that it did without the use of the Internet (although many key demands remain unmet). The rebellion provides an important example of the power of the Internet as a weapon in the hands of the economically and politically marginalised, albeit one that requires some links between grassroots organisations and those – often in NGOs and Universities – with greatest access to the technology. It also rather dramatically illustrates the point that the Internet may have an important bearing on mainstream politics even where penetration rates remain low.

Reforming the rules for party competition

For many political actors, the rules of the institutional game that they are playing will determine the extent to which they embrace new technologies and seek to use them for their own purposes. Where the rules of the game are not favourable for the advancement of technologies, they are unlikely to be widely assimilated. At least for those that wish to play within the rules of the game – if only to change the rules – institutions provide (dis)incentives to behave in a particular fashion. In Mexico in the early 1990s, there were few inducements for parties to pursue a serious policy of engagement with the Internet.

A *prima-facie* case can be made that the biggest boost to the use of the Internet politically came from the 1996 political reform, COFIPE.[20] Earlier reforms had done much to make the electoral system freer, but that of 1996 made substantial progress in levelling the playing field. It did this through massive increases in public financing and guaranteed access to the media, for all parties. To give an indication of the type of figures involved, parties were jointly allocated 3 billion pesos for 2000, that is, over US$300 million. This is not only a ten-fold increase on the 1994 allocation, but an amount substantially in advance of the norms prevailing in many richer countries.[21] 30 per cent of this money is shared equally among all parties and 70 per cent is distributed in proportion to congressional representation. Newly registered parties receive 2 per cent of the total, which allows them to get a foothold in the system if they can keep their registration (set at 2 per cent in any federal contest). Exactly the same formula applies to access to the media, the political coverage of which is also more generally monitored by IFE.

Although the amounts of money involved are impressive and courted substantial controversy, the impact on competition was palpable. In 1994, the PRI had outspent its rivals by a factor of twenty (de Swaan, Martorelli and Molinar Horcasitas, 1998: 165). In 2000, strict campaign limits and limits on private donations alongside the increases in public financing provided a more equitable spread of resources. The PRI's share of party financing fell to 30.3 per cent. All parties now had the resources to develop and communicate their messages far more effectively, including the opportunity to invest in ICTs. Bruhn (1999: 106) concludes for the

PRD that 'campaign strategies depended heavily on the financial base offered by institutional change'.

Thus, on both finance and media grounds, the opposition has been able to compete on something like a level playing field. No matter how sophisticated a campaign the opposition might have liked to have run in the past, the structural obstacles were too difficult to surmount. In 1997 and 2000, by contrast, opportunities for successful campaigning existed. As Moreno (1999: 143) concludes:

> In the process of increasing political competition that Mexico is undergoing, if campaign information is not necessarily about specific policy proposals and programmes, it is definitively about the presence and strength of the opposition parties. The lack of this information obviously limited the voters' political options before 1997.

In short, the institutional environment was not propitious for the development of the Internet as a party and electoral tool prior to 1996, but became so after 1996. We now turn to examine some of the manifestations of party Internet activity, paying particular attention to the party system and the 2000 election.

Parties and campaigns

Mexican election and party websites evince a degree of comprehensiveness and technical sophistication that is comparable with that of many established democracies. We have already raised some clues as to why this might be the case: public financing means that the parties have sufficient resources; the Internet is mainly used by the young, whose membership and votes will be open to capture in subsequent elections; rapid growth is anticipated; parties wish to be seen as in touch with the latest technological developments; parties have a keen eye on their overseas audiences; and technology and expertise can be harboured from the United States more easily by Mexico than by other Latin-American countries. Despite very low levels of penetration, parties gave serious thought to their web presence in the 2000 election and there has been ongoing development subsequently.

Party presence

Election laws dating back to 1946 require parties to have national registration in order to compete in federal contests and presidential candidates must come from these nationally registered parties or alliances.[22] There were six presidential candidates in 2000, two of whom represented alliances of two and five parties respectively, making eleven parties in total. Both alliances – the Alliance for Change (AC) on the right and the

Alliance for Mexico (AM) on the left – developed a separate web presence in addition to that for each party.

Because the universe of competing parties is fixed by the national registration requirements, all official and non-official political sites provide links to each of these parties. On official sites, such as IFE's, parties were simply listed in alphabetical order. On most sites, however, the big three parties – PRI, PAN and PRD – were listed first, usually in that order, a reflection of opinion-poll ratings rather than support in the previous election (where the PRD gained more seats than the PAN). Once the alliances were approved, links to alliance websites were included.

In an obvious sense, the Internet has facilitated a general increase in exposure for minor parties, whose voice has rarely been heard through the conventional media. All minor parties, including the new Social Democracy (DS) and Centre (PCD) parties had web presence, with basic information on the party's background and principles and its candidate's proposals available. As mentioned, these parties were not differentiated in any way on official sites. In the past, fringe parties have tended to be either pro-government satellite parties or parties of the left that have struggled to find a stable organisational identity. The Internet at least presents some opportunities for genuinely independent minor parties to develop a public presence.

It is not just the presence of minor parties, however, that has been at issue in Mexico. Until quite recently, information about, and the public presence of, the opposition generally was limited. Whereas the concern in established democratic contexts has been the informational balance between minor parties and the established parties, in a democratising context it is more the balance between a ruling party on the one hand and the opposition as a whole on the other. In order to try to make their voices heard, both the PRD and the PAN have invested substantial resources in creating and maintaining comprehensive websites that provide voters and analysts with information on alternatives to PRI rule. The Internet evinced greater exposure for all opposition parties than had previously been the case with exposure on radio and television.

However, the impact of the Internet in providing the public with greater information on the opposition pales against the impact of the new rules on media access, which are among the most tightly prescribed of any system.[23] Television and press coverage under the PRI had been heavily skewed in favour of the ruling party, even following initial political liberalisation. Repression, threats to withdraw advertising revenue, and self-censorship kept journalists in line.[24] Following COFIPE, coverage has been far more balanced both in terms of the amount of time allocated to each party and in the general lack of bias exhibited in political reporting.[25] With over 90 per cent of Mexicans reporting that they receive their main political information through television – the vast majority through Televisa's empire – changing the rules of the game in this area was critical. Thus, although we might anticipate the Internet becoming more significant for the party system in later years, its impact cannot be easily assessed in the context of wide-sweeping changes to the presence of the opposition on conventional media. In other words, opposition exposure would have increased with or without the Internet.

Comprehensiveness and sophistication

A divide between the three major parties and the minor parties is clearer in terms of the amount of information provided and the technical prowess of the sites than it is in terms of presence and access. The PRI, PAN and PRD have many more resources to dedicate to ICT development. Their sites were, and continue to be, marked by both comprehensiveness of information provided and sophistication of presentation. They provide detailed information on party background and development; basic party documents; a daily 'press room' for press releases; election proposals; links to party committees and organisations; and information on congressional candidates, as well as details on parallel local and gubernatorial contests.[26] Minor parties were able to provide some basic information, but they lacked the comprehensiveness of the major players, and their sites were not maintained so regularly. Nevertheless, even minor-party sites are more than adequate as sources of information in terms of design, clarity and level of information.

All party sites were relatively sophisticated, with those of the three main parties incorporating Flash technology and utilising audio-visual features. The basic provision of text-based materials was often available through the more user-friendly PDF format, and campaign videos and speeches were available for download with QuickTime (PRI) and RealPlayer (PAN) technology. All of Fox's campaign spots, for example, were available for download from the campaign website. Within the three-party block, both the PRI and the PAN appeared to have embraced the spirit of the technology more enthusiastically than the PRD; the latter was more inclined to concentrate on its text-based messages, whereas the former parties experimented more with audio-visuals. However, there is little discernible difference across the three parties on this criterion today.

It is unlikely that this dominance of the major parties had much of an impact on competition, however. Although there is no reliable data available, it would be surprising if more than a fraction of the low user base had sufficient computing power to benefit fully from the audio-visual add-ons, at least at anything more than a frustrating download speed. For this reason, sites maintained text-only versions, which at least allowed for the provision of basic information to would-be voters. However, it is clear that in incorporating the latest software into website design, parties were not primarily looking to average voters: they were looking to domestic academics and journalists; to foreign observers (English-language versions are again prominent); and to impress tomorrow's opinion formers and voters, that is, the young.

Parties, alliances and candidates

One interesting set of questions relating to parties and the Internet in all political systems concerns the extent to which they focus upon the leader at election time. In parliamentary systems, of course, the leader is not directly elected as a prime minister, but seeks to be returned as one of a number of single- or multi-member constituency representatives. In such circumstances, it may be interesting to discern differences among parties in the extent to which they place the leader centre stage in their websites, and how these change over time. In presidential systems, such as the Mexican, this question is more pronounced since there are separate elections for the president and the legislature. Where these elections occur simultaneously (as in Mexico), relations between the candidate and the party form an important part of the political dynamic. A further complicating factor in the 2000 election, already raised, was the fact that a number of parties came together to form electoral alliances. In seeking to examine the impact of the Internet in such circumstances, therefore, we are concerned with a complex web of relationships between the candidate, the party and the alliance partners. What can we discern of these relations in the 2000 election?

One point to be made is that separate websites were maintained for each of these constituent units. For example, the Alliance for Change maintained a website providing information on the campaign, common candidacies and election proposals. This site linked to those of the two constituent parties – the PAN and the PVEM. Special pages on the candidate, Vicente Fox, existed through these sites, although information provided through his own party (the PAN) was more detailed than that through the PVEM. All of the non-allied parties maintained separate pages on their candidate, biographical details, election proposals and so forth. Indeed, given that these parties were not anticipating returning more than a handful of congressional representatives, their sites were largely monopolised by the candidate and his programme.

In this sense, the web may be seen as a tool to promote particular candidates, rather than parties *per se*. In other words, the web may reinforce an identifiable tendency in the region to focus on personalities to the detriment of policies. Many analysts view such a focus as one source of the rise of 'neo-populists' in the region, with media-friendly candidates effectively by-passing mediating institutions such as parties and riding roughshod over legislatures and judiciaries. A case can be made that Fox's candidacy in Mexico exhibited populist characteristics. Much of his campaign was fronted by a civic organisation, *Amigos de Fox*, whose membership base far outstripped that of the PAN and which is credited with generating the momentum that put Fox into position as the best-placed opposition candidate to challenge the PRI, and thereby garner the anti-PRI vote.

The website maintained separately by Fox comprised an effective focus for a campaign that began some three years before the election. The site contained daily press releases; videos of Fox's television spots; a weekly campaign summary (available in Word format); full archives of press releases, policy statements and the candidate's campaign diary; as well as biographical details and campaign pledges. It was through this site that the clearest experiments with interactivity were made. For example, the candidate entered chat rooms with users, while interviews with radio stations were relayed live online, with opportunities to email the programme while on air. Fox has maintained this weekly programme – *'Fox en vivo, Fox contigo'* ('Fox live, Fox with you') – in the presidency, and transcripts of the programme are available for download as well as a full archive of recordings. Thus, as well as being a tool that parties may use to communicate (and receive) information, the Internet may also be used by individuals seeking to by-pass party structures.

In the case of Fox's campaign for the presidency, there is little doubt that the candidate took centre stage and the party a back seat. The use of the Internet as a campaign tool was more pronounced by the candidate than by the party. We should reiterate, however, our earlier point, that behaviour in 2000 was fundamentally shaped by the question of the regime's future. We might anticipate a closer link between the party and candidate now that that question has been resolved.

Campaigning in Mexico

A rapid 'Americanisation' of campaigning has been evident in Mexico since 1996, which I have elsewhere labelled a shift from a 'tortilla' model of campaigns to a 'coca-cola' model (Wallis, 2001).[27] Parties have focused more heavily on communicating messages through the media than on traditional set-piece rallies around the country. Critics charged that Fox's campaign, in particular, was little more than a marketing and PR exercise. However, it would be a mistake to suppose that traditional campaigning is finished. Fox paid careful attention to his TV and radio spots, but he also undertook an indefatigable tour of the country, filling plazas and pressing the flesh in remote communities. Moreover, finance reform boosted party organisations and has facilitated an increase in traditional techniques, such as door-to-door canvassing. These efforts are supported by increasingly sophisticated database systems and telephone canvassing, both based on developments in party ICT capability.

In terms of attempting to capture undecided voters, party and alliance websites provided constituency-level information on candidates, previous results and trends in support. However, there was no evidence of parties narrowcasting and there was only limited use of websites as a recruitment tool for new members. However, a marked difference with the case in many established democracies comes from the emphasis placed on youth. All major parties have a youth organisation, and they provide separate web presence for these organisations, as well as joining details. Chat rooms are available on some of these pages and there are specially designed pages for children on the PRI website, featuring graphics, cartoons and games. The greater demographic imperative in Mexico explains the focus on capturing the hearts and minds of the young at the earliest opportunity.

There is some evidence of opportunities for interactivity, rather than a one-way flow of information from the top down. We have already mentioned the use of chat rooms. Some parties provided opportunities for voters to send their opinions to the party or candidate through electronic forms. There were general opportunities for 'comments or suggestions' on all relevant sites, although in the main these are simply directed to webmasters.

Independent political discussion sites

Finally, one further feature of the 1997 and, especially, the 2000 campaigns has been the proliferation of independent political websites, lists and discussion groups, such as *presidenciables.com* and *Elector2000.com*, as well as pages within the sites of the mainstream press, such as *Reforma* and *Proceso*. All of these sites provided voters with a comprehensive array of information on parties and candidates, as well as offering analyses and comments from specialists and users alike. Because of the requirement that parties and alliances have national registration to compete in elections, there is a set number of parties, all of which are listed on these sites, although most placed the PRI, PAN and PRD first – usually in that order. Conferencing facilities for the exchange of views in reaction to the latest political developments were also available. In addition, a number of sites provided instant gauges of public opinion by asking users to state their voting intention electronically. It goes without saying that such instant electronic responses are poor indicators of overall public opinion, given the skewed nature of the user group and the lack of checks on multiple voting. Nevertheless, the opposition Alliance for Change outpointed the PRI by a substantive margin on these indicators, in contrast to opinion polls showing their candidate to be at best neck-and-neck. Many sites also track published opinion-poll trends, featuring polls-of-polls and user-friendly graphics.

Conclusions

The development of these sites is indicative of a general information explosion that has occurred in Mexico as the shackles of the dictatorship have gradually been released. Many of the sites are unsurprisingly biased, and many contain scathing criticisms of politicians, but they also evince engagement among the citizenry with the political process. In a democratising context, of course, technology should not be required to invigorate engagement with the political process, but it may have a critical role to play in consolidating that engagement and providing alternative sources of information and analysis. There is evidence that this is already happening in Mexico.

Engagement with the Internet among party-political actors in Mexico was contingent upon changes in the institutional rules of the game. Although a democratising force in some respects throughout the 1990s, its move into mainstream democratic politics required the reforms of 1996. As we have stressed repeatedly, political behaviour has been so clearly structured by the issue of the regime's future in recent years, that future projections on the role and use of the Internet by Mexican parties and candidates must remain tentative. However, as we have also stressed, the embracing of the technology by parties is very real and the demographic and technological outlooks such that we may confidently anticipate a more central role in subsequent elections.

Notes

1 'Electronic democracy' remains a useful shorthand for what Hoff, Horrocks and Tops and collaborators prefer to term Technologically Mediated Innovations in Political Practice (Hoff, Horrocks and Tops, 2000b). To a Latin Americanist, 'Americano-centric' implies a continent-wide centrism that does not square easily with the focus in the literature. 'US-centric' would be more politically correct.

2 Theories of the pathology of established democracies are summarised in Kaase and Newton (1994). Whether ICTs are viewed as a mechanism by which to reinvigorate 'politics as usual' or as a contribution to a radically new way of conducting politics depends upon whether political changes in the advanced democracies are viewed through the pessimistic lenses of the 'crisis of democracy' (Crozier, Huntington and Watanaki, 1975) and 'overload' (King, 1975; Olson, 1982) schools prevalent in the 1970s and 1980s, or through the more optimistic lenses of radical democracy (Laclau and Mouffe, 1985) or the 'silent revolution' (Inglehart, 1977) schools, among others. Three of Bellamy's (2000) four models of electronic democracy look to ICTs to stimulate representative democracy, while only Cyberdemocracy articulates a new vision of politics.

3 Ironically, the sub-set of established democracies has often been defined by membership of the Organisation for Economic Cooperation and Development (OECD), which Mexico joined in 1992.

4 I follow the 'industry standard' definition of a completed democratic transition offered by Linz and Stepan (1996: 3) as: 'when sufficient agreement has been reached about political procedures to produce an elected government, when a government comes to power that is the direct result of a free and popular vote, when this government *de facto* has the authority to generate new policies, and when the executive, legislative and judicial power generated by the new body does not have to share power with other bodies *de jure*'.

5 A review of the literature on the institutional correlates of governability and democracy in Latin America can be found in Foweraker (1998).

6 Based on Purchasing Power Parities.

7 These figures are taken from eMarketeer's *eLatinAmerica Report*, summary available at http://www.emarketeer.com. Accessed 7 March 2001.

8 Peru, for example, fostered an extensive public booth network – the Red Científica Peruana – to overcome the dual constraints of low income and low telephone penetration (Latin American Newsletters, 2000).

9 Indeed, Latin American Newsletters (2000) complains of 'hopeful estimates' that 'add or lose a market the size of France' to the region.

10 Taken from *'Recopilación de estadísticas y conteos Febrero del 2001 sobre nombres de dominio, hosts y servidores de web en México y el mundo'*. Available at: http://www.nic.mx/nic-html/Conteos/0102survey.html. Accessed March 7 2001. Their figures are summarised from those of the Internet Software Consortium (www.isc.org).

11 eMarketeer, *eLatinAmerica Report, op. cit.*

12 It is true, as Domínguez (1999) argues, that 'normal', policy-based competition has become more pronounced in the Mexican system as partisan attachments weakened and assessments of government performance became more commonplace. But further developments in 'issue-based' voting were surely contingent upon the question of democracy being resolved first, that is, upon a clean transfer of power.

13 The post-revolutionary regime dates to the 1917 Constitution and developed its classical features with the establishment of the official party in 1929 and the creation of corporatist interest mediation structures within that party in the 1930s.

14 Later admissions that the system had been 'forced to fail' have been made (Domínguez and McCann, 1996: 152). Half of the ballots remained uncounted and were subsequently incinerated.

15 There are eight citizen-councillors and one president.

16 IFE organised through this programme a 'children's election' that took place at the same time as the real election in almost 50,000 of the country's 113,000 voting booths.

17 One of the major groups involved in the 'anti-globalisation' protests that are presently haunting world leaders is the Italian revolutionary movement, Ya Basta!, which takes its name and inspiration from the Zapatistas.

18 At least some of the communiqués in this 'netwar' were supposedly (initially at least) distributed through a laptop carried on Subcomandante Marcos's back and powered by a car battery, but the majority were rather less prosaically produced by hand and smuggled through army lines for sympathisers to spread the message electronically. The concepts 'netwar' and 'cyberwar' are discussed in Arquilla and Ronfeldt (1993).

19 There has in fact been a long-standing ceasefire in Chiapas, although sporadic

violence has persisted. It remains true, however, that the Zapatistas have used violence to achieve political ends, which has presented a dilemma to many would-be sympathisers.
20 Federal Code of Electoral Processes and Institutions.
21 The riches so embarrassed the PAN in 1997 that it felt compelled to return some of the money, while the PRD established a fund for families of murdered activists and a scholarship scheme (Bruhn, 1999: 106), alongside more conventional campaign uses.
22 Democratisation moved the registration decision from the control of the interior minister to IFE.
23 There are no specific provisions in the 1996 legislation for ICTs, beyond the general requirements for IFE to disseminate information and support civic education and development.
24 Government advertising constitutes approximately 40 per cent of the revenue for the press. Prior to 1989, the government maintained a monopoly of newsprint, which provided a further lever on the press.
25 The total time allocated to parties for the year 2000 was 1,620 hours of radio time and 419 hours of television time. This time is allocated according to the same 30:70 formula that applied to public financing, with new parties each allowed 4 per cent of the total. On this formula, the PRI had 25.5 per cent of coverage, against 21 per cent for Fox's Alliance for Change. In addition, more general reporting on television and radio news was monitored by a *Comisión de radiodifusión* that reported to IFE's General Council, with updates published (on IFE's website) every few weeks. For the period 19 January to 3 June 2000, the PRI had more mentions on all forms of radio and television than any other party, with 33.3 per cent of the total, against 28.4 per cent for the Alliance for Change and 20.7 per cent for the Alliance for Mexico – a vast improvement on previous elections. Over 90 per cent of news coverage, however, was deemed to be neutral by the reporting body, which has representation from all the parties. See *Comisión de Radiodifusión, Informe Acumulado*, presented to IFE General Council July 2000.
26 All gubernatorial candidates and most mayoral candidates develop web pages available through the main party pages.
27 Fox, as the exemplar of the modern approach to campaigning, comes from a business background with Coca-Cola.

References

Arquilla, J. and Ronfeldt, D. (1993) 'Cyberwar is coming!', *Comparative Strategy* 12(2): 141–165.
Bellamy, C. (2000) 'Modelling electronic democracy: Towards democratic discourses for an information age', in Hoff, J., Horrocks, I. and Tops, P. (eds), *Democratic Governance and New Technology: Technologically mediated innovations in political practice in Western Europe*, London: Routledge, 33–54.
Bruhn, K. (1999) 'The resurrection of the Mexican left in the 1997 elections: Implications for the party system', in Domínguez, J. and Poiré, A. (eds), *Toward Mexico's Democratization: Parties, campaigns, elections and public opinion*, London: Routledge, 88–114.
Cleaver, H. (1998) 'The Zapatistas and the electronic fabric of struggle', in Holloway, J. and Peláez, E. (eds), *Zapatista! Reinventing Revolution in Mexico*, London: Pluto Press.
Crozier, M., Huntington, S. and Watanaki, J. (1975) *The Crisis of Democracy: A report*

on the governability of democracies to the Trilateral Commission, New York: New York University Press.

de Swaan, M., Martorelli, P. and Molinar Horcasitas, J. (1998) 'Public financing of parties and electoral reform', in Serrano, M. (ed.), *Governing Mexico: Political parties and elections*, London: Institute of Latin American Studies, 156–169.

Domínguez, J. (1999) 'The transformation of Mexico's electoral and party systems, 1988–97: An introduction', in Domínguez, J. and Poiré, A. (eds), *Toward Mexico's Democratization: Parties, campaigns, elections and public opinion*, London: Routledge, 1–23.

Domínguez, J. and McCann, J. (1996) *Democratizing Mexico: Public opinion and electoral choices*, Baltimore: Johns Hopkins University Press.

Ferdinand, P. (2000) *The Internet, Democracy and Democratization*, London: Frank Cass.

Foweraker, J. (1998) 'Institutional design, party systems and governability – differentiating the Presidential regimes of Latin America', *British Journal of Political Science*, 28: 651–676.

Hoff, J., Horrocks, I. and Tops, P. (2000a) 'Introduction: New technology and the "crises" of democracy', in Hoff, J., Horrocks, I. and Tops, P. (eds), *Democratic Governance and New Technology: Technologically mediated innovations in political practice in Western Europe*, London: Routledge, 1–10.

Hoff, J., Horrocks, I. and Tops, P. (eds) (2000b) *Democratic Governance and New Technology: Technologically mediated innovations in political practice in Western Europe*, London: Routledge.

Huntington, S. (1991) *The Third Wave: Democratization in the late twentieth century*, Norman: University of Oklahoma Press.

Inglehart, R. (1977) *The Silent Revolution: Changing values and political styles among Western publics*, Princeton: Princeton University Press.

Kaase, M. and Newton, K. (1994) *Beliefs in Government*, Oxford: Oxford University Press.

King, A. (1975) 'Overload: The problems of governing in the 1970s', *Political Studies*, XXIII: 283–296.

Laclau, E. and Mouffe, C. (1985) *Hegemony and Socialist Strategy: Towards a radical democratic politics*, London: Verso.

Latin American Newsletters (2000) *The Internet in Latin America: Special report*, London: Latin American Newsletters.

Linz, J. and Stepan, A. (1996) *Problems of Democratic Transition and Consolidation*, Baltimore: Johns Hopkins University Press.

Mainwaring, S. (2000) *Rethinking Party Systems in the Third Wave of Democratization: The case of Brazil*, Stanford, CA: Stanford University Press.

Mainwaring, S. and Scully, T. (eds) (1995) *Building Democratic Institutions: Party systems in Latin America*, Stanford, CA: Stanford University Press.

Mizrahi, Y. (1998) 'The costs of electoral success: The Partido Acción Nacional in Mexico', in Serrano, M. (ed.), *Governing Mexico: Political parties and elections*, London: Institute of Latin American Studies, 95–113.

Moreno, A. (1999) 'Campaign awareness and voting in the 1997 Congressional elections', in Domínguez, J. and Poiré, A. (eds), *Toward Mexico's Democratization: Parties, campaigns, elections and public opinion*, London: Routledge, 114–146.

Olson, M. (1982) *The Rise and Decline of Nations*, New Haven: Yale University Press.

Rose, R. and Chull Shin, D. (2001) 'Democratization backwards: The problem of third-wave democracies', *British Journal of Political Science*, 31: 331–354.

Wallis, D. (2001) 'Outfoxing Leviathan: On the campaign trail down Mexico way', *Journal of Public Affairs*, 1(3).

Whitehead, L. (1995) 'An elusive transition: The slow motion demise of authoritarian dominant party rule in Mexico', *Democratization*, 2(3): 246–269.

10 Online groups and offline parties

Korean politics and the Internet

Rod Hague and Seung-Yong Uhm

The power of the Internet is making itself felt ahead of South Korea's parliamentary elections in April, to the displeasure of the aging political establishment. Civic groups, armed with the Internet, are breaking the iron triangle of politicians, bureaucrats and conglomerates are becoming a major force by attracting grassroots support.

(*Financial Times*, 18 January 2000)

Introduction

This chapter is intended to investigate three propositions about current developments in the political uses of the Internet in South Korea (hereafter, Korea). First, are political parties or citizen movement groups better at utilising the Internet to mobilise public support, and building popular trust in their performance? Second, do online citizens consider citizen movement groups (hereafter CMGs) to be more reliable than political parties in representing their interests? Third, how should political parties respond to pressures from, and challenges by, CMGs? Should they ignore civic groups, attempt strategies of coalition or co-option with them, or compete with them for public support? This question is particularly important in a consolidating democracy, with potentially sharp disparities between democratic aspirations and political reality (Rose *et al.*, 1999). Thus, our main focus is a comparison of political parties and CMGs in terms of how they use the Internet, as well as their online relationship with citizens. Where demands from civil society exceed the capability of political institutions (as they are very likely to do), and where regime performance falls short of satisfying public expectation, under what conditions do people decisively turn away from democratic governance? So far in Korea, people have not responded to the gap between democratic ideal and current practice by rejecting democracy itself (Rose *et al.*, 1999). But the relationship between Korea's political institutions and civil society in general remains problematic, in particular that between political parties and CMGs. These relationships are arguably crucial to resolving disparity between citizen expectations and party performance in the supply of political services.

Our main contention is that, for all the cyber-optimist predictions and an astonishingly rapid penetration of Korean society by the Internet, no significant transformation in the fundamental structure of Korean party politics has yet occurred. As Nixon and Johansson (1999) pointed out, the Internet cannot change party politics unless there is willingness on the part of political practitioners to accept change and adapt to it. Dominant patterns endure unless and until there is a vision of, and motive for embracing, a radically reformed party politics. Korean political parties have adopted the technology of the Internet but have not significantly adapted their practice, far less their nature, to exploit its potentialities. Party websites are largely decorative and symbolic channels of political communication, at best supplemental to other modes and processes of communication (Norris, 2001). While the Internet provides parties and other political organisations with a way of furnishing a variety of information for users without intermediation by other media, it does not thereby contribute to reforming party structure or revitalising party politics. Our reading of the situation is that in personality-dominated and highly centralised parties like those in Korea, the Internet figures as a means for political marketing rather than for electronic democracy. This judgment largely accords with that of Gibson and Ward (2000) on British party activity. Despite the technological advantages of a low-cost and interactive medium, the Internet seems to provide insufficient benefits for political organisations to restructure their operations around it. This reluctance no doubt derives from a nexus of psychological, structural, and institutional reasons.

We also argue that, contrary to the vision of participatory grassroots democracy flourishing in cyber space, users are unlikely to see themselves empowered by the Internet to the extent that pressure for political reform is stimulated by the actions of individual citizens. Our impression is that online participants in Korea seem more inclined to ventilate complaints, often related to their personal interests, in an emotional manner than to engage in reasoned discourse on matters of public importance. The relative anonymity of Internet communication tends to lower the quality, and often the validity, of electronic political messages. Individuals have varied motives for using the Internet, and these are mostly not to do with politics: user surveys indicate that only a tiny proportion of the Internet-using population are politically oriented.[1] One might surmise that the amount and scale of individual online political engagement is minuscule, and simply insufficient to measurably influence the political process. The Internet seems chiefly to provide individuals with opportunities for personal political catharsis. Such a conclusion could, however, be over-pessimistic.

We are not denying the longer-term potential of the Internet to alter the political landscape. The main reason, in our view, is that the Internet helps solve the collective-action problem for aggrieved or discontented citizens. Citizens who may be individually powerless, or nearly so, can mobilise into groups reflecting their common purpose. These groups, built around shared values, skills and information, can readily become significant alternatives to political parties. In the wired society, the transaction costs for individuals wanting to join a cause they espouse fall close to zero. Political parties opposed to self-reform can begin to feel pressure from civil society. The Internet is a potent vehicle for generating collective power through CMGs and NGOs, if the underlying predispositions are out there in the grassroots (Pickerill, 2000). The Korean experience thus parallels that elsewhere (Dutton, 1999). The Internet provides civic organisations with expanded opportunities to inform and educate the public, to mobilise political support, and to articulate distaste for or scepticism towards mainstream party politics.

Civic and environmental groups are thus increasingly going online, developing and demonstrating their organisational skill, and coming up with fertile ideas for exploiting the Internet (Pickerill, 2000). The threshold costs of online participation being significantly lower than for conventional modes of participation (Bonchek, 1995), individuals are more likely to associate themselves in some degree with organisations articulating values they share. Korea's major political parties are being pressured by an increasingly organised, mobilised, and expressive public. Through civic and environmental groups, the Internet facilitates the exercise of collective power from the grassroots.

Given the sluggishness of formal institutions in adapting themselves to a changing societal, political, and technological environment (Dutton, 1999), alongside a public distrustful of party politics, the Internet has opened up public space for those groups nimbler and more adept at using the new media to educate, organise and mobilise segments of the public (Pickerill, 2000).

There can be few purely online organisations in politics, if only because the ultimate goal of any serious political organisation is to bring about changes in the real world. This applies even to online movements in Korea like the Cyber Party (http://www.cyberparty.or.kr) or the Progressive Network Movement (http://www.jinbo.net). The question is how much does the Internet contribute to achieving the goals of an organisation or in bringing about fundamental changes in patterns of political activity rooted in the real world? These issues are closely related to the origins and given structure of political organisations. Political parties, among the most important symbols of democratic governance, are endowed in varying degree with 'brand' loyalty among their followers, plus ideological and operational resources, that reduce their need to rely on a relatively untested medium of communication, whatever its apparent advantages. CMGs or NGOs, by contrast, have stronger incentives to employ the new medium in an attempt to expand their reach and influence. CMGs may be just as keen on garnering public support as political parties. However, whilst public support for the latter is most crucially evidenced in elections, support for the former is less visible, and may be volatile or very narrowly focused. Their nature arguably prompts CMGs to use the Internet more actively. We do not seek here to consider the motives of CMGs for active engagement in online campaigning. Rather, we seek to assess the impact of their online activities on party politics; whether it contributes to reforming and revitalising political parties or, on the contrary, weakens the function of political parties. Our position is similar to that of Bimber (1998), who has argued that the Internet accelerates issue-group formation and action, but does not revolutionise and qualitatively transform democracy.

Korea: technology on fast forward, party democracy on hold

South Korea has experienced not only rapid penetration by the Internet but also fast political development as a consolidating democracy. About 52 per cent of Korea's population uses the Internet regularly (defined as at least once a month), while just under half of all households are linked to the Internet by broadband connection (ADSL, Cable, or ISDN) (KRNIC, 2001).

Korea's democratic transition began in 1987 when general-turned-dictator Chun Doo Hwan conceded citizen demands for direct election of the president, amending the constitutional provision by which the head of state was previously chosen through an Electoral College subject to heavy government manipulation (Park, 2000; Kim, 2000a, 2000b; Steinberg, 1998). Despite widespread public perception that the democratic reform agenda remains unfinished, rapid democratic development in Korea since 1987 cannot be denied (Chung, 1998; Kim, 2000a, 2000b; Park, 2000). Currently, we might summarise, democracy in Korea is being consolidated behaviourally, attitudinally, and constitutionally (Lee, 2000; Kim, 2000a, 2000b).

However, under consolidating democracy, the legacy of the authoritarian era still continues to distort the party system (Kim, 2001). The political parties played only a limited role in the democratisation of Korean politics, partly because of the tactics of the military regime of the period. Even after the transition to democracy, and despite their apparently 'catch-all' style, the parties fell well short of representing the full range of social interests in Korea and in their ability to resolve social conflicts (Kim, 2001). The typical Korean political party is personality-dominated. Parties are boss-centred. Each party rallies around a particular boss as the source of its vigor (Park, 2000); without a dominant leader, the party's life-force ebbs away. Some analysts argue that Korean political parties have not yet matured to the point where they can function both as symbolic embodiments of and practical institutions for democratic governance (Kim, 2001). We should be cautious, however, before assuming that mass political parties are pre-requisites for a functioning democracy (Sartori, 1976). Even in mature liberal democracies, the evidence concerning the centrality and vitality of political parties for regime stability and effectiveness, their current significance for governance and future prospects, seems too mixed to warrant such an assumption. At any rate, since modern political parties first emerged in Korea in 1948, public support has rested more on personal loyalty towards a certain leader or on geographical background than on ideology or social class (Park, 2000; Steinberg, 1998).

Boss politics has thus been dominant in the party system. Although factions may exist within a party, power in the party tends to gravitate towards one person. A party without a strong leader as its focal point most likely becomes fragile and may fall apart (Park, 2000). As leading politicians seek opportunities for political power, reconfiguration of political parties in the run-up to elections is commonplace. Figure 10.1 demonstrates how the party system has been reconfigured, as three contemporary political leaders have manoeuvred: Dae-jung Kim, the current president; Young-sam Kim, a former president; and Jong-pil Kim, a former prime minister.

The major Korean political parties diverge only modestly in ideology or policy direction. The political parties represented in the National Assembly are all centrist or conservative, the ideological horizon of Korean politics having been substantially reduced since the partition of the Korean peninsula (for example, see Park, 2000; Kim, 2001). While it is sometimes said that Korean elections lack major debate on substantive policy, there are modest but significant differences between the major parties on economic management (for example, in policy towards the *chaebol*, the conglomerates that dominate Korean economy, and also in policy towards North Korea and unification of the Korean peninsula). In the past, the parties would mount huge campaigns to mobilise their supporters in elections. As in other countries, campaign activities are often now stage-managed for the benefit of the TV cameras. Broadcasting time and advertising space in the print media are allocated to the parties at election time by the Central Election Management Commission. Elections tend to focus on personalities, however, particularly of the party leaders and presidential candidates. This is no surprise given that a party's identity in the public mind rests mainly on its leader's personality. The frequent breakdown and formation of political parties leaves little time or opportunity for distinctive policy lines to become associated in voters' minds with particular parties

What factors contribute to electoral choice in Korea? Voting patterns undoubtedly have a regional cast (Park, 2000). Voters tend to support the candidate of the party whose leader comes from the voter's region of

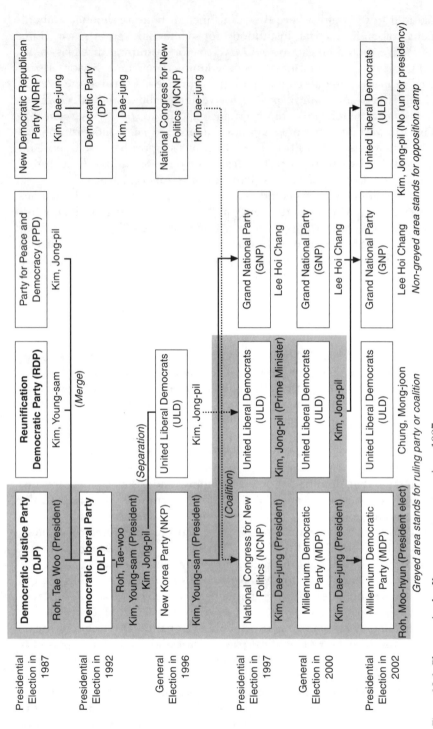

Figure 10.1 Changes in the Korean party system since 1987

origin. In the event that no significant party on the ballot is led by a politician from the voter's own region, negative regional voting occurs as voters cast their ballots against candidates whose party is headed by a politician from a region perceived to be a rival (Steinberg, 1988).

Personality dominance, bossism, and lack of ideological distinction all contribute to the instability of the party system. Prominent political leaders make and unmake political parties all the time. Members of the National Assembly change party affiliation according to political convenience or the state of their relationship with the leaders. Ever-shifting parties, which may not last long enough for voters to develop stable attachments, confuse ordinary citizens, resulting in widespread disillusionment with existing parties (Park, 2000). A sense of frustration among the public is revealed in several indicators. The turnout in the general election in 2000 was 57 per cent, the lowest ever recorded. In a survey conducted shortly before the 2000 general election for the National Assembly, over half of those intending not to vote in the election said that this was because voting never resulted in any change (Office of Information, 2000).

On the other hand, partly owing to proactive policies by the government towards the development and distribution of information and communications technologies, the Internet has been permeating Korean society very quickly. Hopes of using the Internet to boost efforts for democratic reforms have arisen among politicians as well as citizens and academic analysts. In theory, the nature of Internet technologies enables individuals to exercise their right more effectively to bring their personal opinions and interests before fellow members of the public, bypassing the traditional media and political parties as formers of public opinion (Savigny, 2002). The Internet's potential to lower transaction cost facilitates efforts even by those with few resources to organise and mobilise political support on a scale that would be impossible without it (Bonchek, 1995).

However, in reality, demand for political information is relatively low. In a regular large-scale survey conducted by Korea Network Information Centre (KRNIC), less than 1 per cent of respondents said that they frequently accessed political-party and governmental websites. This finding possibly understates usage of political websites – it may not include, for instance, people visiting political websites for the entertainment or personal advice services they generally offer. While we may accept that few people use the Internet chiefly for political information or involvement, another study (Kim and Yoon, 2000: see Table 10.1) reports a higher proportion of users acquiring political information through the Internet, either as a most important or next most important use. While it is not possible to scrutinise in more detail the kinds of political information sought, it is assumed that a variety of interests in public affairs or online civic life are merged into this figure. Although sample size in this survey, at 1,143

Table 10.1 Survey of Korean Internet users: main purposes of Internet use

	Most important use of Internet	Next most important use of Internet	Average of most important and next most important use
Entertainment/Games	27	12	19
Investment/Financial	26	13	19
Business	20	12	16
Newspapers/Magazines	16	13	14
Political information	9	21	15
Educational information	2	30	17
Total	100.0%	100.0%	100.0%

Source: adapted from Kim and Yoon (2000).

Note
Percentages have been rounded.

respondents, was smaller than the KRNIC surveys, the gender and age profile was broadly similar: 64 per cent male, 36 per cent female; 55 per cent aged under 30; 34 per cent aged 30–40; 11 per cent aged over 40.

Interestingly, this study also reported that respondents who had looked at party or candidate websites in the last national election were more likely to have voted than those who had not done so (Kim and Yoon, 2000).

Internet-driven change in Korean party politics

To combat widespread public disenchantment with political parties and politicians, all the major political parties and many Members of National Assembly (MNA) have gone online. Eight party websites can be identified, though only five of the parties concerned have members in the National Assembly. Among these websites, only those of the leading parties, the governing Millennium Democratic Party (hereafter MDP; http://www.minju.co.kr) and the main party of opposition, the Grand National Party (hereafter GNP; http://www.hanara.or.kr), can be considered sophisticated and professional websites with extensive content and a variety of menus and sub-divisions. The MDP and GNP websites stand out from those of other parties by their better quality of design and content, confirming the point that online politics tends to mirror the distribution of political resources offline (Davis, 1999; Margolis and Resnick, 2000). Taking advantage of the fast-growing broadband connectivity throughout Korea's population, the two major parties are running Internet broadcasting sites, managed by specialised technicians and reporters in order to deliver real-time video news. Both parties are so well aware of the main audience group for web services that they put substantial resources into 'infotainment', intended to attract the younger generation, whose orientation is presumed to be slanted towards entertainment and games. They also put considerable effort into building virtual communities wherein web users share relatively non-political information but which are also intended to provide supportive messages for the party's line. To promote these online communities, groups of contributors and active participants are organised among younger party members. Each party has dedicated teams of professionals to create and manage its website. Thus, the designers of the major Korean party websites do seem to be aware of the relative unpopularity of political websites, and have developed features and content providing for relatively 'nonpolitical' uses and gratifications (see Table 10.2).

The MDP and GNP websites have been compared elsewhere in terms of their design and contents (Kim, 2000a, 2000b; Chung, 1998), but several comments seem pertinent here. First, the strategies of the parties for online political activities are similar rather than distinctive. This is perhaps not surprising. Korean political parties tend towards the 'catch-all' variety, with limited ideological differentiation. There is also a common driver within the environment of web-based politics. The demographic distribution of Internet users confines all parties to the same target audience of predominantly younger age-groups. Electoral supporters of GNP, however, are typically rather older and more conservative. Nearly 40 per cent of its supporters are in their forties, and a similar proportion are

Table 10.2 Website content of the two leading Korean parties

Categories	Millennium Democratic Party (Min-Joo Dang)	Great National Party (Hannara Dang)
Host provided menu (top-down stream of information)	Greeting from party leader Introduction to party Organisation and politicians Policy committee section Secretary general section Woman's world News room Policy library	Greeting from party leader Introduction to party Organisation and politicians Hannara today Hannara vision Comments and press release Policy library Internet TV
User participation (upwards stream of information)	Open bulletin board system Online petition Online poll	E-sponsoring E-petition Policy proposal Open bulletin board system
Online special (interactive)	E-Minjoo (democratic) Channel for weekly news letter	Speaking truth (Chamsori) Cyber spokesman, youth monitor, cyber discussion email club
Soft contents entertainment	Game, movie, humour, cultural event, weather, etc.	Humour, game, book, cultural events, IT news

white-collar workers or self-employed (Kukmin Ilbo, 2001). Given the fact that over 50 per cent of the Internet population are in their twenties and thirties, however, the GNP has little choice but to aim its online presence at younger age groups, even though it can not expect to harvest many new adherents this way. With nearly 30 per cent of its supporters in their twenties, the MDP, by contrast, has a rather younger age profile, and so the Internet reaches potentially deeper into its electoral territory (Kukmin Ilbo, 2001).

Second, both major parties offer and manage interactive services in the same way. They operate public bulletin boards, which are often filled with irate and sometimes highly abusive criticism. While these messages might indicate pervasive anger and disappointment among citizens, they are also attributed to 'black' campaigning by the supporters of other parties. Contributions to party bulletin boards can be anonymous (including an email address is optional). Other contributors give false email addresses. A striking contrast will be drawn later with online contributors to CMGs.

Contributors to bulletin boards are warned that abusive messages will be deleted. Because abusive messages are so numerous, webmasters are more concerned to expunge contributions incompatible with the dignity of the party's cyber-presence than to engage contributors in discussion. They are not consistently attentive in this task, however; now and again the webteams lose control of the agenda on the party's public bulletin board (Stromer-Galley, 2000). Consequently, although bulletin boards provide channels for public communication with the parties, the quality of interaction thus generated is distinctly limited. Party websites, in fact, are no more interactive than government ministry websites, and often less so. While ministry websites allow for discussion between ministers and individual citizens, no party website provides an interactive space in which the head of a party, or other senior officials, can discuss issues with citizens.

Interaction with party followers is limited in other ways. No major party website, at the time of writing, provides Intranet facilities for core members. While opportunities for supporters or the general public to offer party headquarters their opinions on party policy are at present constricted, the MDP has recently innovated in this direction, but with a separate, specialised interactive website. The main-party websites are essentially transmission belts, justifying party decisions, broadcasting political messages linked to the party line and disseminating material to local activists, media professionals and political junkies. The main differences from TV and newspaper coverage is that messages on the party website are typically longer, use multimedia and, of course, are unmediated by media professionals independent of the party. Korean parties do not appear to be running websites to bridge the gap between citizen and the state more effectively, nor to encourage the public to assert its views and interests more actively, but chiefly as a channel of reinforcement, persuading voters to follow the party line. This is hardly surprising. Despite predictions of semi-direct democracy (Toffler, 1980) or the vision of the electronic *agora* (Rheingold, 1993), the potentialities of computer-mediated communication have hardly begun to affect the perspectives acquired by politicians in the pre-Internet age. In Korea, most politicians would seem to be dedicated followers of fashion when it comes to ICT. The idea that computer-mediated communication could be used to enrich inner-party democracy might well be viewed by politicians as a threat to their leadership and freedom of action.

Korean party websites, moreover, perform no significant role at present in elite recruitment (though see the conclusion to this chapter). Korean election law stipulates, rather vaguely, that the nomination of candidates for public office be made through a democratic procedure within a party. However, the realities of candidate selection rarely live up to legal precept. In practice, the process of choosing candidates is distinctly top-down. Typically, *ad hoc* screening committees are set up at national headquarters for would-be candidates, and these committees are routinely expected to select candidates favoured by the party's leader. Websites have not so far been used to facilitate bottom-up nominations from the nation-wide party membership or primary-style contests.

The relationship between those who lead the party and those who manage the website is part of the problem. Websites tend to be designer-led and run by professional webteams rather than actively managed by the politicians whose photographs and biographies adorn the pages. An outcome of professional specialisation is that webteams, typically in the middle or lower reaches of the party hierarchy, may be outside the inner-party loop of strategy discussion and policy formulation, and are only brought in at a relatively late stage to handle presentational aspects. Party leaders thus remain relatively detached from the party's web-based activity, only weakly involved and possibly uninterested in it.

A further aspect of political usage of the Internet involves that by individual politicians. Davis (1999) argues that while politicians with substantial political resources tend to use information technologies proactively, those politicians with fewer resources rarely develop websites. We would argue that the structure of political risks and opportunities also figures strongly. American congressional politicians, for instance, seeking re-election within a highly individualised electoral environment, routinely maintain personal websites of a sophisticated, professional standard. With their personal fate more strongly tied, in most cases, to that of their party, British MPs are following suit more slowly. Personal websites are *de rigueur* only among Liberal Democrat MPs, can be found for about a quarter of Labour MPs, but are still rare among Conservatives (Uhm and Hague, 2001).[2] Members of the Korean National Assembly (MNAs), by contrast, have been quick to adopt the Internet. As of July 2001, 87 per cent of

MNAs were running personal websites. The primary purpose of such websites seems to be that of personal advertising and image-building, not least of politicians qualified for the information era. Some individual sites are more interactive than the official party websites, with politicians (or others on their behalf) answering questions and engaging in discussion. The websites of some individual politicians, for example those of the party leaders, register more hits than the official party websites. They are primarily tools of political marketing, rather than of interactive democracy, enabling individual politicians to engage in permanent personal campaigning.

Korean MNAs are elected by two routes: 227 (83 per cent) by electoral district under first-past-the-post and 46 (17 per cent) by a national pool, which tops up the legislative assembly proportionally to party support nationally. Table 10.3 shows correlations between web-page ownership and selected factors. Given a generally high level of website ownership by MNAs, most of the correlations are uninformative. The main point of interest is a fairly strong association (phi = 0.435) between website ownership and method of election, that is, between MNAs elected by district and those chosen proportionally. Website ownership, at 95 per cent, is higher among members representing electoral districts, whereas among MNAs chosen under the proportional system it is just under 80 per cent. This difference, we would argue, reflects rational calculation. District MNAs have stronger incentive than proportionally elected MNAs to demonstrate to their electorate an awareness of the new communication channel. They also stand directly to gain if the new medium is efficacious in gathering or consolidating support.

A milder but indicative correlation (phi = 0.23) emerges between geographical background and website ownership. Inhabitants of metropolitan regions are more likely to be better-educated and to include more regular IT users. MNAs representing such areas are more likely to be early adopters of websites. There is little or no difference in the propensity of

Table 10.3 Correlation between MNA home-page ownership and other factors (Phi Co-efficient)

Factors	Home-page ownership
Election method (electoral district or proportional)	0.435*
Geographical background (Seoul region; large city; small town or rural)	0.23*
Age at last election	0.19*
Number of terms served	0.09
Educational background	0.03
Ruling or opposition party	0.02

Note
*Significance level: 0.01.

MNAs to set up individual websites depending on their age, number of terms served or whether in government or opposition parties.

The role of citizens' movement groups

One of the most striking trends in Korean civil society since 1988 has been the proliferation of the CMGs (*Simin Udongtanche*). These initially encompassed a wide variety of social organisations, such as religious groups, environmental organisations, women's groups, consumer movement groups, organisations for reunification, movements for educational reform, and organisations of the handicapped. From just forty-seven groups identifiable in 1988, rising only to sixty-nine by 1993, the number of CMGs was estimated at over 4,000 as of January 2001, a phenomenally explosive growth. Though varied in their origins and aims, these groups tend to focus their energies on making the legislative process in the National Assembly more transparent to citizens, pressing for democratisation within the political parties, on efforts to reduce political corruption and regionalism. They have generally sought to promote, deepen, enrich and institutionalise public participation in civic life, though also prone to 'conflictual engagement' with the elites dominating Korean society (Kim, 2000a).

In a number of respects, the CMGs are different from the anti-government and often anti-capitalist and anti-American popular movements that played a significant part in the breakdown of the authoritarian regime. First, the CMGs are largely led by, and disproportionately composed of, individuals with professional backgrounds: teachers and lecturers, lawyers, doctors, scientists and technologists. Second, in terms of their approach, the CMGs emphasise gradual institutional reforms based on rational discourse and logical analysis, rather than the emotionally charged hostility to the established order often displayed by people's movement groups. Third, the CMGs rely mostly on legal and non-violent methods, such as publicity drives, lectures, and the distribution of pamphlets, rather than street protests and demonstrations favoured by the people's movement groups. Fourth, in regard to issues, the CMGs are concerned with fair elections, consumers' rights, the fight against corruption, the environment, and gender inequality rather than far-reaching systemic change. Compared with the parties, the CMGs have shown themselves rather adept at conflict resolution: for instance, the Citizens' Coalition for Economic Justice successfully intervened in the long-running dispute between pharmacists and medical practitioners, which the government had failed to resolve (Kim, 2001). There are clear signs that CMGs are themselves becoming contenders for power or, more accurately, becoming training grounds for, and pools of, potential candidates for office. Several CMG leaders have been elected to the National Assembly and have sought formal relationships with both parties and the National Assembly.

Some CMG members see this permeation of the political elite as part of the effort for political and institutional reform, but the strategy is deeply controversial within the CMG community.

In fact, during the pro-democracy struggle against authoritarian regime, civil-society groups largely exercised hegemony over political parties (Kim, 2000b). After the authoritarian breakdown, however, the focus of Korean politics steadily shifted towards party politics, marginalising civil society in general, and in particular the people's movement groups that had played a leading role in the fight against authoritarianism, in the forefront of pro-democracy demonstrations. In addition to a growing sense of inability to control their new governors, voters became more disillusioned and frustrated. Throughout the politics of democratic consolidation in Korea since 1988, CMGs have focused their efforts on monitoring the electoral process, and improving both the scale and effectiveness of political participation. In the National Assembly elections of April 2000 various organisations combined to form Citizens' Solidarity for the National Assembly Elections, and engaged in a nationwide campaigning to reject unfit candidates. Citizens' Solidarity reviewed the backgrounds of legislative candidates and identified eighty-six who had been involved in antidemocratic acts, including corruption, tax evasion, draft dodging and other illegal or immoral activities. The Central Election Management Committee (CEMC) co-operated by disclosing on its website (http://www.nec.go.kr) the military-service records of candidates running for office, including any criminal convictions. The Citizens' Solidarity blacklist was published online, and civic society groups waged a vigorous campaign, in the media and online, for voters to reject these unfit candidates. Two-thirds of candidates on the Citizens' Solidarity blacklist failed to be elected. Interestingly, some analysts claimed that these activities deepened voter disillusionment with politics, leading to the lowest-ever recorded voter turnout at 57 per cent (Ra, 2000).

Table 10.4 shows the electoral outcomes for blacklisted candidates in the April 2000 Korean elections for the National Assembly. The highest rate of defeat for these candidates was in Seoul and neighbouring satellite cities, which together comprise 25 per cent of the national population. More people in their twenties and thirties (who are more likely to be IT literate than older age groups) inhabit this metropolitan area compared with other regions. Internet penetration is higher than other local cities, with over a fifth of the national Internet population living in the city of Seoul itself, and just under a fifth in neighbouring province of Kyunggi whilst the average proportion of the Internet population resident in other regions of the country is about 5 per cent. Opportunities for higher education are much more available in the Seoul metropolitan region than elsewhere in the country, creating a more educated electorate, which also fosters a faster take-up of IT, as well probably diluting regionalist sentiment and regional particularism in the voting booth. The digital divide in

Table 10.4 Korean National Assembly Elections, April 2000: electoral outcomes of candidates blacklisted by Citizens' Solidarity

Region	Number of candidates blacklisted	Number of blacklisted candidates defeated	Defeat rate
Seoul Metropolitan region	20	19	95%
Choong-chung region	23	18	78%
Kyung-sang region	35	16	46%
Chun-ra region	8	6	75%
Total	86	59	69%

Note
Significance level: 0.05.

Korea at present is thus largely one between the metropolis and the provinces.

Table 10.4 indicates substantial but lesser success for the Citizens' Solidarity blacklist in two other provinces, Kyung-sang, which backed the former ruling and current opposition camp (GNP), and Chun-ra, which backed candidates of the current governing parties (MDP and its coalition partners). A keen sense of regional rivalry characterises these provinces, with regional particularism continuing to shape electoral choice, whereas in another province, Choong-chung, with lesser regional attachment, over three-quarters of the blacklisted candidates failed to be re-elected. Whereas regional particularism generally remains significant in Korean electoral behaviour, voters in the most economically and educationally advanced region are less likely to demonstrate this tendency in their voting.

Lacking funds and physical resources on the scale of the major political parties, CMGs make a virtue of necessity by heavy reliance on online activity. Given the profile of their leadership and active supporters, drawn largely from Korea's well-educated professional class, this of course is not surprising. The gap between the top leadership and web management evident within the major political parties is far less apparent among CMGs: in many cases, the leadership is the web-management team, though some CMGs have established additional subordinate organisations, specialising in cyber activities or cyber-campaigning. What such websites lack in professionalism may be compensated for by relevance of content, shared concerns and immediacy of communication throughout the group. Websites of CMGs are not necessarily more interactive than those of political parties. As illustrated in Table 10.5, the direction of communication is predominantly downwards, from webmaster to user, though there is a members' forum, in addition to a public bulletin board, in which two-way and multi-way interaction can take place.

Table 10.5 Contents of the website of Cyber Citizens' Solidarity for Participatory
            Democracy

Menus	Content description	Direction of communication
Introduction	History Organisation Membership registration Fund raising	Down and up
Information service	Volunteer activities General information	Down
Issue library	Important issues Activities	Down
Community	Open BBS Exclusive members forum	Up
Help desk	How to use the website	Down

There are strong indications that CMGs are trusted more than other social and political organisations. Table 10.6, based on a large-scale survey of the Korean public carried out in December 2001, shows a stark contrast in public attitudes towards civil movement organisations, on the one hand, and towards political parties on the other. CMGs emerge as the most trusted institutions in contemporary Korea, more than the military, religious, medical and legal institutions, with political parties as the least trusted.

In other opinion surveys conducted on behalf of the government, many respondents regard citizens' movement groups as more seriously committed to political reform than other organisations, including political parties (Office of Information, 2000). When asked who would take the leading role of promoting the sense of fair elections, over one-third of respondents named citizens' movement groups. A quarter of respondents said

Table 10.6 'Which of the following institutions do you trust the most?' Selected
            social and political institutions (%)

	Trust very much	Trust somewhat	Don't trust very much	Don't trust at all
Civic movement groups	6	59	30	5
The military	7	56	33	5
The news media	2	46	44	8
Civil servants	1	42	46	10
Political parties/National Assembly	1	10	36	54

Source: Korean Barometer (Survey of Korean Attitudes and Value Systems), December 2001 (Office of Information and World Research, Seoul, Korea). Translation by the authors. Percentages have been rounded.

that they would be willing to inform citizens' movement groups of any illegal activities in election campaign, slightly fewer than those who responded that they would report any misdeeds to the Central Election Management Commission.

Further evidence about the levels of trust enjoyed by different kinds of political organisations is displayed in Table 10.7. Both political parties and citizens' movement groups encourage the authors of messages on bulletin boards to include their email address, even if these are optional. Revealing one's email address may be done even when one does not exactly trust other participants in cyberspace, including the webmaster, but where the participant intends to continue with the dialogue. We take trust in this instance simply to mean an individual's belief that others will not knowingly or willingly do him or her harm (Newton, 1997). Many messages sent to party websites are written by people wanting to ventilate their complaints, rather than to exchange ideas. The language of these contributions is often extremely rude and defamatory. A notable contrast in Table 10.7 is between the unwillingness of contributors to party bulletin boards to reveal their identities with their preparedness to do so in contributions to the bulletin boards of two leading CMGs. On the Internet, of course, anonymity does not, however, guarantee that individuals are safe from detection by the authorities. Furthermore, even though contributors may present an email address, the information may be fake. None the less, the contrast in perceived levels of trust between political parties and CMGs is striking.

In theory, the nexus of ICTs termed the Internet, and accumulating experience in employing those technologies, could help revitalise the role of parties in representative democracy, to carry out their intermediary role more effectively, and strengthen public trust in representative institutions. This review suggests that party-political usage of the Internet in Korea has so far largely failed to exploit its potentialities. Despite elaborate and

Table 10.7 Bulletin-board contributors optionally disclosing an email address: Korean political parties and citizen groups compared

Web hosts	June 2001	July 2001	August 2001	Average rate of optional email disclosure
Millennium Democratic Party	49/349	59/350	54/398	13%
Great National Party	61/380	54/378	38/403	13%
Citizens' Coalition for Economic Justice	172/189	186/201	190/214	91%
Peoples' Solidarity for Participatory Democracy	188/193	175/187	187/193	96%

extensive party websites, and a very high rate of website ownership by legis-lative politicians, few significant changes are visible in critical areas of party politics, such as democratisation of party structure, policy formation or the practice of political recruitment. Party websites in Korea tend to function more as broadcasting media than as narrowcasting or interactive channels. The websites of individual politicians, though sometimes more interactive than the official party websites, function primarily as vehicles for personal advertising and profiling. Party strategies for handling the interactive potentialities of the Internet are relatively unsophisticated (Coleman, 2001).

Until very recently there has been a dearth of ideas and impetus for organisational reform other than relatively cosmetic developments such as open Bulletin Board Systems and the provision of email links to party leader or webmaster. There are now, however, some indications of organi-sational response. First, the GNP's new website *Chamsori* ('speaking truth'), while run separately from the main party site, features interactive operation and the idea seems to be to provide a host forum in which a variety of social issues can be aired, moderated by a cyber-spokesperson adopting a more informal and familiar tone. *Chamsori* includes an interac-tive menu called Youth Monitor, with similar aims, to detect the issues of most concern to young people in Korea, ostensibly allowing fresh ideas and alternatives to filter up for consideration by the party. Given the low state of popular trust in the parties, it remains to be seen how seriously this initiative will be treated by those it is intended to attract.

The December 2002 presidential election

Korean democracy is presidentially centred, with a strong presidency com-bining the roles of head of state, chief executive and party leader (though sharing the role of head of government with the prime minister, nomi-nated by the president and confirmed by the National Assembly). A president backed by a party majority in the National Assembly undoubt-edly controls the major levers of governmental power. With the president elected for a non-renewable five-year term, the pivotal event in the Korean political calendar is the presidential election, and the stakes of power embedded in it. This contest, we contend, is catalysing developments in the party and wider political system, including political exploitation of ICTs. With the three dominant figures of the last decade ('the three Kims' – retiring president Kim Dae Jung, former president Kim Young Sam, and ageing ULD leader Kim Jong-Pil) no longer at centre stage, the field for the forthcoming presidential election in December 2002 was left unusu-ally open.

If in the past elections and parties have been leader-dominated, with only limited public scrutiny of candidates' credentials and fitness for public office, this has now begun to change. One of the CMGs, the Cyber

People's Solidarity for Participatory Democracy, established an online database collecting information about likely major contenders for the presidency, giving biographical details and career experience. The database offered a structured comparison of the potential candidates' public statements and declared positions on all the key policy issues facing Korea (relations and reunification with the North, government policy towards the *chaebol*, reform of the financial sector, relations with Korea's major international trade and security partners, and so on). Since CMGs enjoy far higher public trust than the parties, this potentially gives them considerable scope as mechanisms for political quality assurance. One observer described CMGs as the 'new governors', emerging from the failure of party politics to consolidate Korean democracy. The role of CMGs as public watchdogs seems closely analogous to that of consumer organisations seeking to educate the public so that purchasing choices are better informed, using publicity to expose malpractice and poor quality and to drive up the standard of competition between producers. It is perhaps not too fanciful to suggest that the Korean CMGs are imposing a degree of quality control over the candidate choices offered to the electorate. At the same time, through the provision of detailed and accurate information to a well-educated electorate, the CMGs are seeking to reduce the regional and emotional bias that has previously characterised Korean electoral choice.

There is some evidence that the major parties are responding to the changing electoral environment. Both the governing party and the main opposition party more or less simultaneously announced the introduction of a primary election to select their candidate for the presidential race. These primaries gave all MDP and GNP party members a vote in choosing their party's presidential candidate. The total party memberships involved, however, were rather modest (35,000 for the MDP, and just under 25,000 for the GNP). A novelty was that each of the two main parties gave non-party members a vote in its presidential primary. These non-party members were chosen randomly through sample surveys, and were equal in number to each party's total membership. The GNP, in addition, earmarked a fraction of the total primary electorate for e-voting in its presidential primary. Internet users could register with the party, and a proportion of those registering were then randomly selected to be representative of 'netizens' in the general population. In the MDP primary contest also, a small proportion (2.5 per cent) of the total vote was reserved for Internet voters. These innovations provide the clearest indication yet that both the major Korean parties, faced with widespread popular distrust, are attempting to broaden the basis of popular involvement in their key decisions, and thereby secure greater legitimacy for the candidate each presented to the Korean nation in the presidential election. The presidential election of December 2002 arguably saw the Internet come of age in Korean politics. Reformist presidential candidate Roh

Moo-hyun based his campaign strategy on reaching a youthful electorate (nearly half of all voters are under 40 years of age) by means of the Internet and cell phones. Roh was backed backed by Nosamo, an online support group, which recruited around 78,000 members and helped him win the first MDP primary and then the presidency. The most dramatic impact of the new technology came on election day itself, the Roh campaign team making more effective use of internet and cell phones to get out the vote. Exit polls indicated that about 60 per cent of younger voters voted for Roh, who captured 49 per cent of the poll overall and emerged the victorious candidate after a recount.[3]

Conclusion

The December 2002 presidential election revealed crucial differences in the ability to use Internet and cell-phone technologies for election purposes. The victorious candidate realised that younger voters were much more at home with these technologies than older voters and exploited this difference skilfully. Our broader assessment, however, remains that there is a structural lag between the prevailing stance of the political parties and the expectations of an increasingly well-educated population, particularly in the metropolitan region. The CMGs have arguably emerged in response to this structural strain, using the Internet as a primary channel of communication to both articulate and disseminate critiques of current political practice and policy. The major parties are, of course, trying to hold on to their existing supporters on the one hand, and seeking additional support from floating voters on the other. The CMGs, meanwhile, are seeking to wean voters away from traditional regional attachments and persuade them to be rationally independent in making electoral choices. They are, moreover, undermining the credibility of party-led campaigns by providing more accurate and objective information about candidates. There is now added impetus since the civic movements groups have demonstrated a capacity to mobilise votes, as well as opinions, around their critiques. Gibson and Ward (2000) have argued that the impact of the Internet is more evident in modernising than in democratising British party politics. A similar point can be made in relation to Korea, with the difference that Korean democracy is less securely established, structurally and attitudinally, at both mass and elite levels and is more conditional upon economic performance (Lee, 2000). The remarkably rapid diffusion of the Internet throughout Korean society offers opportunities for institutional reform, to deepen and consolidate this crucial experiment with democracy in East Asia. So far, however, there is only modest evidence to support the notion of an emergent new style of Korean party politics in the Internet era.

Website references

Central Election Management Party (CEMC): http://www.nec.go.kr.

Citizens Coalition for Economic Justice: http://www.ccej.or.kr.

Cyber Party: http://www.cyberparty.or.kr.

Cyber People's Solidarity for Participatory Democracy: http://www.people-power21.org.

Great Nation Party (Hannara Dang): http://www.hannara.or.kr.

Korea Network Information Centre (January 2001) 'Survey on the Number and Attitudes of Internet Users in Korea', Seoul, Republic of Korea: http://www.nic.or.kr.

Millennium Democratic Party (Minjoo Dang in Korean): http://www.minjoo.or.kr.

Progressive Network Movement: http://www.jinbo.net.

Ra, D.S. (2000) 'Study on the Application and Operation of Internet Communication in the 16th General Election in Korea' (16 Dae Chongsun-eso Natanan Network Hwal-yong mit Un-yong-e Kwanhan Yonku). Cyber Culture Research Centre: http://www.cyberculture.re.kr.

Notes

1 Regular updated surveys of Internet usage and behaviour in Korea can be found at: www.nic.or.kr/ (the Korean Network Information Centre).

2 The evidence for the UK does not entirely support this argument. While the Liberal Democrat party is certainly less well financed than its major party opponents, it was among the early adopters of email communication. Of the three main UK parties, the Liberal Democrats are currently the only party in which individual websites are the norm for its elected representatives at Westminster, in the Welsh and Scottish Assemblies and in Europe. See Uhm and Hague (2001).

3 Media accounts of the election focused on the election day announcement by Chung Mong-joon (head of National Alliance 21) withdrawing his support for Roh, a development which threatened to split the reformist vote and throw the election to conservative GNP candidate Lee Hoi-chang. According to the media, shocked and angered Roh supporters were then galvanised in action. Websites supporting Roh recorded around three million hits during polling day, some five to six times more than average. But personal communication to the authors suggests that Roh's MDP campaign team had planned an intensive vote mobilisation effort, put into effect as tracking exit polls indicated a tightening race on election day. Text messages were sent to cell phones of almost 800,000 people urging them to vote. With GNP supporters concentrated among elderly and generally less techno-savvy voters, this kind of strategem was less practicable.

References

Bimber, B (1998) 'The Internet and Political Transformation: Populism, Community, and Accelerated Pluralism', *Polity*, 31(1): 133–160.

Bonchek, M. (1995) 'Grassroots in Cyberspace: Recruiting Members on the

Internet', paper presented to the 53rd Annual Meeting of the Midwest Political Science Association.

Chung, J.M. (1998) *Party Politics in Post-Industrial Society and Development of Korea's Political Parties (Hooki Sanop-sahoi euii Chongdang-chungchi wa Hankook eui Chong-dang Balchon)*, Seoul: Han-ool.

Coleman, S. (2001) 'The 2001 Election Online and the Future of E-Politics', in Coleman, S. (ed.) (2001), *Cyber Space Odyssey, The Internet in the UK Election*, London: Hansard Society.

Davis, R. (1999) *The Web of Politics; The Internet's Impact on the American Political System*, New York: Oxford University Press.

Diamond, L. and Shin, D.C. (2000) *Institutional Reform and Democratic Consolidation in Korea*, Stanford, CA: Hoover Institution Press.

Dutton, W.H. (1999) *Society on the Line: Information Politics in the Digital Age*, Oxford: Oxford University Press.

Gibson, R.K. and Ward, S.J. (eds) (2000) *Reinvigorating Democracy?: British Politics and the Internet*, Aldershot: Ashgate.

Kim, S. (2000a) 'Civic Mobilization for Democratic Reform', in Diamond, L. and Shin, D.C. (eds), *Institutional Reform and Democratic Consolidation in Korea*, Stanford, CA: Hoover Institution Press.

Kim, S. (2000b) *The Politics of Democratization in Korea: The Role of Civil Society*, Pittsburgh: University of Pittsburgh Press.

Kim, S.J. (2001) 'Civil Movement, National Assembly and Political Parties' (*Shimin undong kwa Kukhwi, Chung-dang*), *Civil Society*, Vol. 3, Research Institute of Civil Society and Joong-ang Ilbo, Seoul, Korea.

Kim, Y.C. and Yoon, S.Y. (2000) 'Political Application of the Internet and the 16th General Election of Korea', *Journal of Korean Political Science*, 34(3).

Kukmin Ilbo (2001) 'Survey on Current Affairs and Public Attitudes to the Presidential Election', Kukmin Daily, Seoul, Korea, 7 December 2001.

Lee, S.J. (2000) 'Mass Perceptions of Democracy', in Diamond, L. and Shin, D.C. (eds), *Institutional Reform and Democratic Consolidation in Korea*, Stanford, CA: Hoover Institution Press.

Margolis, M. and Resnick, D. (2000) *Politics as Usual: The Cyberspace 'Revolution'*, Thousand Oaks, CA: Sage Publications.

Newton, K. (1997) 'Social and Political Trust in Established Democracies', in Norris, P. (ed.), *Critical Citizens: Global Support for Democratic Governance*, Oxford: Oxford University Press.

Nixon, P. and Johansson, H. (1999) 'Transparency Through Technology: The Internet and Political Parties', in Hague, B. and Loader, B.D. (eds), *Digital Democracy: Discourse and Decision-Making in the Information Age*, London: Routledge, 135–153.

Norris, P. (2001) *The Digital Divide*, Cambridge: Cambridge University Press.

Office of Information and World Research (2000) 'A Survey of Citizens' Attitudes Towards the Establishment of Culture for Fair Elections', *Korean Barometer*, Seoul, Korea, February 2000.

Office of Information and World Research (2001) 'Survey of Korean Attitudes and Value Systems', *Korean Barometer*, Seoul, Korea, December 2001.

Park, C.W. (2000) 'The Asian Update's Korea's 16th National Assembly Elections', *Asian Society*, 1–17.

Pickerill, J. (2000) 'Environmentalists and the Net: Pressure Groups, New Social

Movement and New ICTs', in Gibson, R.K. and Ward, S.J. (eds), *Reinvigorating Democracy?: British Politics and the Internet*, Aldershot: Ashgate, 129–150.

Rheingold, H. (1993) *The Virtual Community: Homesteading on the Electronic Frontier*, New York: Addison-Wesley.

Rose, R., Shin, D.C. *et al.* (1999) 'Tensions Between the Democratic Ideal and Reality: South Korea', in Norris, P. (ed.), *Critical Citizens: Global Support for Democratic Governance*, Oxford: Oxford University Press.

Sartori, G. (1976) *Parties and Party Systems: A Framework for Analysis*, Cambridge: Cambridge University Press.

Savigny, H. (2002) 'Public Opinion, Political Communication and the Internet', *Politics*, 22(1): 1–8.

Steinberg, D. (1998) 'Korea: Triumph Amid Turmoil', *Journal of Democracy*, 9(2): 76–90.

Stromer-Galley, J. (2000) 'Online Interaction and Why Candidates Avoid It', *Journal of Communication*, 111–132.

Toffler, A. (1980) *The Third Wave*, New York: Bantam Books.

Uhm, S.Y. and Hague, R. (2001) 'Political Participation in a Virtual Community: Korean and UK Compared in Political Context', paper presented at ECPR Workshops, Grenoble, April 2001.

11 Extremism on the net

The extreme right and the value of the Internet

Nigel Copsey

Introduction

A long-lasting association with the horrors of Nazism has stymied right-wing extremism ever since the Second World War[1] and, in most countries, right-wing extremists have found themselves marginalised from mainstream society. Without political and social respectability, extreme-right groups have been forced to operate as political pariahs, largely restricted to the political fringe with little space or opportunity to propagate their ideology. Within this domain, where far-right ideology has been disseminated, for the most part it has been through printed media (typically newspapers, magazines and newsletters). Frequently of low quality and variously subjected to legal restraint – such as laws against incitement to racial hatred and Holocaust denial – this material has seldom circulated beyond a narrow band of followers. Yet as one observer has recognised, it is 'in the nature of radicalism and extremism to propagate by all available means' (Whine, 1997: 209), and whilst this is not strictly true (some extremists stop short of advocating violence), advances in modern technology have been seized upon by right-wing extremists eager to widen their audience. Since the 1980s, far-right activists, mainly in North America, have used cable television, radio, faxes and 'dial-a-hate' telephone messages. But what is now on offer is beyond compare: a truly global communications medium of an estimated 400 million users. The Internet is, as Stern (2001) says, 'the most remarkable communication advancement of our time because it is easier, cheaper, quicker, multimedia, immense, and interactive'. That right-wing extremists should avail themselves of the opportunities presented by the rapid expansion of the Internet should therefore come as no surprise, especially when material on the net remains largely free from the restraints imposed by national laws, censorship and regulation.

In this chapter, we will explore the incursion of the extreme right into cyberspace. What this requires, at the outset, is a definition and conceptualisation of right-wing extremism. From here, we can trace the origins and development of right-wing extremist activity on the net. The central questions to be considered are: why and in what ways has the extreme right increasingly targeted the Internet? What is its value to right-wing extremists?

The attention of most scholars and journalists in this field has been caught by the proliferation of racist 'hate-sites' in North America. In view of the fact that these sites far outnumber right-extremist sites that originate elsewhere, this is not surprising. However, in keeping with the overall theme of this book, our attention must be directed towards the impact of the net on political parties. Consequently, a section of the chapter will focus on the 'cyber experience' of Britain's leading extreme-right electoral party, the British National Party (BNP). The BNP has not been chosen at random; comments it made in 1995 that 'the Internet is the most significant development for politics since the invention of television'[2] suggest that it attaches great significance to the Internet. Following this 'virtual encounter' with the BNP, our final remarks concern whether extreme-right activity on the net constitutes a significant threat to liberal society. In what ways can such activity be countered?

Defining right-wing extremism

Defining the extreme right is a challenge in itself. To start with, the fact that authors make use of varied terminology to describe the extreme pole of right-wing activity gives rise to obvious difficulties. Even a brief glance at the specialist literature reveals numerous other terms in play such as radical right, far right, ultra-right, fascism, neo-fascism, neo-nazism and even national or new populism (Cheles *et al.*, 1991; Merkl and Weinberg, 1993; Betz, 1994; Taggart, 1995; Betz and Immerfall, 1998). Frequently, these terms are used interchangeably; at other times, strict conditions are applied. But be that as it may, since the term 'extreme right' remains the most commonly accepted umbrella term (at least by European scholars; the term 'radical right' having circulated more widely in North America) we will stick with it.

There is, as Mudde (1996: 228) says, 'a broad consensus in the field that the term right-wing extremism describes primarily an ideology in one form or another'. Yet, as Hainsworth (2000: 4–5) recently observed, the form that this ideology takes cannot be reduced to a uniform type that is identical in every case. Instead, the extreme right should be viewed as a broad 'political family' that possesses an ideology that is comprising common constituent parts but that, in terms of actual practice and emphasis, is subject to significant variation. When approached in this way, it then becomes possible to further divide right-wing extremism into a variety of subgroups.

One way of proceeding is to follow the lead of Mudde (1996: 229) who identifies the ideological core of right-wing extremism through a literature review that uses a rate of recurrence technique. What this means is that he selects those ideological features that are repeatedly mentioned by at least half of the authors of twenty-six separate definitions of right-wing extremism. Adopting this approach – and for the purposes of this chapter – the defining features of the extreme-right political family turn out to be: nationalism, racism, xenophobia, anti-democracy and the strong state. Consequently, any group that matches this ideological profile can be regarded as extreme right. That is not to say this method does not have its problems. For instance, in terms of relative importance, how do we rank these different elements? What happens if all five features are not present? But a detailed discussion of these methodological concerns remains outside the range of this chapter.[3]

Moving beyond these common features, the extreme-right political family can be quickly broken down into a number of subgroups or categories according to organisation and/or ideological orientation. If classified by organisational type, probably the most familiar are the electoral parties such as Le Pen's *Front National* but it is possible to identify other types as well – extra-parliamentary groups (for example Ku Klux Klan), skinhead gangs (for example Blood and Honour), terrorist groups (for example the German Hoffmann Military Sports Group active from 1974 to 1980), international groups (for example *CEDADE* – the Spanish Circle of Friends of Europe), publishing houses and even think-tanks (for example the French *Nouvelle Droite*). When ideological orientation is our means of classification, closer inspection soon reveals a wide range of tendencies: from those who deny, relativise or minimise the Holocaust – the revisionists – though to nationalist and anti-immigrant populists, neo-Nazis, white supremacists, religious fundamentalists, revolutionary nationalists, pan-European nationalists, conservative revolutionaries and crypto-fascists (Griffin, 1991). What all this shows is that the political family of right-wing extremism is multifaceted and embraces a wide spectrum of organisations and tendencies.

Right-extremist use of the Internet: its origins and development

Without doubt, the most conspicuous right-extremist presence on the Internet has been in the domain of the World Wide Web (WWW). Since the first appearance of Don Black's *Stormfront*[4] in March 1995, the number of right-extremist homepages has rapidly increased. Although difficult to determine with any accuracy – web pages frequently have short life spans – recent estimates of the number of far-right homepages range from hundreds of sites to as many as 3,000.[5] Yet the earliest use of computer systems by right-wing extremists actually dates back to the mid-1980s. In 1985, the Los Angeles based Anti-Defamation League reported the creation of a bulletin board system (BBS) by white supremacists in the United States. This venture, sponsored by the Aryan Nations, required activists to dial a series of home computers using a modem and appropriately supplied software (Marks, 1996: 148–150). But this BBS was not linked to the Internet and had relatively few users. To secure access, one had to become acquainted with the telephone number(s) and this typically meant locating these numbers in relevant far-right publications. As a result, distribution of material was largely restricted to those who were, as Bernstein says, 'in the know'.[6] Not surprisingly, when overshadowed by the arrival of more sophisticated Internet technology, with its promise of reaching millions, these bulletin boards soon fell from favour.

According to Bernstein, right-wing extremists in the United States have been the quickest to move away from these old-style bulletin boards and adopt new Internet technologies.[7] The development of right-extremist activity on the net has therefore been uneven: Europe has been slower to respond and this can be partly explained by the fact that Internet technologies originated in the United States where computer hardware and cost of access[8] is also comparatively cheaper. But the experience of Germany in particular, where bulletin boards remained popular with right-wing extremists, also shows the importance of country-specific factors, above all legal and constitutional restraints.

In 1994, a popular computer magazine exposed an active system of far-right bulletin boards in Germany known as the *Thule* Network.[9] This BBS, which gave rise to continuing concern, was thought to be drawing in some 1,500 right-wing extremists. A nodal point for extreme-right activity, it was distributing information on demonstrations, magazines and books, providing contact numbers for a variety of leading activists and posting details of anti-fascist opponents, hostile judges and unsympathetic journalists (Whine, 1997: 215). Moreover, since *Thule* was not linked to the Internet[10] and access to its most secure sections could only be obtained through a series of passwords and identity checks, it was also highly secretive. Consequently, like its forerunners in the United States, it had only a small circle of users but what is interesting in this case is that this limited access was deliberate. A wave of neo-Nazi and skinhead violence in Germany in the early 1990s had resulted in a clampdown on neo-Nazi activity by the German authorities. This had resulted in numerous groups being banned and many far-right militants being placed under surveillance.[11] What the *Thule* Network therefore offered – in a country in which displays of Nazi symbolism, incitement to racial hatred and Holocaust denial are all illegal – was an opportunity for extreme-right militants to retain their anonymity and still remain part of a neo-Nazi subculture without running the risk of prosecution. Operating in such hostile conditions, it makes sense that German right-wing extremists were relatively slow to respond to the possibilities of the Internet. None the less, in 1996 the more 'respectable' organisations of the German extreme right, such as the *Nationaldemokratische Partei Deutschlands* (National Democratic Party of Germany) and *Die Republikaner* (The Republicans), did start to establish their own WWW homepages. Even so, their initial forays were very cautious; content was deliberately sanitised to prevent any legal action from being taken.

As we shall see, it has been the opportunities afforded by the web that have received most interest from right extremists but it is also clear that other Internet technologies have not been ignored. Electronic mail (email) allows extremists to instantly communicate on a variety of levels (one-to-one, one-to-many, many-to-many) and proves especially valuable for internal networking purposes, particularly when sympathisers are geo-graphically dispersed. Email is also a relatively secure medium most of all when encryption techniques are put into effect. What is more, it is open to misuse. Under the protection of a variety of systems that keep secret the identity of the sender(s), right-wing extremists have carried out numerous 'mail bomb' attacks on opponents; victims are targeted with abusive language, multiple mailings and exceptionally large files (Back *et al.*, 1996: 13).

Aside from electronic mail, increasing numbers of right-wing extremists were also drawn to the USENET area of the Internet during the early 1990s. Within a succession of 'newsgroups', the USENET provides a forum for online discussion but it can also be used as a vehicle for disseminating extremist propaganda. Each 'newsgroup' has a subject set for discussion; the more controversial subjects are listed under the 'alt' (that is, 'altern-ative') category and within this particular domain, right extremists are attracted to groups such as alt.skinhead and alt.politics.nationalism.white. However, since these discussion groups are open and often unmoderated, right-wing extremists have found their efforts frequently thwarted by opponents who have flooded these discussion groups with opposing points of view. A recent glance at alt.politics.nationalism.white, for instance, revealed a series of postings from the Anti-Defamation League.[12] As a result, right-wing extremists are now favouring discussion groups on their own websites where access can be controlled more effectively.

The value of the Internet

Notwithstanding the use of these other net technologies, what has really captured the enthusiasm of the extreme right has been the development of the World Wide Web especially when, during 1995, it became the most used part of the Internet (Eatwell, 1996: 65). That the average Internet user will most frequently connect with the WWW field and that, through it, a potential audience can be reached on a scale far in excess of what conventional forms of printed media could reach, largely accounts for the web's popularity amongst right-wing extremists. As *Stormfront*'s Don Black says, 'Whereas we previously could only reach people with pamphlets, or by holding rallies with no more than a few hundred people, now we can reach potentially millions of people.'[13] At all times eager to promote their extremism, the web offers the far right a display place that is open to all those who either by intention or by accident visit it – in the case of *Storm-front.org*, around 20,000 visits per week.[14] Worryingly, a British study under-taken between January and February 1998 demonstrated the relative ease with which extremist sites can be accessed. This was the case even when known organisations and uniform resource locators (URLs) were not specified in the original search. Common terms in right-wing extremist vocabulary – 'revisionist', 'paki' and 'nigger' – were input into three differ-ent search engines (*AltaVista*, *Northern Light* and *Infoseek*). Of the first ninety results that were then examined, each search engine found fewer than ten extremist sites, but 'surfing' site-to-site using hypertext links accessed hundreds of others (Brophy *et al.*, 1999: 10–12).

With such ease of access, the real concern is that once individuals are exposed to far-right propaganda on the net, in so doing some will be inspired to embark upon a 'career of extremism' by signing up to a particular group. But this is only part of the problem since in isolated cases individuals may be inspired to act alone. The consequences of this can be horrific – the case of the racial terrorist campaign conducted by lone bomber David Copeland in London in 1999 should serve as a grave warning to us all.[15] Yet it would be wrong to be too alarmist; the far right is all too aware that the number of 'hits' on an extremist web page does not necessarily correspond to the number of sympathetic inquiries. Many vis-itors will be opponents, researchers, journalists or students (for instance, of those that accessed one major revisionist site in 1995, 32 per cent could be traced to academic institutions) (Eatwell, 1996: 66).

This notwithstanding, what clearly draws right-wing extremists to the web is the promise that it will act as a central vehicle in the drive for new recruits. Yet in actual fact, the web's attractiveness to right-wing extremists is multi-layered. Here, we are indebted to Eatwell (1996) who in a previ-ous study, was able to break its appeal down under four general headings:

- low cost, potentially high-quality presentation, set-up and distribution;
- audience variety and the ability to tailor messages;
- the ability to create an effective sense of community;
- the ability to bypass national laws and boundaries.

As we take each of these headings in turn, the real value of the net reveals itself in the ways in which it compensates for right-wing extremism's struc-tural weaknesses.

In the first place, the cost of establishing a presence on the WWW is low; start-up costs can easily be met by individuals, let alone organisations. This is especially advantageous for marginalised groups that frequently exist on very limited resources. What is more, the web also allows propa-ganda to be disseminated through a variety of high-quality formats and although the sophistication of homepages fluctuates, in general, the tech-nical sophistication of extremist sites has improved significantly. For instance, the British National Party's initial web presence in 1995 amounted to little more than elementary downloadable text; the current version, as we shall see, is far more sophisticated and makes use of the latest multimedia technology.[16] Eatwell (1996) makes the important point that extremist propaganda frequently suffered from poor presentation in the past and this emphasised its lack of respectability. Yet in many cases, what is being presented today is of equivalent standard to mainstream and commercial output. Moreover, with downloadable publicity, the costs of distributing far-right propaganda can be kept to a minimum.

The web, as we have seen, makes available to right-wing extremists a platform to a far wider and varied audience. But the web also affords the opportunity to target messages at specific audiences. Whine believes that extremists are particularly eager to influence youthful and impressionistic audiences.[17] Indeed, research carried out in Britain suggests that the most active Internet users tend to be those aged less than 25 years.[18] Across the Atlantic, researchers examined right-extremist sites over a two-week period in the summer of 2000 and came across several US extremist sites that had been designed specifically for children and teenagers: the World Church of the Creator's *Creativity for Kids* included downloadable 'white pride' colouring book pages and crossword puzzles, on offer from *Stormfront for Kids* was a free download of a white supremacist computer game, while *Hammerskin Nation* offered free MP3 downloads of 'white power' music. Thankfully, however, their findings were reassuring: the majority of material on the most important far-right sites had not been authored for a specifically youthful audience. At this stage, the evidence from the United States suggests that targeting remains far less aggressive and systematic than is frequently claimed (Ray and Marsh, 2001). In the case of the World Church of the Creator, for instance, its children's site was never updated.[19]

Since sympathisers of fringe groups frequently feel isolated and cut off from mainstream society, another way in which the web profits right extremists is by empowering them with a sense of community. The web compensates by providing a sense of cohesiveness and common purpose. In promoting this 'cyber-community' of extremists, the online discussion groups provide most immediacy. However, by connecting the user to many other sites of right-extremist reference, websites also create the impression that there exists a global ideological network of like-minded people. As Stern (2001) says, 'Each hate group no longer communicates in isolation: it uses the Internet to advertise and to create the illusion that hate is not practiced in isolation at the fringes, but is part of a strong worldwide movement.' This sense of community can work at various levels. For some, it may encourage participation in real organisations and networks that exist outside the Internet. For others, however, especially those that are more geographically isolated, the 'lone wolf' mentality can be sustained by providing an enclave where shared views are repeatedly reinforced and legitimised.

Through its capacity to transcend national laws and boundaries, the Internet adds a further dimension to the extreme right's armoury. In this way, the net serves as an exceptionally expedient weapon. In particular, this holds true for European-based extremists where material – such as Holocaust denial – that is protected under the First Amendment in the United States is prohibited in certain countries such as Germany and France. But with its global reach, this material can now be accessed on the web by almost anyone. In order to ease this further, right-wing extremists have started to disseminate their material in a variety of languages – Gary Lauck's neo-Nazi NSDAP/AO, for instance, which is based in Lincoln, Nebraska, offers material over the WWW in many languages including English, German, French and Spanish.[20] As for those right extremists based in countries such as Germany that are intent on disseminating what are, under German law, criminal texts, the recent trend has been to establish their homepages with foreign providers based in North America in order to evade prosecution.

Although overlooked by Eatwell (1996), one additional advantage that the web holds for right extremists is its capacity to raise revenue. We see this in a variety of ways. There are those sites that ask for donations or charge annual subscriptions, but the most significant development has been in the growth of online merchandising, particularly white-power music. It has been estimated, for instance, that around 50,000 white-power CDs are sold every year in the United States (Ray and Marsh, 2001). Once these CDs are listened to, the real concern is that youngsters will then attend white-power concerts where actual recruitment could take place. Amongst the most important online outlets are *Resistance Records*, operated by activists from the US-based neo-Nazi National Alliance, and *Vinland Records*, a company based in the US that has raised money for the Aryan Nations' legal defence fund.

> The advantages of these websites are obvious. The companies can cut out any middlemen by selling by credit card directly to the purchaser. Potential buyers can even listen to sound clips from the CDs. Goods which would never be on display in the shops in many countries, either through preventative laws or the nazis' distribution problems, are available direct by mail order at the touch of a button.[21]

Yet David Goldman, a monitor of extremist sites since 1995, remains sanguine:

> this music operation is going to be compromised by Napster or other music-sharing software that allows the free sharing of music. As a result, all these groups selling racist CDs to finance their operations

may find that it becomes a money-losing proposition. The technology [to swap music via the net] is already there, and stopping it is like trying to put the genie back in the bottle.[22]

Into cyberspace with the British far right: virtual encounters with the British National Party

Thus far we have reflected on the extreme-right political family and the value of the net in the broadest sense. At this point, and in accordance with the overall concerns of this book, the focus will be narrowed down in order to look carefully at how the Internet has impacted on an extreme-right political party – in this instance, the British National Party. Unlike its continental counterparts, such as the French *Front National*, the Italian *Alleanza Nazionale* and the Belgian *Vlaams Blok*, the British National Party's electoral performance has been dismal. Since it was formed in 1982, it has experienced little relief from an otherwise miserable existence on the electoral fringe. Struggling to break out of a 1–4 per cent electoral ghetto has been the norm and a local council by-election victory in the Millwall ward of London's Tower Hamlets in 1993 provided no more than temporary reprieve – the seat was lost in 1994. At the 1997 general election, only three BNP candidates captured more than 4 per cent of the vote although in 2001, the BNP did achieve its best ever general election performance with seven candidates capturing between 4 and 5 per cent, two candidates between 5 and 10 per cent and three candidates gaining over 10 per cent of the vote.[23] Even so, its claim that it has now entered the political mainstream remains extravagant. No BNP candidate has ever won a seat in a parliamentary election; as for party membership, this was estimated to be little more than 2,300 in May 2001.[24] What the BNP therefore provides is a typical example of a party that is still largely confined to the right-extremist fringe. In view of that, we are in a position to consider two issues. The first is the impact that the net has had on internal party strategy; the second is its external effect on BNP support and status.

The BNP first unveiled its website in the autumn of 1995. Comparatively quick on the uptake, not only was the BNP the first British right-wing extremist organisation to establish itself on the WWW, it also beat the mainstream Conservative Party on to the Internet by several weeks. The prime instigator of this move was the forward-looking Michael Newland, the BNP's erstwhile press officer.[25] The belief within the BNP – held particularly strongly by the leader at that time, John Tyndall – was that a key factor in the continued failure of the BNP was opposition by the mainstream media, whether in terms of 'conspiracies of silence' or out-and-out condemnation. With the Internet promising a rapidly expanding user base within only two years, the net offered an ideal opportunity to bypass this media 'censorship'. The first problem, however, was locating a provider that would be willing to host the BNP's proposed site. Concerned that British ISP companies would say no to its racist material, Newland managed to establish a web presence for the BNP by renting space from a provider overseas. In actual fact, his fears proved unwarranted – by the middle of 1997, various domestic right-extremist groups had established their websites through British ISP companies (for example, International Third Position on *PIPEX* and the British Hammerskins on *DEMON*).[26]

As an early arrival on the net, the layout of the BNP's original website was understandably basic. The homepage was titled 'British National Party News Service' and merely provided a textual summary of the BNP's newspaper, the *British Nationalist*. Indeed, when compared to the printed version, the quality of its net adaptation was distinctly second-rate (the only graphic was a plain Union Jack and there were no photographs). Within weeks, however, Newland had quickly added to the website with a new library section (basically a selection of recent articles from the BNP's monthly magazine *Spearhead*), a list of BNP regional branches with post-office box contact addresses, and a links section that revealed a connection to the more extreme *Stormfront* site. But as a tool for recruitment purposes, it had obvious limitations. Above all, it was a very uninspiring site. The text offered nothing qualitatively different from conventional BNP propaganda. Moreover, the links that were provided to more extreme sites (which became more numerous by 1997 and even included Holocaust denial sites) hardly facilitated its quest for political respectability. Although the BNP did start to use its website in support of its electoral campaigns (in 1997 the BNP published what it believed to be the most important sections of its election manifesto on its web page and also provided a sample copy of its 1997 general election address), the impact was negligible. Despite being hailed as a 'tremendous advance' by the BNP, its appearance on the net did nothing to arrest the party's gradual decline after 1994. By 1998 party membership had slumped from 2,000 to little more than 1,000.[27]

The contrast between this original website format and the latest version (www.bnp.org.uk), redesigned in July 2001, is striking. The upgrade boasts a glossy, 'branded' appearance that immediately catches the eye. The homepage banner has new party chairman, Nick Griffin, scrupulously presented in suit, shirt and tie, flanking a flowing Union Jack, and the populist comment – in the style of the *Front National* – 'Everyone is against the BNP – except the people!' Indeed, what reveals itself very quickly is the debt of inspiration to the French far right. This is evident from the picture of a triumphant Griffin parading onstage at the BNP's Red, White and Blue Festival (an event modelled on the FN's festival) through to the design of the homepage itself (it is practically identical to the site of Bruno Mégret's *Mouvement National Republicain*).[28] Naturally, the latest technology gives rise to greater sophistication and where once the BNP could only offer textual summaries of its printed publications, now material is offered in virtual formats that can be easily read and downloaded free of charge through *Adobe Acrobat Reader* software. Particularly impressive is the option to listen and view a number of interviews between BNP representatives and the mainstream media through its audio/video facility. Beyond these cutting-edge features, the site is obviously intended to serve as a tool for recruitment with a variety of user-friendly contact options on offer. But it is also noticeable that in seeking to present itself as a legitimate political party, more thought has gone into checking that content is free from fascist association. Consequently, the particularly unsavoury links to Holocaust denial sites, neo-Nazi organisations and to Aryan dating pages (!) have been removed. Moreover, no online discussion fora are provided or links to regional party sites. This all means that content and information is unidirectional and controlled from the centre.

The recent transformations to the BNP's website – achieved by a different party activist, Simon Darby[29] – need to be placed in the wider context of developments in overall party strategy. Speaking for those 'modernisers' within the BNP who thought that a more moderate and respectable image would deliver the type of electoral success experienced by extreme-right parties on the continent, Cambridge-educated Nick Griffin ousted John Tyndall as party chairman in 1999.[30] In terms of party policy, the most significant change has seen the core policy of compulsory repatriation abandoned, but Griffin's restructuring of the BNP has also extended to organisational renewal. As part of this, Griffin has assigned prime importance to the Internet where what matters first and foremost is the way in which the BNP is seen by mainstream society. Therefore, its main function is to give out the message that the BNP is a credible, modernised and legitimate constitutional party. Even so, this has not precluded other, less legitimate uses of the net. For instance, during September 2000, the BNP sent out a secret email to supporters encouraging them to effectively hijack the fuel-tax protests whilst at the same time launching an anonymous fuel-protest website. This had almost the same address as another fuel-protest site and was clearly designed as a copycat site. Once exposed, however, this duplicitous exercise backfired and genuine protesters rounded on the BNP.[31]

As for the value of the BNP's official website, much will depend, of course, on the extent to which the general population engages it. The party claimed, in early 2001, a rate of between 1,000 and 1,400 hits a day.[32] This rate was bettered during the general election period when, after successfully challenging the BBC to establish a link to its website, Griffin claimed that a total of 500,000 pages were downloaded from the BNP site.[33] In a further move, in July 2001, Simon Darby threatened Birmingham City Council with legal action if it continued to use software that blocked access to the BNP's website in the city's libraries. Following publicity in a local newspaper (with a circulation in excess of 100,000), the City Council backed down.[34] But presumably the damage had been done. Those that had never considered searching for the BNP site prior to this publicity might now have considered a search out of curiosity. If all this gives the impression that the Internet is providing the BNP with a powerful weapon in its drive for political respectability, a number of factors should be borne in mind.

The first concerns the size and socio-economic profile of the Internet-user population. The most recent statistics show that for the period January to March 2001, 9.2 million households had access to the net in the United Kingdom; this amounts to over one-third of all households.[35] As for social class and Internet use, however, a report from March 2000 showed a clear disparity between upper-middle- and middle-class use (48 per cent) and semi- and un-skilled working-class use (7 per cent). The report warned that although net penetration would pass 60 per cent of the population by 2003, over 20 million citizens could be left unconnected or excluded.[36] Yet this has gone unnoticed by the BNP. Its political strategy, as defined by Nick Griffin, is to target those wards in high ethnic-minority areas where it polled particularly well at the 2001 general election (for example, Oldham, Burnley) and these wards are likely to be relatively deprived, white working-class districts. What this means is that they are precisely those areas that are most affected by the so-called 'digital divide'. As a result, over the foreseeable future, the BNP's Internet audience will not necessarily correspond to its target constituency. A second factor relates to website popularity. Evidence from the United States suggests that political sites do not make it into the top 100 or even top 1,000 most visited destinations.[37] Finally, as mentioned previously, the number of website hits does not necessarily reflect the number of potential sympathisers – for all the 500,000 BNP pages that were downloaded during the 2001 general election, the party's average vote was only 3.9 per cent across the thirty-three seats that it contested. Indeed, from what we have seen, it is hard to see how the party's website could, on its own, deliver the level of support necessary for the BNP to extricate itself from the political fringe. But what remains a possibility is that the Internet might contribute to the creation of some *partial* legitimacy. One can only speculate here but perhaps the mainstream media's willingness to engage with the BNP between April and July 2001 was *in part* the consequence of journalists visiting the BNP website and taking its 'respectability' at face value.[38]

Conclusion

Evidently, the net is a valuable resource for right-wing extremists. In the past, distribution of far-right material was more often than not constrained by limited circulation, poor quality and a variety of legal restraints. By comparison, the present-day generation of right extremists is privileged. On offer today is a global communications medium that is increasingly accessible, can deliver high-quality presentation and remains relatively free from regulation. But has the arrival of this new medium effected any increasing acceptance of right-wing extremism? The maxim here is do not overestimate the danger, because, according to Stern (2001), 'While (extremist) websites make information available to millions of people, users must access these sites. Most will not.' In this sense, what really matters is not the supply of material but its demand. The call for extremist material over the WWW is clearly limited and will, in all probability, remain so unless a crisis of contemporary capitalism triggers a radicalisation of Western democracies. Indeed, when located in overall net activity, the volume of traffic to extremist websites is small beer. Whilst it is undeniable that right-extremist sites have flourished in recent years, there is no evidence to suggest that the Internet has led to a massive surge in support for right-wing extremism in any country. In this respect, the experience of the BNP is nothing out of the ordinary.

All that said, the fact remains that within the broad spectrum of the extreme-right political family, there resides a harder element that is uninhibited in its extremism. Its material, like child pornography, is frankly abusive and may well cause offence and distress to those that encounter it. Regardless of the extent of demand for such material, the point needs to be made that any material that openly incites racial hatred and discrimination is an affront to human dignity. This has no rightful place in a democratic society, whether it is to be found inside or outside the Internet. But the net is, of course, an international medium and therein lies the real problem of control. The only realistic solution to this is an international agreement but there are, as one net activist put it, 'more than 150 countries on the net and more than 150 ideas about what should be legal or illegal' (Brophy *et al.*, 1999: 50). We need only compare the US perspective (which allows freedom of speech under the First Amendment) with the German view (which has strict laws governing right-extremist propaganda) to appreciate the difficulties involved.

Without international agreement, the default position is to explore numerous other avenues within the national context. One option is to follow the legal route whereby legal responsibility for such material is placed with either the content provider (for instance, a website that publishes a hypertext link to such material), the service provider (for example, *America OnLine, CompuServe*), the network provider (that is, those that supply the technical infrastructure) or the access provider (for example, a university or a cybercafé). But legal approaches are fraught with problems – for instance, is an ISP a publisher or a carrier of material? A more productive approach might be to exert pressure on the ISPs to self-regulate; when this happens, however, right-wing extremists simply find other ISPs abroad and in some cases even become providers themselves.[39] Where technical solutions are sought, these largely involve software filtering and whilst this might be effective in the home, the example of the BNP shows that this can be self-defeating in the public arena. Whatever route is preferred, we run into numerous difficulties. Clearly there is no easy answer.

That uninhibited extremism continues to afflict the net is without doubt a depressing fact. Whilst it may not be drawing many towards its orbit, there is certainly an isolated few that may be inspired – through the most extreme content – to follow a more violent course of action. On the other hand, the net could also serve as an end in itself with the consequence that extremist activity in the 'real world' actually declines. But perhaps the real danger comes from other elements in the extreme-right political family – like the BNP – that are using the web in order to moderate the way in which they are seen. Those organisations that use the net in this (more intelligent) way represent the greater threat to liberal society since it is political legitimacy that allows right-wing extremism to gain a foothold in the party system. Once this is achieved, extreme-right parties are in a position to mobilise support around a range of populist issues at the same time as presenting themselves (disingenuously) as legitimate political actors. Without the support of the Internet, this has already happened in countries such as France. Regrettably, now that the net has been added to the range of the far right's tactical options, the possibility of it happening elsewhere is likely to increase.

Notes

1 Those right-wing extremist political parties – such as Le Pen's *Front National* or Fini's *Alleanza Nazionale* – that have recorded significant electoral success have done so through denying allegiance to fascism.
2 *Spearhead,* October 1995.
3 For a discussion on possible solutions to this problem, see C. Mudde, *The Ideology of the Extreme Right,* Manchester: University of Manchester Press, 2000, pp. 178–180.
4 Don Black is a leading US right-wing extremist who has led David Duke's Knights of the Ku Klux Klan.
5 L. Back, 'On the dark side of cyberspace', *Searchlight,* No. 307, January 2001, p. 22.
6 See L. Bernstein, 'Hate on the Internet', *Searchlight,* No. 249, March 1996.
7 Ibid.
8 In Europe, cost of access is cheaper in Finland but it is at least double or more than double the US rate in France, Austria, Belgium, Germany and Spain. See *Achieving Universal Access,* London, Booz, Allen & Hamilton, March 2000, p. 19.
9 The *Thule* Network's name is derived from the 'Thule Society', a Nazi vanguard organisation from the 1920s of which Rudolf Hess was a leading member.
10 An Internet address was established in June 1996 and was operated through a provider in Canada.
11 Between November 1992 and September 2000, seventeen neo-Nazi organisations had been banned.
12 Alt.nationalism.politics.white newsgroup, accessed 15 August 2001.
13 Quoted in *The Guardian,* 25 June 2001.
14 *The Guardian,* 25 June 2001, p. 50.

15 Copeland found the 'recipe' for his nail bombs on the Internet.
16 http://www.bnp.org.uk (15 August 2001).
17 M. Whine (1997) 'ICTs and Political Extremism', paper presented to the Electronic Democracy Conference, University of Teesside, 17–18 September 1997.
18 *Achieving Universal Access*, p. 12.
19 See *The Southern Poverty Law Center's Intelligence Report*, Issue 101, Spring 2001, pp. 44–45.
20 http://www.nazi-lauck-nsdapao.com (15 August 2001).
21 S. Silver 'The Web of Lies', *Searchlight*, No. 280, October 1998.
22 *The Southern Poverty Law Center's Intelligence Report*, Issue 101, Spring 2001, p. 45.
23 *Searchlight*, No. 313, July 2001, p. 7.
24 According to *Searchlight*, No. 311, May 2001, p. 7.
25 Newland stood for the London Mayoral election in 2000 but at the time of writing he is no longer with the BNP.
26 *Searchlight*, No. 263, May 1997, p. 5.
27 *Local Elections 1998 including London: Briefing Pack Including Analysis and Results of Extreme Right Candidates*, London, CST Elections Research Unit for the Board of Deputies of British Jews, p. 3.
28 See http://www.m-n-r.com (15 August 2001). Bruno Mégret was a former leading member of the French *Front National* who split from Le Pen in 1999 and has since formed the National Republican Movement.
29 West Midlands Regional Organiser.
30 Griffin is an opportunist. In the 1980s he had previously led a radical faction within the National Front; as late as 1995 he had criticised those elements within the BNP who were intent on chasing 'the elusive rainbow of respectability'. See *Searchlight*, No. 246, December 1995, p. 5.
31 See *Searchlight*, No. 306, December 2000, pp. 14–15.
32 *Searchlight*, No. 310, April 2001, p. 8.
33 This claim was made in his speech at the Red, White and Blue Festival in August 2001.
34 See *The Voice of Freedom*, August 2001, p. 11.
35 Government statistics online. Available at: http://www.number10.gov.uk.
36 See *Achieving Universal Access*, pp. 12–13.
37 *Interactive Week*, 22 May 2000, online. Available at: http://www.zdnet.com (26 August 2001).
38 Media interest in the BNP increased dramatically following 'race riots' in Oldham in May 2001. The following month, the BNP captured 12,000 votes in Oldham.
39 For instance, the NPD has operated a service provider – '*NPD.net – National Provider Deutschlands – Das Deutsche Netzwork*'.

References

Back, L., Keith, M. and Solomos, J. (1996) 'Technology, Race and Neo-Fascism in a Digital Age: The New Modalities of Racist Culture', *Patterns of Prejudice*, 30(2): 3–27.

Betz, H.-G. (1994) *Radical Right-Wing Parties in Western Europe*, Basingstoke: Macmillan.

Betz, H.-G. and Immerfall, S. (eds) (1998) *The New Politics of the Right: Neo-Populist Parties and Movements in Established Democracies*, Basingstoke: Macmillan.

Brophy, P., Craven, J. and Fisher, S. (1999) *Extremism and the Internet*, British Library Research and Innovation Report, No. 145, February.

Cheles, L., Ferguson, R. and Vaughan, M. (eds) (1991) *Neo-Fascism in Europe*, Harlow: Longman.

Eatwell, R. (1996) 'Surfing the Great Wave: The Internet, Extremism and the Problem of Control', *Patterns of Prejudice*, 30(1): 61–71.

Griffin, R. (1991) *The Nature of Fascism*, London: Pinter.

Hainsworth, P. (ed.) (2000) *The Politics of the Extreme Right*, London: Pinter.

Marks, K. (1996) *Faces of Right-Wing Extremism*, Boston: Branden Publishing Co.

Merkl, P. and Weinberg, L. (eds) (1993) *Encounters with the Contemporary Radical Right*, Boulder, San Francisco and Oxford: Westview Press.

Mudde, C. (1996) 'The War of Words: Defining the Extreme-Right Party Family', *West European Politics*, 19(2): 225–248

Mudde, C. (2000) *The Ideology of the Extreme Right*, Manchester: University of Manchester Press.

Ray, B. and Marsh II, G.E. (2001) 'Recruitment by Extremist Groups on the Internet', *First Monday*, Available at: http://www.firstmonday.dk (6 August 2001).

Stern, K. (2001) *Hate on the Internet*, online. Available at: http://www.ajc.

Taggart, P. (1995) 'New Populist Parties in Western Europe', *West European Politics*, 18(1): 34–51.

Whine, M. (1997) 'The Far Right on the Internet', in Loader, B. (ed.), *The Governance of Cyberspace*, London: Routledge, 209–227.

12 Conclusions

The net change

Paul Nixon, Stephen Ward and Rachel Gibson

Introduction

The contributions from this book at first sight seem to show how little political communication using ICTs appears to differ from its more traditional forms. Despite the range of case studies involved, the diversity of the focus and the differing political traditions, there are broad similarities of experience in the areas studied. However, our message is not simply one of confirming the status quo. Parties are beginning to adopt new ICTs more extensively and new practices are emerging gradually. Some subtle differences can be detected among parties and party systems in their use of ICTs. In exploring such findings, this concluding chapter brings together the issues discussed in this volume, highlighting some of the main points to emerge from the contributions. In order to assess these overall findings we return to the three broad areas discussed in Chapter 1, namely: campaigning and style of politics; electoral outcomes and the balance of power between parties; and internal organisation and democracy. This leads to a final assessment of the determinants shaping parties' web strategies and the development of their use of new ICTs.

Party campaigning and elections: the impact of the Internet on the style of politics

One of the central issues of the book is how far the emergence of new ICTs could bring about a new style of politics or new trends in campaign communication and whether such trends represent an 'Americanisation' of campaigning, particularly in liberal democracies.

Symbolic politics

One of the first patterns to emerge from the studies here is the symbolic value of Internet use. All the case-study chapters confirm a rapid growth of party online activity over a short period from the mid- to late 1990s. As Villalba shows in the case of France, once one party moved to build a net presence the others quickly followed, fearing to be left behind. This has become important as an expression of modernity. Parties wish to be seen as being up to date, modern in their outlook and in touch with technological change. This aspect of a projection of modernity is most strikingly seen in Chapters 4 and 8, concerning the Mediterranean states and Romania respectively, where confidence in democratic politics is not yet fully established and the use of the Internet is one way to try to distance parties operating in the new, democratic arena from the old discredited politics. In a sense, the very notion of an Internet presence for Romanian parties can be viewed as an affirmation of new values and an absolute rejection of old-style politics and the values associated with them. The new form of discursive space on the Internet can also be viewed as somehow clean and untainted by previous events. This is theoretically space open to all, although in practice the comparatively low levels of Internet access reduce such openness.

Internet campaign communication style: more of the same?

In Chapter 1, we highlighted four possible developments in campaign style: information-heavy campaigning; increased interactivity; increased personalisation and targeting of party messages; and the possible decentralisation of campaigning. Our evidence from the different case studies suggests a rather mixed picture.

- *Substantive campaigning.* Content analysis from many of the places analysed in the chapters (US, Mediterranean, France, Australia and Korea) indicates that the primary purpose of party websites has been the provision of standard information about party organisation and policy and, in some cases, personality. Much of this information is available elsewhere offline, so in a sense parties are not providing much that is new but more of the same in a different format for those who want it.
- *Interactive campaigning.* Again the content analysis suggests that innovation in the form of interactive campaigning is much less well developed and where interactivity does occur it is controlled by the parties rather than the voters. As Villalba argues in Chapter 6, the commonest interactive opportunities available on websites tend to be unidirectional rather than allowing two-way communication. For example, whilst email contacts on party websites offer the appearance of openness and interactivity, as Mocan *et al.* found in Romania, there is no guarantee that parties will actually respond to email enquiries. It appears that, since websites offer parties a greater ability to communicate directly with voters without interference from intermediaries, parties are then reluctant to cede that new-found control of the communication process to voters.

- *Personalised campaigning.* The chapters note some limited efforts to target political campaigning segmentally and new technologies have facilitated such differentiation (see Chapter 5), in particular aiming at broad groups of voters (young people and expatriate voters in particular), rather than providing messages for individuals. However, at the same time, this notion of niche marketing has run alongside an increasing standardisation of political campaigning at a national level. As Hague and Uhm point out in Chapter 10, although parties recognise the possibilities of targeting and tailoring their campaigns for individuals, many still focus on the catch-all principle of building broad coalitions of voters, rather than trying to differentiate their message to a wide variety of niche groups.

- *Decentralised campaigning.* Several chapters suggest that the Internet has promoted individual candidates/personalities. Wallis argues that, in the case of Mexico, the 'web may be seen as a tool to promote particular candidates, rather than parties *per se*'. Similarly, Margolis *et al.*, Hague and Uhm, and Villalba all note the increasing use of the Internet to project the image not just of a party but of individual politicians. Indeed, Margolis *et al.* note that, in many cases, US candidate websites actually failed to mention the party name. However, it is unlikely that this trend of personality politics is promoted directly as a result of the increasing use of the Internet. As Hague and Uhm, and Wallis recognise, the pre-existing political framework and culture is often the key, that is, where personalities were already prominent in a political system they use the Internet to further the process of candidate based politics.

At one level, therefore, from the evidence presented here, party presence on the Internet seems to represent largely an additional element to a party's repertoire of action along with more traditional communication forms rather than a transformation of the fundamental relationship between political parties and the public, as some earlier advocates of cyber democracy hoped. As noted by Cunha *et al.* in Chapter 4, the Portuguese Communist Party's information official argued that the reason for a net presence was 'to get the message to the public and party positions to Internet users', which, as Cunha *et al.* point out, facilitates the party by 'enabling them to take advantage of the potential the technology gives them to circumvent the media altogether and to appeal to voters directly'.

Nevertheless, there is evidence that web campaigning is not simply about information provision and that the parties are beginning to explore new online-marketing strategies, which provides some evidence of 'postmodern' campaigning set out in Chapter 1. In Chapter 5, on the UK, Bowers-Brown shows how new marketing techniques are being applied to political activity. He contends political parties have the opportunity to adopt the Internet as a personalised marketing channel. The parties are also giving more attention to news management and message development. Bowers-Brown notes how UK parties are adopting political marketing strategies in which 'policy, party and personnel are regarded as malleable factors rather than the values of the potential voter'. He argues that the evidence leads one to believe that political parties are, indeed, using the Internet not just to communicate information but also to build relationships, thus emphasising the importance of trust and reputation. This move towards a more relationally focused approach is highlighted through varying levels of interactivity, which are, as Bowers-Brown notes, limited but growing.

Americanisation and Internet campaigning: it's all the same?

At the start of this chapter we indicated the broad similarities of experiences across the countries discussed here. One of the main debates in campaign communication literature in recent times has been the notion of Americanisation or standardisation of campaigning techniques in liberal democracies. Given the apparent US dominance of the Internet, it was suggested in Chapter 1 that new ICTs might lead to further Americanisation.

Certainly, there is some direct evidence of parties looking to the American experience. As Bowers-Brown indicates in Chapter 5, both the main UK parties spent considerable time with their US counterparts studying the online campaigns of US presidential candidates. Similarly, Wallis notes that Mexico's geographical proximity to the US means that campaign techniques have a tendency to transfer across the border. Yet, it is difficult to tell whether Internet campaigning is really any different from traditional communication methods. British parties have regularly studied US campaigns for some time prior to the emergence of the Internet. Examining US presidential candidates' e-campaigns is merely an extension of that practice.

It is also clear that parties and candidates do not simply look to the US wholesale as part of their learning experience. Often parties watch the experiences of their global sister parties. As Copsey points out in relation to the BNP's website, much had been drawn from the experiences of French far-right parties. The far right in particular have established strong online networks.

Finally, as Cunha *et al.* argue in their chapter on the southern European states, although there are distinct similarities between parties' use of the Internet in liberal democracies, political context and culture matters in the adoption of new ICTs. There were differences both between southern European countries and other liberal democracies and the countries themselves. The particular political and institutional rules within countries help shape Internet use by parties (see below).

Party systems and inter-party competition: the impact of the Internet on outcomes

In Chapter 1 we asked whether the impact of the Internet would, or could, change campaign outcomes and thus the balance of power between political parties. Does it make some parties more competitive than previously? Will its utilisation upset party systems uniformly? In particular, several chapters in this volume have provided additional evidence for the equalisation versus normalisation debate.

There is broad agreement amongst the contributors that the Internet can provide fringe parties with a presence. As Wallis states, in relation to Mexico, opposition parties have been allowed more exposure because of the Internet. However, the overall benefits of such exposure for outsider/fringe parties are dubious. Margolis *et al.* provide comprehensive evidence of the dominance of the US Democrat and Republican parties in cyberspace and, of course, the traditional media through their preexisting resource advantages. Whilst the domination of major players is less pronounced in multi-party systems, parliamentary parties still lead the way, as was demonstrated in Chapter 4. Although cyberspace allows fringe parties a presence, as several chapters indicate (see Chapters 4, 8, 9 and 10), the vast majority of the electorate still receives its political information via traditional broadcast methods. Even where citizens are using the Internet for political information they do so through sites such as AOL or the BBC, which they see as having authority and impartiality – when in fact much of the reporting is based upon information released in varying forms by the political parties themselves. This is also true of fringe or emergent parties, but they often lack the resources to update the information as quickly and may not have the same levels of access to, or daily interactions with, journalists. Thus the major parties often set the agenda, with the fringe parties struggling to get the same level of recognition and having to provide far 'juicier' stories in order to attract attention. In essence, a political catch 22 is at work here: at present, fringe parties need to gain recognition through traditional political means in order to obtain the resources needed for online developments, and such resources that are available are often swallowed up by traditional parties.

Nevertheless, although the web is unlikely to bring significant electoral gains for outsider parties, as Copsey shows in Chapter 11, the value of the Internet to fringe parties in other respects should not be overlooked. He describes how parties of the extreme right have used the Internet as a significant part of their repertoire in order to circumvent legislative constraints upon their actions, taking advantage of the international nature of Internet information exchange and the lack of concerted responses from governments. This has enabled them to publish their material to as wide an audience as possible. Moreover, Copsey indicates that a relatively professional website can make small parties appear larger than they actually are and bolster their legitimacy. This is easier on the Internet than with traditional forms of communication, where print costs and lack of access to TV, radio and the press are major barriers.

We can see that whilst some small advances may well be made by parties from outside the mainstream, the notion of the positive effect of the equalisation thesis is questionable, although, as Cunha *et al.* warn in Chapter 4,

> in no sense will this be an unqualified process: institutional and party system features, as well as ideology, will count at least as much as sheer size when it comes to what the parties are able and willing to do with the technology so that, given the right circumstances, the technology's potential to act as a 'party-competition leveller' is likely to remain very much a real one.

In sum, it seems that the Internet may widen the competitive playing field and allow more players to play the game but its role as a leveller in the electoral game is much more questionable. It may allow fringe parties to survive but, currently, it hardly allows them to thrive.

Participation and intra-party democracy: the impact on party organisation

In Chapter 1 we suggested that 'Internet-based technology might have a greater impact internally within parties'. We noted the shifting general circumstances of political organisation and mobilisation: decreasing levels of party membership; a fall in activism from both apathy and a centralising of political campaigning; and the shift to 'catch-all' parties and a concomitant realignment of financing away from individual members towards state and institutional donations.

Individual-level participation online: voters, members and parties

The potential to transform political parties through new technology is immense. For example, the net, at least in theory, offers non-geographically limited spaces for discourse and organisation. Yet, as almost all the contributors have noted, the potential for increased discursive activity between the party elites and the membership using the Internet has, to date, not been fulfilled. This is not to say that parties are ignoring the new technologies internally. As Bowers-Brown indicates, public websites are sometimes only the tip of the iceberg, with larger parties employing sophisticated electronic internal communication channels, especially during election campaigns. However, so far, new ICTs have been used less for internal participatory purposes and more for campaigning and administration. Parties have been wary of opening up electronic-participation channels with either members or the public for several reasons. First, the quality of debate in open fora is, as Hague and Uhm argue, low. Unless electronic discussion is moderated, and sufficiently well organised, then bulletin boards and chat rooms are often more akin to graffiti walls than meaningful arenas for discussion. Moderation requires considerable resources (finance and staff), which is often beyond the means of many small parties. Second, most electronic channels for party discussion are information exchanges, rather than substantive policy debating arenas, and are at best only additional consultative channels. This is not surprising since, as most of the chapters here confirm, use of the Internet remains the pursuit of those already politically active, and parties are concerned not to give undue advantage to often already privileged groups. Furthermore, as one UK party e-campaigns manager indicated,[1] party rules and constitutions were created before the emergence of the Internet and to make electronic consultation decisive would require significant changes to their organisational framework, ethos and rules.

Collective participation and internal democracy: the sub-national level

Whilst many parties have created internal electronic arenas for their members and staff, as Chapters 3, 6, 7 and 10 (USA, France, Australia and Korea) confirm, the independent spread of new ICTs throughout party structures is variable. As we suggested in Chapter 1, in candidate-centred systems such as the USA, or systems where parties are less well established, such as Korea, there is a greater incentive for individual representatives to provide their own campaign sites. However, in more party-oriented systems, local parties' and party representatives' use of the technology remains haphazard. In Australia, as Gibson and Ward found, the state sites often mirrored the national-party sites rather than producing any diversity. In France, Villalba argues that 'opposition and dissent to the main party line remains low despite the supposed openness of the Internet. When it does exist, it does not manage to modify the content of party policy'. Both these chapters confirm the suggestion outlined in Chapter 1 that, because of the centralisation of resources in parties, any Internet-assisted organisational change is generally driven top down and more likely to benefit party elites than grassroots activists. Overall, it seems that new ICTs are more likely to enhance some of the pre-existing trends in internal party democracy such as individualisation of participation and even more centralised control of campaigning.

Shaping party Internet use: the key components

As was noted at the outset of this chapter, party experiences and use of new ICTs have been broadly similar across countries. However, within this general pattern, we have also seen subtle differences between both countries and individual parties. In assessing parties' approach to new ICTs, rather than looking for simplistic 'one size fits all' determinist explanations of party online campaign strategies, we need to assess a complex balance of different variables. From the evidence presented here, party ICT usage derives from the interplay of three broad areas, as outlined below.

- *Systemic-technological.* The level of technological development, access to the Internet and the diffusion of the technology throughout a country clearly stimulate some level of activity from parties. The threshold may actually be quite low since, even in countries such as Romania, where access is comparatively low, parties still create websites. In Chapter 7 (on Australia), it was tentatively suggested that uneven patterns of technological diffusion within a country can shape different levels of enthusiasm from state level parties. Villalba indicates that in France the development of their own Minitel system arguably inhibited the rapid uptake of the Internet. Overall, technological development may help explain initial uptake of, and general attitudes towards, new ICTs but not necessarily determine how the technology is used.
- *Systemic-political/social.* The chapters have all noted the importance of a range of political-social factors in shaping patterns of online party activity, including: the degree of federalism; electoral laws (particularly those relating to party finance and access to the traditional media); the electoral cycle; and the type of electoral system and party competition. Pre-existing political patterns clearly spill over into cyberspace, as was indicated in many of the chapters. For example, it is apparent that elections are one of the main stimuli to online innovation (see Chapters 3, 5 and 9). In this respect, the peculiarities of the US political system could be seen as helping drive political campaigning online, since its federal, candidate-based system provides many more elections and consequently more opportunities for innovation with ICTs. By contrast, more centralised systems with national elections every four to five years (such as the UK or France) provide fewer opportunities for experimentation.
- *Individual internal party influences.* Three sets of factors (resources, incentives and philosophical outlook) seem important here. As we have noted above, resources (finance and staff time) play a key role in the levels of sophistication of parties' Internet strategy. Incentives basically focus on the potential advantages to be gained for a party in using the new ICTs. Specific online target audiences produce important inducements in encouraging parties to direct resources into Internet-based technologies. Finally, as Löfgren and Smith (Chapter 2) argue, philosophical outlook or ideology can play a role in the use to which new media are deployed. For example, evidence from Chapter 7 (on Australia) suggests that the Greens do put more emphasis on openness and participation in their sites, in keeping with their ideological identity.

Conclusion and prospects

Overall, one can reasonably argue that the initial phase of party website development is over. For the most part, the early years of Internet use (1994–1998) were about symbolically creating a presence online. Currently, Internet strategies are being integrated into the mainstream of party communication and campaigning activity. So far, parties have concentrated their interest on employing new ICTs to increase their campaign effectiveness, rather than for participatory purposes, as cyber-democrats might have hoped. As this volume has revealed, parties have been cautious in using the new technology, just as they have been with other technologies such as television in the 1950s (see Chapter 5). Nevertheless, although parties' use of the Internet has often been derided as dull and propagandist, their caution is understandable. In most countries, Internet access and political web use are still minority interests and, as several authors point out, because websites require citizen initiative to use them, the broadcast media remain far more important in getting one's message across to a large audience. As has also been seen, parties are limited by their internal rules and structures. Chapters 9 and 10 (on Mexico and Korea) both indicated that new social-movement organisations (NSMs) and citizen groups were arguably more imaginative and active than parties, lending some support to Bimber's (1998) notion of 'accelerated pluralism' outlined in the introduction to this volume. In part, this reflects the fact that there is more to lose for parties if they make errors with their ICT strategies. NSMs do not stand in elections and are generally under less journalistic scrutiny and, consequently, their online failures are less obvious. Moreover, political parties' hierarchical structures mean that staff responsible for ICT strategy have less of a free hand than those involved with loose protest networks.

Despite not being able to conclude from the evidence presented here that the Internet has radically altered political parties and the way in which they operate, it is clear that some changes are discernible. Nor do we agree that new technologies necessarily erode the functions of political parties *per se*, creating either a utopian direct democracy or a dystopian demagogy. Political parties are using the Internet, although not to its full potential. Whilst the Internet has not proved to be the saviour of party systems experiencing declining public interest and participation, it has contributed to a partial regeneration of democratic ideals in newly democratised countries such as Romania. We can also see that the patterns of its use are at least causing political parties to re-assess the ways in which they communicate with the public, either directly, via a website, or indirectly, through other media. So far, then, change has been more along the lines of administrative and communications modernisation.

The Internet may eventually help alter the style of party politics but have a less radical effect on party competition. The net gain for parties is that it provides a flexible and sophisticated communication channel with the public but this in itself does not solve the problem of voter antipathy towards parties – it provides the means but not the end. However, it is worth remembering that based on past experience of dealing with the emergence of communications technologies, parties remain resilient organisations. It seems likely that they will adapt to the latest communication challenge presented by the new media. The Internet, therefore, is unlikely to be either the saviour or executioner of political parties: their future lies in the hands of the parties themselves and their relationship with voters.

Note

1 Interview with one of the editors, 7 May 2002.

Reference

Bimber, B. (1998) 'The Internet and Political Transformation: Populism, Community and Accelerated Pluralism', *Polity*, XXXI, 1: 133–160.

Index